P9-CFI-014

Anarchy and culture

Anarchy and culture

The problem of the contemporary university

Edited by *David Martin*

New York
Columbia University Press

Published in 1969
by Columbia University Press
New York

© Routledge & Kegan Paul Ltd, 1969

Library of Congress Catalog Card Number: 74–80271

Printed in Great Britain

Contents

Our Contributors

David Martin	*Reader in Sociology, London School of Economics and Political Science*
Richard Layard	*Lecturer in Economics and Deputy Director of the Unit for Economic and Statistical Studies on Higher Education, London School of Economics and Political Science*
A. H. Halsey	*Professorial Fellow, Nuffield College, Oxford*
M. Trow	*Professor of Sociology, University of California*
John King	*Lecturer in Statistics, the City University*
Rowland Eustace	*Institute of Social and Economic Research, University of York*
Ernest Rudd	*Reader in Sociology, University of Essex*
Robert Chester	*Lecturer in Social Administration, University of Hull*
Geoffrey Martin	*Ex-president, National Union of Students*
Alan Shelston	*Lecturer in English, University of Manchester*
Paul Rock Frances Heidensohn	*Lecturers in Sociology, L.S.E.*
Stephen Hatch	*Research Officer in Higher Education, Institute of Education, University of London*

Ernest Gellner   *Professor of Philosophy (Department of Sociology) L.S.E.*

John Dunn   *Fellow of King's College, Cambridge*

Bernard Crick   *Professor of Politics, University of Sheffield*

John Sparrow   *Warden of All Souls College, Oxford*

Donald G. MacRae   *Professor of Sociology, L.S.E.*

Peter Wiles   *Professor of Russian Social and Economic Studies, L.S.E.*

L. C. Sykes   *Professor of French, University of Leicester*

Foreword

A book like this faces several dilemmas: to document and to describe; to theorize and explain; to think and comment; to lament (or rejoice) and prescribe. It does all in varying degrees. Some pieces are highly personal, others almost wholly analytic or descriptive. The focus is on Britain because our own culture presents quite specific patterns, yet international comparisons are included where these seem helpful. An attempt has been made to achieve a fair spread of political commitment and personal attitude along the waystations between culture and anarchy, although the representatives of the radical wing were in the event unable to produce contributions in time. The main lack is a contribution from a natural scientist. Many contributors are sociologists who at this stage can do little more than indicate the range of explanations and guess at the most relevant ones. Prolonged research is now in hand and we shall have to wait for it. Meanwhile, here is interim documentation and interim comment.

David Martin

David Martin

The dissolution of the monasteries

For many years after the technocrats built the Great City the monks and the technocrats lived in peace. Indeed the monks hardly ever came into the City (except to visit their wine merchants) and preferred to live quietly in their stately houses. These were in green pleasant places, often close by the banks of a stream.

Almost everybody felt kindly towards the good old monks. They were occasionally quaint and precise about somewhat minor matters but otherwise did no man any harm. In any case they were greatly admired for their ability as cultivators. Their level of cultivation was very high. It was widely held that three years spent in the monasteries provided an excellent breathing time before the real business of life should begin. Young people would lie by the streams, join in the rites, speak about spiritual things with the monks, and every now and then engage in a little cultivation.

The monks were careful scholars and in accordance with an ancient vow of intellectual chastity bent all their energy to make their studies pure. In the study of numbers, for example, they achieved extraordinary heights of purity. Anything which was 'applied' smacked of the Great City and contravened the ancient vow. All the same many were still not content with the standards of purity and entered more ascetic orders devoted to pursuits which were not only useless but which could obviously be recognized as such.

Meanwhile, in the Great City there was a great need for knowledge and many people prepared and ready to seek it. The technocrats believed that knowledge was to be sought after in monasteries and asked the good monks to build new foundations, to allow into their midst many youths who had spent all their lives in the Great City. These had maybe never even seen the long black robe of a monk, much less witnessed a performance of the ancient rites. Nevertheless, such youths prepared themselves by continuous spiritual exercises rising gradually from levels to degrees, happy in the promise that when they had spent their time with the monks they would become great men in the City. As for the monks they were full of sad foreboding, but they began to raise the new foundations, just as the technocrats had commanded them.

So the young men and women from the Great City sat at the feet of the monks and learnt many things, but most of all they learnt how to live in a monastery. Many indeed so loved the cloistered calm of their mentors that they wished never to leave it. Others stayed awhile and on their return to the Great City set up lay brotherhoods to cultivate themselves, just as did the good old monks. Yet others returned to the world only to find that the technocrats had deceived them and that they were not to be great men in the City but minor officials in distant provinces. And the more it became noised abroad that the technocrats were deceivers in this important matter, the more youths there were who wished never to leave the life of the cloister.

So the monasteries became full to overflowing, the ancient rites were disrupted and in many places ceased almost to be practised. The monks were blamed for serving the technocrats who had so deceived them; the technocrats were blamed for disturbing the hallowed ways of the ancient rule.

So it was that when the technocrats heard of all these things they began to build new houses, no longer in secluded valleys but in the Great City itself. In these houses appeared orders of friars[1] whose business it was to think on the ways of the Great City and on the ancient knowledge of the monks, so that both should be brought together in harmony. They took no vows of purity and so were feared and despised by the monks. Because most of them lived in the City many were not experts in cultivation. On this account they could not be allowed in the more magnificent of the old monasteries. Instead, they brooded on the Great City, on the foolish cultivation of the monks and on the deceptions of the technocrats. And the youths who came to them brooded likewise.

Many were the things the friars preached about in the Great City, but the technocrats did not hear them. So the time came when the youths who sat listening in the great preaching houses said to the friars: to preach is not enough, more is required of you. No one here has taken the ancient vows and it is now time to turn knowledge into activity. How can he who has never himself acted truly know?

The friars themselves were divided. There were those who respected cultivation and did not hate the ancient vow even though they had never taken it themselves. Others left the preaching houses in anger and pro-

1 Social scientists.

claimed the dawn of a new time as spoken of in the work of the old Abbot Herbert Marcuse:[1] when the monasteries should be dissolved, the Great City destroyed and all belong to the brotherhood. Such men gave themselves over to wild courses, singing bawdy songs, writing in a most scurrilous fashion and rushing about like so many sturdy beggars from place to place.

Seeing that vagrants did so greatly increase, and that the friars could barely control the perversity of the multitude the technocrats thought how they might bring all these things to an end. A few sturdy beggars were held in surety, but at this their fury only increased. Friars who had spent early years in the monasteries were charged with the oversight of the preaching houses, but to no effect. New houses were established where nothing was to be taught but how youths should prepare themselves for the life of a minor official in the provinces. And the technocrats spoke with the friars how they might mend their preaching, no longer ranging in wild debate and heady talk, but attending only to one matter at a time and most soberly ascertaining the facts. Some were even cajoled into imitating the technocrats by converting seminars into laboratories and exchanging black robes for white coats. All was to no avail, and the vagrants only became the more tumultuous. . . .

The end of the monks

Monachatus non est pietas. Monkishness is not true piety. This was the Protestant principle and it is also the policy of protesters in the contemporary university. The monastic insistence on contemplation and the academic commitment to objectivity are analogous, both in the nature of their aim and in the claim to a specialized, detached role. In the case of the academic his role requires a respect for criteria of objective validity, a careful sifting of evidence, and a disinterested stance *vis-à-vis* the world of man and nature. Such a stance does not require a disavowal of responsibility towards the world, especially perhaps towards the world of man, but it does mean that with regard to his own subject the academic should try to be neither the paid spokesman of an agency such as the state, nor the ideological representative of a cause.

Contemplation, discipline and objectivity are all under attack. To the extent that they reflect the tradition of 'remote and ineffectual' dons the attack has some justification. Academics belong to an open not a closed

---

[1] Spokesman of the Joachimite heresy. Actually, of course, Marcuse's message is not very hopeful.

order, they are open brethren not exclusives. Moreover, no one doubts the loudest claims to objectivity often conceal the most subtle corrosions of bias. All the various intrusions of subjectivity have been recently much advertised. Yet this seems no reason to positively praise distortion in the interests of commitment or for letting the social imagination run riot simply because it is creative, dynamic and forward looking. These forms of radical subjectivity may correct an imbalance, but are in themselves quite opposed to the notion of a balance. Just as *sola fide* – faith alone – struck at the heart of monastic disciplines, so radical subjectivity strikes at the heart of academic disciplines. Intellectual antinomianism leads to an anarchy where there is no agreed basis of discussion and only the confrontation of viewpoints.

Universities, like monasteries, become corrupt, and fine ideals are used to cover the more insidious corruptions. Nobody need be surprised at that, except those who have no adequate measure of corruption in general. Monasteries and universities need reformation and reform, since they can all too easily remove the fuse from explosive ideas, become inextricably linked to a particular system of ownership, reflect a very partial viewpoint, drift into total irrelevance and so on. Yet without the monastic principle of partial detachment from society there would be little possibility of that catholic fusion of disparate disciplines with overall critical perspectives. Without monasticism, however deformed by a rigid demarcation of subjects, there is no 'universitas', no catholicity, but only expertise of varying kinds in polytechnics. Monasticism and vital criticism paradoxically require each other. Without monks no catholicity; and where catholicity is absent the end of the monks is near. Vocation becomes vocational. Or as Weber put it, the 'call' becomes the calling – the job. Men have to be very careful how they move towards the world because it generally has more power to absorb than they to reform.

The paradox can be illustrated by one young sociologist who said he had no intention of becoming a junior manager. As with so much current protest it is never quite clear whether the objection is to being a junior or being a manager, or indeed to the fact that nowadays a university education does not automatically lead to élite positions. Nevertheless, he had a fundamental objection to being incarcerated in a restrictive secular role with no 'spiritual' returns consonant with his horizons. Of course he also objected to the monastic concept of the university. Yet without the catholic perspectives of a university, and the ecumenical sweep of sociology, he could never have found the language of protest. Without that language he would have been a delinquent not a reformer.

Most reformers are like Martin Luther: ex-monks. They strive not only to reform but to destroy institutions without which they could not have come into existence. It is true that just as Protestants universalized monasticism by taking it into the world, so the protesters wish to universalize the university. The 'free university' is the monastery in the world, rebuilding that world under its immediate impact and responding to its most pressing problems. This is secularization. It is also the quickest way to be absorbed by the world, because once the vital energies of the moment are sapped and euphoria converted into boredom then the institutional framework of monastic life is needed, and not only institutionalization but discipline. Discipline is necessary and so are disciplines. The virtue of the old rule is discovered only when it is nearly lost.

No one denies that most universities exist in a social vacuum. The social seclusion of universities parallels the geographical seclusion of the monasteries. Indeed we still build universities in cathedral towns as if we have some feeling for their deep affinity. Curiously enough, it is this interstitial character which enables the prophet of revolt, Herbert Marcuse, to allot students a special role as the bearers of contemporary dynamism. The point is that they are not overwhelmed by secular cares and workaday restrictions of perspective. This enables them to think and act with wild abandon. So it is all very well for the reformers to repudiate the monastic principle by suggesting that opportunity for thought is useless without action, indeed that thought not based on action is itself emasculated. Without the monastic principle they would hardly have occasion for thought. The unity of theory and practice is the sort of half-truth always seized upon by reforming heretics and admittedly made the more persuasive when an ideal of the objectivity of thought is converted into an acceptance of a static 'objectivity' in the world, indeed into a world of 'objects'.[1]

So there is another parallel truth running in exactly the opposite direction which accuses the activist of using the social seclusion of the university as a false base for moral posturing and for emotional dishonesty in defiance of objective, practical limitations. Even activist students are still contemplatives so long as they are at university: and some of them show remarkably little desire to leave its protective cloisters for the world. The conservative criticism has a justification. Students have no experience of life or of the precarious basis of such civilization as we have. They are

1 One should note in passing that the notion of the objectivity of truth is parallel to the concept of the transcendence of God. At every point current theological arguments find their analogies in the ideological dispute over the university.

BAC

supported in conceptual luxury by a wider society which they then abuse in total defiance of all conceivable likelihoods. Students moralize freely because they moralize at other people's expense, in both senses of the word expense. And it is even odder that the most chronic moralizers should be sociologists, because their sense of outrage can only be based on an incapacity to understand any sociology. This is why they turn sociology into ideology and justify themselves by claiming there is no difference.[1]

Not everybody can become an academic any more than the whole of life can become a seminar. Both the commercial right and the moralizing left are against the seminar mentality. Yet there must be people who accept the life of the cloister as their specialized vocation, if only because the politics of witness ought to depend on people who know the difference between true and false witness. 'Thou shalt not bear false witness' is one of the rules of monasteries and universities alike; it is as fundamental as the call not to be conformed to the world. Monks do not want everybody to have a vocation, but they do claim a right to a special vocation themselves. A civilization is lost when it dissolves its monasteries because the chief end of a monk is patient humility before the truth.

Ritual and the priesthood of all believers

The Protestant Reformers stood by the priesthood of all believers. Modern protesters stand by the participation of all students. The Reformers overthrew the Fathers; students overthrow their own fathers, and indeed, paternalism in general. Many of the Reformers were against ritual and so are many of the protesters, because ritual is an organized pattern of roles: father and son, priest and layman, teacher and student.

According to one student leader, teachers should merely be available to meet the collective requests of students when approached. The theory of the anti-university is that everybody 'says his bit and passes on'. This suggests that we may need no continuing university at all,[2] but rather a communal meeting-place where casual thoughts and maybe casual insults can be exchanged, roughly on the principle of the T group. . . . The result is the institutionalization of impertinence in every sense of the word. It is incidentally interesting that when *teachers* behave in this *ad hoc*, spontaneous way the demand is for *planned* seminars and for *office* hours, i.e. *more* bureaucracy.

1 Part of the trouble stems from the fact that sociology is the documentation of original sin by those who believe in original virtue.
2 This is what radical theologians want to do to the Church.

The attempt to achieve a chaotic, revolving role structure applies even to the roles of leader and led. No 'leaders' must be allowed to emerge since leadership is a socially conferred role: the preferred mode is an alternating pecking-order of charismatic potency. And by a parallel development the abolition of horizontal lines between teacher and student requires the abolition of vertical lines between one subject and another.[1] The role of expert disappears, partly because expertise leads to mystification and so to power. Thus not only is bureaucracy rejected but also the division of labour: Weber *and* Durkheim. The shattered frame of the social cosmos is restored to the dynamic unity of a total *Gemeinschaft*. Marx *and* Tönnies.

Yet clearly not everybody belongs to this total *Gemeinschaft*. The true social cosmos (Luther's 'invisible church') consists of those whose eyes have been opened. It has no membership because that would confer a constricting identity. Hence, when I asked a girl if she belonged to the R.S.A. I found myself having to reformulate the question in terms of whether or not she was in the R.S.A. ambience! Even this degree of identification is plainly seen as near contamination. Radical students fear all categorization, by society or by sociologists.[2] By the same token there is no agreed dogma, even though there is plenty of dogmatism. Like some of the early Protestants there is a tendency to dissolve doctrine in psychology. One makes up doctrine as one goes along. This has the dual advantage of enabling very different and even opposed groups to work together and of avoiding criticism of the programme. Both doctrine and identity are given a hidden character, an adolescent inwardness, a youthful fluidity, preserving them from the adult intelligence and from middle-aged amusement. Like most people students fear hatred less than they fear laughter.

The priesthood of all believers is best symbolized in an established right to use a shortened version of anybody's Christian name at first acquaintance. Surnames belong to one's old secular persona: shortened Christian names belong to the brotherhood – Mike, Hank, Dave, Brett or whatever it may be. This is formalized in another established right to intrude fundamental dialogue without notice – as a man might look over the breakfast table and say 'Are you saved?' The point is that privacy, like tolerance, is seen as neglect, perhaps indifference, even contempt. So privacy is near-Fascist and even tiredness and sleep are reprehensible because they are closely related to apathy. Basic decencies associated with convention and social distance, are disregarded, whether or not they are based on status.

---

1 Not something incidentally to which I oppose blanket objections.
2 Teacher: 'Are you a second-year student?' Student: 'Don't objectify me.'

Everyone has the right to treat anyone else as his brother whether his brotherly attentions are wanted or not. Intrusion becomes an art. The first sign of apathy, tolerance or indifference must be countered by a 'provocation' or a 'happening': these are the only true sacraments of revolutionary activism.

The major sacrament of counter-revolutionary apathy is a sherry party. The waters of Jerez are the gateway to Lethal forgetfulness, leading to compliance, convention, indifference, politeness, sensitivity, privacy. Good girl protesters have been known to declare that lips which touch sherry shall never touch theirs. It induces phantom consciousness. Academics who use it become ghosts in the machine – the machine of their role and of the bureaucracy. It helps them to fiddle while Vietnam burns. It is the class drink, the poisoned chalice. Oxbridge people are 'unreal' because they are known to drink it. N.U.S. diplomacy is stigmatized as 'sherry diplomacy' because it is unreal. The biggest insult when radicals occupied a Senior Common Room at one university was to be politely offered sherry.

All this is linked with an ancient malady to which students are becoming increasingly prone: hypertrophy of the ontological itch. No wonder there is a fringe of drug-taking. Certain social types are stigmatized as ontologically deprived. Though students claim every other deprivation, often on very slender grounds indeed, at least they do not suffer the ultimate deprivations of unreality. Indeed, they ask for more reality than is currently available. The deprived are the suburbanites who mow their lawns on Sunday, are disciplined in their work, dress carefully, enunciate clearly, marry institutionally and have two children. Real people do not speak, but ejaculate elementally. Their marriages are undocumented and they have no lawns to mow.

Sin

Protestantism and protest are concerned with sin: personal, or universal, or specifically white European bourgeois sin. The saved are those who have been made aware of sin, redeemed from false consciousness. Sometimes protesters sit and collectively beat their breasts for bourgeois decadence; it is not clear what it has to do with them, but they evidently enjoy the penitential mood. They are not so much concerned with the specific local sins of capitalist society as with its structural sinfulness. This is in tune with the best Protestant theology, except that the Protestant reference is universal.

It also explains their attitude to violence. Capitalist civilization is, in their view, endemically violent and the object of protest is to unleash this institutional violence into public view. Similarly, capitalist society is manipulative and so-called 'police brutality' converts the psychological manipulation into physical manipulation: darkness visible. Because bourgeois society plans sin it is – at least according to one revolutionary sect – wrong to plan the acts which bring it into the open. True provocation must arise spontaneously. This gives delinquency a theoretical justification: merely to throw a pebble at a hotel is malicious damage, but to throw it at the bourgeois mentality inside is an act of spontaneous moral revulsion. Ideological delinquency represents 'situation ethics' with a vengeance,[1] or if you like 'situation sin'; and it leads not to penitence but to the penitentiary.

When sin is structural, either in Adam or in the social system, any 'piecemeal social engineering' is by definition and by vocabulary merely manipulative. It tinkers with what properly deserves destruction. Even acts of charity become improper. A gift to a Vietnam orphanage can be described as a sop to conscience, almost indeed worse than useless, because it can enable the donor to live less harassed in the system as it is. Good works avail you nothing. Rather, the person whose eyes have been opened must feel free to act in *any* way against the structure, indeed against *structure as such*. *Pecca fortiter*. Luther or Genet.

The way out is through the 'dialectics of liberation', currently transferred to twenty-three gramophone records. In the Old Theatre at L.S.E. this was represented by a play concerned with the achievement of freedom. It began with silence and incense, and then became a morality play in reverse. (Catholicism produces morality plays; radical Protestantism plays against morality.) The message was very simple. We must try every possible combination of relationship and all will remain pure, provided they are not institutionalized: not the dialectics so much as the amateur dramatics of liberation.

This freedom is contrasted with academic freedoms; just as structural immorality is contrasted with piecemeal social engineering. Academics imagine they possess certain limited, institutionalized freedoms, but they are compassed about by a system which renders all of them null and void. They think they are free when – as Luther said – 'freewill is dead'. The teacher lives on a false consciousness from which he requires liberation. In their separated Senior Common Rooms they talk of insurances and

---

1 Another notion shared with the radical theologians: the absence of general moral rules complements the absence of institutions.

mortgages. Students must liberate them from such divisive contexts and all concern with the morrow, if need be by 'occupation'. Those academics who see the student evangelists as mere diseased enthusiasts must remember that they desire nothing worse, or less, than their salvation.

The end of man

The use of theological language in the foregoing analysis is not merely a matter of useful analogy or suggestive comparison. To read Marcuse is reminiscent of reading dialectical theology. The ideas of Sartre on the maintenance of revolutionary *élan* are the problems already faced in the sociology of religion in the development of sectarian consciousness, especially routinization of charisma and the bureaucratization of the spirit. Moreover, the radicals in the Church run parallel to, and often overlap, the radicals in the university. In Germany the religious elements and personnel in the protest have been remarked upon; and there has been a striking absence of the irreligion traditionally current among rebels. This is partly because the radicals in the Church draw on the same phenomenological, existentialist, humanizing, personalist – and ultimately Protestant and Hebraic traditions, as do many radicals in the university. Indeed there is something very proper in the fact that so many of our modern Protestants are Hebrews.

So the crisis runs back to the roots of our civilization: to its vital Hebraic component and to those two institutions which have a special social charter in terms of the injunction to be in the world and not of it. Because Church and university have this intrinsic spiritual element written into their charters they evoke the strongest loyalties and the most vigorous repudiations: loyalty to their aspiration, repudiation of their failures. The middle position between unthinking loyalty and unrealistic repudiation is the monastic and academic tradition, which tries to achieve the highest aspirations in limited enclaves. But this too invites its own corruptions, and creates a demand that the order leave the cloister and march into the world. The social élite must be evicted from the monasteries and the spiritual élite must leaven the lump of the secular world by itself becoming secularized.

Yet the Church and the university not only have spiritual aims but unite them with the task of moral and intellectual socialization. Originally this was done in close partnership until the differentiation of modern society split the roles between them: the university now has little to do with morals, and to the extent that the Church still has a continuing task of moral socialization, this has little to do with intellectual training. Yet, for various historical reasons the Church remains identified as a socializing agency when in fact it is being reduced perilously close to its fundamental *raison d'être*: the realm of the spirit. This is both dangerous and fruitful since all the lesions, disjunctions and backlogs of sudden social change have resulted in the tensions of the spirit becoming partly disembodied from their traditional language and institutional location. Hence the Church only partially reflects these tensions, just as it only partially performs the role of socialization.

The spirit attempts to relocate itself in the university. It cannot be disembodied, but there is an immediate problem of the right relation between spiritual aspects and other social functions. Just as the spirit cannot be disembodied, so no institution can exist *only* to express the spirit, because the spiritual and the secular are woven together not only empirically but also theoretically in the texture of western civilization. For the Church the problem was how to articulate a right relation between moral socialization and the spiritual dynamism of the Gospel. For the university now it is an even more complex task of articulating the right relation between economic and technical imperatives, intellectual socialization, and the urge to moral and spiritual activism.

When the Church was almost entirely bound up with moral socialization Protestantism attempted to break through the system by repudiating the whole structure of moral levels, and disciplines as mere works of the flesh. In the same way contemporary protesters try to wreck the whole system of levels, and degrees, of packaging and processing currently involved in intellectual socialization. Where the Protestants substituted the category of saved and unsaved the protesters substitute the category of true and false consciousness.

Yet the distinction between true and false consciousness, though related to, is *not* identical with, the distinction between truth and falsehood. It is this confusion which results in spiritual hubris, intellectual antinomianism and indiscipline of every kind. A vital relationship is converted into a near identity: learning is not therapy, knowledge is not ideology, because contemplation and action are neither identities nor rivals but complementary.

In a way, of course, all this has to do with the great Weberian themes and we must recognize the valid elements in the current protest. It attempts to counteract acquiescence, consensus politics, the divisive character of multiplying roles, anonymity, the elongated structure of bureaucratic power, indeed the whole process of rationalization conceived apart from overriding human purposes. It rejects knowledge without understanding, processes without community, power without purpose.

Weber argued that an indirect mutation of the Protestant spirit was essential to the birth of the modern world of capitalism and bureaucracy. By a curious irony it is an indirect mutation of capitalism and bureaucracy which produces the protesting spirit, not now canalized and distorted either by the psychic disciplines of capitalist accumulation or by the work disciplines of industrialism, but in a world of increasing automation and leisure able again to ask its own proper question: 'What is the chief end of Man?'[1]

1 Scottish Shorter Catechism.

Richard Layard and John King[1]
Expansion since Robbins

The explosion of higher education

Apart from electronics and natural gas, higher education has probably grown faster than any other major industry in the 1960s. It is bound to occupy a prominent place in the social histories of the period. From 1962–3 to 1967–8 the number of students in full-time higher education in Britain grew from 217,000 to 376,000 and the increase over these five years was greater than over the preceding twenty-five. An impression of the accelerating pace of change can be got from Chart A (p. 15). The universities grew rapidly and were much in the public eye, but in fact the colleges of education and the colleges of 'further education' (the technical colleges and the like) grew much faster and their numbers of students more than doubled in the period.

How has this fantastic explosion come about? It is best seen in terms of the demand and supply of places. Demand has grown particularly sharply over the last five years owing to the coincidence of 'bulge' and 'trend' – the 'bulge' being the increase in the number of young people of the relevant age (owing to the surge in births at the end of the War), and the 'trend' being the increase in the proportion of these who obtain school-leaving qualifications. The 'trend' was already, by 1961, a well-established phenomenon and has continued, though at a sharper rate, since then.

What accounts for this trend? It is impossible to answer this precisely. Doubtless a basic underlying cause is general economic growth. But why exactly does this raise the demand for education? People seek education both for its own sake as a form of 'consumption', and as an 'investment' providing the means to a higher income. As a good in itself, education is felt to add to the interest and grace of life; and when people get richer

1 This is an updated version of an article entitled 'The Impact of Robbins' in the *Higher Education Review*, Autumn 1968, based on a Penguin Education Special by Richard Layard, John King and Claus Moser. The work has been carried out in the Unit for Economic and Statistical Studies on Higher Education at L.S.E. Details on the statistical sources will be found in the book.

they seek more of it, just as they buy more novels or hi-fi sets. The education of a child places heavy costs on his family in terms of loss of earnings, even if tuition is free. And, as living standards rise, people can more easily afford to meet these costs, just as they can afford more of other forms of 'consumption'.

But people also want education as a way to better-paid jobs. And as a country grows richer, the labour market's demand for educated people rises relative to the demand for those with lesser skills – much of modern capital equipment can only be used by educated workers and so on. As a result the number of people for whom education can be financially profitable increases steadily, and more seek to be educated.

But growing national income is not the only cause of this. There are other important social factors at work, which do not depend directly on the growth of income. These factors may tend to raise the place of education in the scale of individual preferences. Perhaps the most important of them is the educational level of parents, which is known to have a potent effect on the educational aspirations and achievements of their children. In this way higher education tends to spread like an infectious disease, multiplying itself from generation to generation. Similarly, the more educated people there are in the community, the easier it is for young people to acquire information about education. Thus the growing public debate about higher education, in the press, radio and television, through parent-teacher associations and in Parliament, depends on a more or less educated public. In turn it informs growing numbers of young people and their parents about the opportunities in a higher education system which might otherwise remain incomprehensible and awesome. Likewise the spread of higher education tends to make possession of a higher qualification a more and more indispensable symbol of status. In these various ways, higher education resembles a snowball steadily growing by virtue of its own momentum. However, the resources of individual families and of public authorities impose limits on this process, and higher education's unparalleled growth since the second world war has happened largely because of the unprecedented rate of economic growth over the period.

An increased demand for places need not of course produce a magic increase in supply. This depends on the response of the suppliers. How has the Government responded? Let us begin with university provision. Table 1 shows the growth in the numbers of young people having two or more G.C.E. A levels and the growth in university entry. From 1957 to 1962 the average increase in the numbers with two or more A levels was relatively small compared with that experienced since. Yet the provision

CHART A   *Students in full-time higher education: Great Britain*

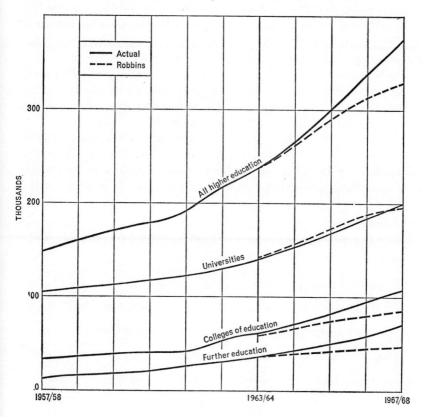

Note: Universities include former Colleges of Advanced Technology.

of university places grew a good deal less fast than the relevant group of school-leavers, and their opportunities declined proportionally. This was the context in which the Robbins Committee was appointed.

There were of course many reasons for the Committee's appointment – the need for administrative coordination between the different sectors, the problems posed by the rising academic standards and aspirations of the colleges of advanced technology and colleges of education, the difficulty of having the Treasury directly responsible for the increasing volume of public expenditure taken by universities, and the widespread feeling that all the parts of the system of higher education should be planned as a whole. But in essence all these problems sprang from the growth in demand for higher education and the consequent inflation of the system. In particular there was increasing public feeling that university entry was becoming more difficult – a feeling borne out by our figures.

There was at the time no clear Government philosophy on how to respond to the increasing flow of applicants. The Robbins Committee supplied a philosophy: the number of places should grow fast enough to accommodate a constant proportion of applicants. To be more precise,

TABLE I

Output of those with two or more A levels, and entrants to full-time higher education. (Persons from England and Wales)

	Numbers obtaining two or more A levels	University entrants (including former CATs)	All entrants	University entrants as % of two or more A levels	All entrants as % of two or more A levels
1956	27,000	21,000	36,000	79	133
1961	43,000	28,000	52,000	65	120
1962	51,000	30,000	57,000	59	112
1963	53,000	32,000	64,000	59	121
1964	61,000	36,000	74,000	59	121
1965	73,000	42,000	87,000	57	119
1966	75,000	43,000	95,000	57	126
1967	79,000	46,000	104,000	58	131

it recommended that the ratio of entrants to the output of those with two or more A levels should, over the period up to 1967, remain constant. As Table 1 shows, this is broadly speaking what has happened. Despite enormous increases in the number of well-qualified school-leavers, the numbers of university entrants and of entrants to all forms of higher education have since 1962 broadly kept pace with them. By the combined efforts of the Government, the local authorities and the institutions themselves, the downward trend in entry rates over the previous five years has been halted and the crisis of the 'bulge' surmounted without any serious aggravation of pressure on places. This in essence is the quantitative impact of Robbins.

It is not of course the whole story by any means. The object of this chapter is to look at the quantitative development of higher education since the Report and at how it has been determined. In particular, we shall compare what has happened with the projections in the Report. These projections involved two types of assumptions – predictive and prescriptive. Here we are asking first, were the predictions right, and, second, have the prescriptions been followed?

In building up its recommendations on places the Report proceeded through the following steps:[1] it forecast the output of 'qualified school-leavers'; it made assumptions about what proportion of these would apply to higher education and what proportion of those who did should be given places. This led to an estimate of entrants. It made assumptions about length of course and overseas students, thus providing an estimate of places. It also made recommendations on staffing and finance. The blueprint which resulted was the first overall plan for higher education in this country.[2]

Before we look at how the plan has worked out, we shall take a look at the Government's immediate reception of the plan and at the public's reaction to the way in which it was constructed.

Reception of the Report

Few official reports in British history, and certainly in educational history, have led to such immediate changes in Government policy. Many of the qualitative recommendations were, it is true, left in abeyance, but the quantitative recommendations up to 1973-4 were accepted in a White Paper published within 24 hours of the Report.[3] It is not cynical to

1 See *Higher Education*, Cmnd. 2154. H.M.S.O., 1963, Chapters VI and XI.
2 In what follows we shall confine ourselves to full-time higher education. On places and also on staffing, we deal with Britain, and on school leavers and entrants with people from England and Wales, as the Scottish data provide no meaningful time series.
3 *Higher Education, Government Statement on the Report of the Committee under the Chairmanship of Lord Robbins 1961–63*, Cmnd. 2165. H.M.S.O., 1963.

compare the treatment received by the Crowther Report published months after a General Election and the Plowden Report published months after another one, with that received by Robbins which came out a year before one. However, there were other powerful reasons for the Government's favourable response. In the first place the crisis of the 'bulge' was so near that there was no time to waste. Moreover, the very setting up of a committee and the debate which follows often completely changes the whole climate of public opinion about the issue being investigated. This is certainly what happened with Robbins. When the Committee was set up there was probably a majority of educated opinion, in the Civil Service and outside, in favour of the view that there was some limit that would soon be approached in the proportion of people who could benefit from higher education. But during the two and a half years of the Committee's work, this 'pool of ability' school of thought was in progressive retreat. The Committee's foreign visits helped to remind people of the lengths to which things seemed to have gone in other countries without loss of quality; and when the Report was published the Committee's Survey of twenty-one-year-olds further strengthened the hands of those who believed in the importance of environment in determining intellectual attainment. Thus by 1963 it seemed quite acceptable to look forward to an endless upward trend in higher education in the foreseeable future, and not, as had been customary, to look for a plateau.[1]

The public reception of the Report was also on the whole enthusiastic. Of the major papers, only *The Times* was noticeably hostile, and, although chided by Sir Geoffrey Crowther for intellectual 'Bourbonism',[2] its hostility did not diminish with time. A part of the trouble was based on a misunderstanding of the term 'qualified school-leavers'. This term had been used in the Report in an entirely neutral sense to mean those holding particular qualifications (e.g. two or more A levels) and not in a normative sense implying that such people were necessarily qualified for higher education. *The Times* in its leaders managed to imply that Robbins had said that all with two or more A levels should go to university if they wanted to. This point was ultimately clarified.[3]

Other critics questioned the appropriateness of numbers obtaining

---

1 It is also relevant that the Robbins figures for 1973–4 were not a great deal higher than for 1967–8, as the latter were swollen by the 'bulge'. This undoubtedly made the Government more willing to enter into a ten-year commitment than it might otherwise have been.
2 *The Times*, 28 October, 1963.
3 See *The Times*: Leaders of 28 September and 5 October 1964, and letters from C. A. Moser and P. R. G. Layard of 29 September and 8 October 1964.

G.C.E. as the basis from which to deduce numbers suitable for higher education, and they implied that this method somehow overestimated future requirements. This criticism assumes that past trends in G.C.E. have not corresponded to trends in numbers suitable for higher education. In fact we believe these two trends have been broadly similar. This was the reason for the claim in the Report[1] that what is being projected *is* a number proportional to those suitable for higher education, and that for convenience only we label this number by familiar qualifications. The method would not be invalidated even if G.C.E. were abolished.

An annual signal for the 'limited pool of ability' school to show itself has been the publication of the figures of vacancies in university departments. It is true that these vacancies, which are almost entirely in science and technology, raise important issues of the balance between faculties, but they normally represent not more than 1 or 2 per cent of all places. Moreover the annual expansion in student numbers is always many times the number of vacancies in the previous year. Though frictional under-utilization of capacity should be cut to the minimum, it is hardly a sign that the general philosophy of expansion is wrong. There is no shortage of well-qualified applicants overall, though there is a mis-balance between faculties.

A more fundamental criticism attacked the whole philosophy of basing provision on the demand of school-leavers for places, rather than on the demand from the economy for the products of the system. The Robbins Committee rejected this latter basis, both because of their desire to meet the 'social' demand from boys and girls, and because of their doubts about techniques of manpower forecasting.

There is a strong case in principle for basing the provision of education on cost-benefit criteria – benefits being defined in the widest possible way to include psychic as well as more directly measurable effects.[2] This would involve calculating the current rates of return obtained by using current income differentials, and also attempting to estimate future shifts in the demand for educated manpower by isolating the variables which affect it.

---

1 *Appendix One*, p. 97.
2 On general issues of objectives in educational planning see Moser and Layard 'Planning the Scale of Higher Education in Britain: Some Statistical Problems' *J.R.S.S.* Series A, 4, 1964; M. Blaug 'Approaches to Educational Planning', *The Economic Journal*, June 1967; and Peter Armitage, Cyril Smith and Paul Alper, *Decision Models for Educational Planning*, Allen Lane, The Penguin Press (forthcoming). Explicitly on social rate of return see Blaug 'The Rate of Return on Investment in Education in Great Britain', *The Manchester School*, September, 1965.

At present a good deal of work is proceeding on both these fronts in our Unit[1] and elsewhere, but it is not yet sufficiently advanced to form a basis for projections derived directly from manpower requirements.

However, it is wrong to underestimate the link between the growth in numbers who would be justified on social cost-benefit grounds and the numbers which would arise on the Robbins criteria of demand for places. For the private demand for places depends, we think, largely on the private rate of return to be got from undertaking higher education, while the number of places justified on cost-benefit grounds depends on the social rate of return. On a number of quite plausible assumptions these two rates of return will move in step;[2] thus private demand will surge forward only when people with higher education can be productively employed and vice versa. One key assumption, however, is the continuation of present policies on subsidies to students. The Robbins Committee judged that, given prevailing attitudes to education, these ought to be maintained for a time, on social grounds. It is clear, however, that if the private price were raised, the private demand would be lower than otherwise. The Robbins Committee have been wrongly charged with being unaware of the fact.[3]

A quite different line of criticism has come from those who think that, though there may be enough suitable students worth educating there will not be enough staff. The Report contained the tautological statement that on certain assumptions a system expanding at a constant or declining rate of compound interest could staff itself. This was admitted to be true, but critics argued that the steady state assumption was irrelevant and that short-run problems were formidable.[4] Calculations in the Report had in fact explicitly pointed to these short-run problems. But events have on the whole disproved these fears, and student-staff ratios have even fallen in most faculties. At the same time teachers' salaries have not in general

1 The Unit for Economic and Statistical Studies on Higher Education at L.S.E.
2 The social rate of return depends on the pre-tax income differential between people with and without higher education and on the social cost of higher education. The private rate of return depends on the above together with the rates of taxation and the rates of subsidy of higher education. Thus the absolute level of private and social rates of return differ. But suppose the demand for educated people, viewed as a function of their relative wages, grows at a given rate, that proportional tax rates are constant and that social costs and subsidies rise at the same rate as average wages per head. Then the shift in supply of educated people needed to keep the social rate of return constant will also maintain the private rate of return at its present level, assuming no change in the relative importance of 'external' benefits.
3 See the *Robbins Report* para. 645 and *Appendix One*, p. 100, para. 15.
4 See Professor Thwaites at The Home Universities Conference, December 1963.

moved adversely to other salaries. The success of the expansion programme is thus due to the fact that in a general sense the Government not only willed the end but also willed the means.

Trends in qualified school-leavers

Now to the trends. As we explained, the Committee's recommendations for places were built up step by step starting with a projection of the output of well-qualified school-leavers. As is well known, this projection has turned out to be too low. The position can be summarized in the tables below.

The 'bulge, was of course predictable, and accurately so – the number of eighteen-year-olds can be forecast more or less right for up to eighteen years ahead. The problem was the trend. Robbins predicted that the proportion of the age group obtaining two or more A levels would rise from 6·9 per cent in 1961 to 8·8 per cent in 1967. In fact, as Table 2 shows, it rose to 10·9 per cent. Thus the actual increase over the six years was 4·0 per cent of the age group – an average of over 0·6 per cent a year, compared with a forecast of 0·3 per cent. These figures are shown in Table 3 together with the comparable figures for the earlier years.

The really striking point is that in the earlier years the average increase was under 0·4 per cent. Thus the 1960s have seen a sharp upswing in the tendency to get A levels. The upswing has been much greater for girls than boys, and the error in the Robbins prediction was greater for girls

TABLE 2

Percentage of the age group obtaining two or more A levels and percentage staying at school aged seventeen. (England and Wales)

			Percentage	
			1967	
	1954	*1961*	*Actual*	*Robbins*
Obtaining 2 or more A levels				
Boys	5·7	8·7	13·0	*11·1*
Girls	2·9	5·1	8·6	*6·3*
Boys and girls	4·3	6·9	10·9	*8·8*
At school aged 17				
Boys	8·6	13·1	17·4	*16·8*
Girls	7·1	10·2	14·6	*12·6*
Boys and girls	7·9	11·7	16·0	*14·8*

Cac

TABLE 3

Average annual increment in the percentages of the age group obtaining two or more A levels and staying at school aged seventeen. (England and Wales)

	1954–61	1961–67 Actual	Robbins
Obtaining 2 or more A levels			
Boys	0·43	0·72	0·42
Girls	0·31	0·58	0·21
Boys and girls	0·37	0·67	0·31
At school aged 17			
Boys	0·65	0·72	0·64
Girls	0·44	0·75	0·41
Boys and girls	0·54	0·74	0·53

than boys. In fact from 1961 to 1967 the average annual increment in proportions with A levels was almost as high for girls as for boys. And if we express the increment as a percentage rate of growth (on the 1961 base) it is much higher – an 11 per cent rate of growth for girls compared with 8 per cent for boys. Bit by bit the sex gap is closing.

These results have amply confirmed the warning of the Robbins Committee that their projection of places needed should be regarded as a minimum, and their view that the projections were particularly conservative in the case of girls. We are not able to say, except in terms of arithmetic, why the trend in achievement has been so much higher since 1961 than before; but it may well be that the Report itself and the atmosphere it created has contributed to the outcome.

Arithmetically we can examine the two components in the forecast of output: first, the numbers staying on at school, and second, the proportion of these who get good qualifications. If we do this, we find that the Robbins estimates of the trend to stay at school have been relatively accurate (especially in 1965 and earlier) – the growth in the percentage staying on to each age being fairly well in line with that predicted by linear extrapolation of the experience of 1954–62. This illustrates an interesting fact about the British (and many other) educational systems. Suppose we want to predict the numbers of seventeen-year-olds at school at a given time. The simplest method would be to project the past trends in the absolute numbers, but in this particular period this would have produced hopelessly wrong results. For the size of the age group (which in this period fluctuated wildly) profoundly affected the numbers staying on in school. However, if we take this as given, the proportion of people of each age who stay at school shows an uncannily stable trend. The mechanism whereby this comes about must be complicated. One can imagine that in any particular year the pattern of attainments among a cohort is independent of its size, and that it is this pattern that determines, via its effect on attitudes of school teachers, parents and children, the proportion who stay on. Even so, it is remarkable that the absolute number appears to be more or less irrelevant, considering that it is the absolute number who have to be provided with desks and teachers and the absolute number who have to find suitable jobs. The stability of these trends in staying on makes it clear that the adjustment of private educational behaviour to market opportunities is subject to important time-lags and that other important long-term influences may also be at work.

Though the Robbins 'staying on' forecast was fairly successful, the A level forecast went wrong; whereas the Robbins Committee assumed that the proportions of leavers of each age who obtain a given qualification would remain constant, they have in fact risen. The reasons are not too clear. The proportions clearly cannot go on rising above 100 per cent, and projections done at the Department of Education and Science since Robbins normally assume that their future rate of increase will be less than in the past. The result, as illustrated in Table 3, is that the projected growth in the percentage of the age group getting A levels has tended to be smaller than that in the past.[1]

Universities

Granted the output of qualified school-leavers, we can now examine the course of university expansion and see how opportunities of entry have been affected by Government policy. As soon as the Government accepted the Robbins target of 197,000 places in universities (including former colleges of advanced technology) for 1967–8, the Chairman of the University Grants Committee wrote to all the universities asking them to say what they thought they could do to help to achieve this target and how much it would cost them. The required increase in places amounted to 40 per cent over four years, yet in their replies, the universities said they

[1] This raises an important statistical question as to whether it is best to make separate projections for the two stages mentioned – first 'staying on' and then the proportion of stayers on who qualify – or whether a more accurate answer might not be obtained by projecting the A level proportions directly. For a number of reasons, we prefer the latter approach, even though it produces the statistical inconvenience of not being able directly to relate the A level projection to that of school population.

could provide some 20,000 places more than were needed – a magnificent response which considerably surprised those who hold a general belief that universities are impervious to social need. The response was undoubtedly influenced by the euphoric atmosphere induced by the publication of the Report, and also perhaps to some extent by the new opportunities offered by such an expansion. It did, however, dispel – one hopes for ever – the picture of universities as exclusive clubs which cannot bear to expand their membership. When we show (later) that other sectors have expanded faster than the universities, the reader should not forget that this is by the wish of the Government and not of the universities.

In the revision of the quinquennial settlement which followed, the universities, in receiving their new recurrent allocations, were asked to provide a total of places equal to the Robbins target. This they have done almost to the letter, as Table 4 shows. The Robbins targets were based on the objective of maintaining the 1961 ratio between entrants and the output of well-qualified leavers. As compared with Robbins, the number of entrants (except in 1967) has been almost exactly as recommended, but of

TABLE 4

Students in full-time higher education. (Great Britain, thousands)

	Universities (including former CATs)		Colleges of education		Further education		All full-time higher education		Percentage of places in universities	
	Actual	Robbins	Actual	Robbins	Actual	Robbins	Actual	Robbins	Actual	Robbins
1957–8	103	—	33	—	13	—	148	—	70	—
1961–2	123	—	42	—	27	—	192	—	64	—
1962–3	131	—	55	—	31	—	217	—	60	—
1963–4	140	*142*	62	*59*	36	*36*	238	*238*	59	*60*
1964–5	154	*156*	71	*66*	43	*39*	267	*262*	57	*60*
1965–6	169	*173*	82	*74*	51	*42*	302	*290*	56	*60*
1966–7	184	*187*	95	*80*	59	*45*	339	*312*	54	*60*
1967–8	200	*197*	106	*84*	71	*47*	376	*328*	53	*60*
Percentage growth 1962–3 to 1967–8	53	*50*	93	*54*	129	*51*	74	*51*	—	—

course the numbers of school leavers with A level has been higher, by as much as 26 per cent in 1967. Thus the proportion of 'qualified school-leavers' entering university has fallen by about 10 per cent of itself since 1961. There is still a good case for getting back to the 1961 proportion.

The recent quinquennial settlement for the years 1967–8 to 1971–2 does not achieve this. It provides for an increase of about 20,000 places over the Robbins targets for 1971–2: 220,000 to 225,000 places being the new official target.[1] But by that year we can expect (using the Department's latest projection) an output of people with two or more A levels some 21 per cent higher than Robbins. This implies that the entry rate in 1971 will be only some 90 per cent of its 1961 value.

There remains, however, the critical problem of the subject balance in the intake.[2] In the late 1950s and early 1960s it was the policy of the U.G.C., reiterated by Robbins, that two-thirds of additional places in universities should be in science and technology. The point of view was that the total size of the universities should be based on a passive response to popular demand, this demand being taken as relatively impervious to policy. On the other hand it was felt that the subject balance within the resulting total could be based on manpower considerations and that attempts to manage demand in this sense could be successful. They have proved a complete failure. The swing away from science in the sixth forms, that began in 1959 and was first noticed in the Robbins Report,[3] has continued; and the universities, faced with a growing proportion of good candidates in arts, have responded in an essentially passive manner. Entry rates in arts and science have moved roughly speaking together and though it may have become marginally more difficult to find a place in arts relative to science, the change does not come out strongly in the statistics. As a result, instead of two-thirds of the extra students in universities (excluding colleges of advanced technology) being in science and technology, the proportion of the extra places provided from 1961–2 to 1966–7 has been only 37 per cent. If we include colleges of advanced technology in both years the proportion was 43 per cent. As Table 5 shows, the proportion of all places in arts subjects has risen from 40 to 44 per cent instead of falling to 37 per cent. How are we to interpret this outcome? It is undoubtedly a failure of planning, since it implies that the capital investment in science has been higher relative to arts than it would have been if the ensuing teaching commitments had been foreseen. This debacle has arisen from the fact that, paradoxically, the universities, which are often thought to be outside social control, are in fact much more centrally planned than the schools. There is no advance planning of the size of sixth forms, still less of their subject balance. One reason for this is, of

1 See *Hansard*, 27 October 1967, Cols. 591–2.
2 On the issues discussed below see also Moser and Layard, *op. cit.*, pp. 510–11.
3 *Robbins Report*, pp. 163–4.

course, that the sixth forms constitute a small part of the school population and substantial changes in them can be fairly easily absorbed. The
main instrument of planning in the educational system is via the control
of capital expenditure, but most sixth forms have no specific buildings,
and therefore those who sanction capital expenditure are not required to

TABLE 5

*Places in universities (including former CATs) by faculty. (Great Britain,
1961–2 and 1966–7)*

	Arts	Pure science	Applied science	Medicine	Agriculture	Total
Number (thousands) Actual						
1961–2	49·3	31·4	24·1	16·6	2·1	123·5
1966–7	81·3	44·4	37·0	18·9	2·5	184·1
Robbins						
1966–7	*68·9*	*52·7*	*43·8*	*19·0*	*2·5*	*186·9*
Percentage Actual						
1961–2	40·0	25·4	19·5	13·4	1·7	100·0
1966–7	44·1	24·1	20·1	10·3	1·4	100·0
Robbins						
1966–7	*36·9*	*28·2*	*23·4*	*10·2*	*1·3*	*100·0*

form a view about the sixth forms; nor, if they had a view, would they
have any ready means of implementing it. There seem two ways out of
this situation: to take an active manpower-orientated policy in the schools;
or to stop taking one in the universities.

The U.G.C. have now overtly opted for the latter. For the first time
they issued (in November 1967) a 'Memorandum of general guidance'
explaining general ideas lying behind the allocations of the final quinquennial settlement announced in the same month.[1] This is what the
statement said about subject balance: 'The Committee have taken the
view that in the light of present A level trends the major increase must be
in the number of arts-based, rather than science-based students.' Among

[1] University Grants Committee, *Annual Survey/Academic Year/1966–67*, Cmnd.
3510. H.M.S.O., 1968, Appendix C.

other paradoxical results, this has had the effect of sharply restricting the prospective growth of the former colleges of advanced technology, which, had they not become universities would now be a major focus of expansion. A different approach informs the Report of the Dainton Committee.[1] They believe that the swing is highly undesirable and that it must be halted by an active policy in the schools. This argument is based largely on the evidence of the Triennial Manpower Survey of Engineers, Technologists, Scientists and Technical Supporting Staff.[2] This survey collects evidence on employers' opinions about short-term demands. Such evidence is difficult to interpret, and it is necessary at least to consider the alternative argument that an accelerated production of scientists and engineers would require an over-investment in those sectors of education.

In short, it is desirable to look at the economics of the swing. This involves knowing the salary differentials between graduates in different subjects, and it is unfortunate that we do not yet have usable statistics on these.[3] But common observation suggests that, if scientists and engineers do command any premium, it is not large.[4] And scientists and engineers cost a lot more to produce than arts graduates. So if each group of graduates were being paid the value of their (marginal) product, it would seem to follow that society's return is just as high in producing arts as science graduates.

But are graduates being paid their economic value? The average salaries of arts graduates are strongly influenced by the salaries of the high proportion of them who are in the teaching profession, this being much less true for science teachers. Now the teaching profession is remarkable in its insistence that teachers shall be paid similarly in all subjects, regardless of the state of supply and demand in different fields. As a result, a shortage of graduate science teachers may lead to a pay rise for teachers of modern

1 Council for Scientific Policy, *Enquiry into the Flow of Candidates in Science and Technology into Higher Education*, Cmnd. 3541. H.M.S.O., 1968 (The Dainton Report). See also Committee on Manpower Resources for Science and Technology, *The Flow into Employment of Scientists, Engineers and Technologists*, Report of the Working Group on Manpower for Scientific Growth, Cmnd. 3760. H.M.S.O., 1968 (The Swann Report), and C. M. Phillips, *Changes in Subject Choice at School and University*, Weidenfeld & Nicolson (forthcoming).
2 Dainton Report, para. 5.
3 A follow-up study of a sample of graduates from the 1966 Sample Census currently being undertaken on behalf of the Department of Education and Science will help here.
4 The case of doctors is different and their high pay explains the still strong demand to study medicine better than the Dainton explanation that the subject is 'in touch with human and social affairs' (para. 151), which was equally true in the 1950s.

languages – the purpose of the rise being to make science teachers' pay competitive with the pay of scientists in industry. This must be an extremely important mechanism for equating the prospects of arts and science graduates. It also brings home the dangers of inferring the true value of a person's work from his actual rate of pay. For this reason the broad conclusions of the Dainton Committee seem to us right and important. The country may not be notably short of scientific specialists, but it is very likely that good returns could be got from increasing the level of general scientific understanding among educated people. Mathematics has a key role in this and the greatest manpower bottleneck in the country now is probably the shortage of mathematics teachers to implement the Dainton recommendation of mathematics for all in the sixth forms.

There is one other major point we should like to make on the question of university expansion. The Robbins Committee looked not only to 1973-4 but also to 1980-1. It estimated the places needed then and obtained from the U.G.C. an estimate of the numbers who could be accommodated in existing universities. (This included the 'new' universities which, contrary to common impression, were conceived before Robbins.) After allowing for the upgrading of some non-university institutions, there was left a gap of 30,000 places which the Committee said should be filled by six further universities, of which one should be a so-called 'SISTER' – a Special Institution for Scientific and Technological Education and Research, designed to strengthen the appeal of technology and to win for applied studies a proportion of the bright lads who are now so predisposed to pure research. In the event the 'overbidding' by the universities in their immediate response to the Report led the Government to think that the U.G.C. might have also underestimated the potential capacity of existing universities in 1980–1. For this reason, and because of its 'binary' philosophy (on which more below), the Government rejected the idea of the six further universities. They also rejected the idea of SISTERS. The higher trend in A level output might, however, make them think again, and the case is particularly compelling for a brand new institution concentrating on really high level technological studies to be founded in the early 1970s.

Finally, at a more detailed level, it is pleasing to note that the proportion of graduates going on to postgraduate studies has grown faster even than the Report suggested, by at least 6 per cent a year (on its 1961 level) as compared with $2\frac{1}{2}$ per cent recommended. But is the recent rate of growth of postgraduate study an unmixed blessing? The U.G.C. think not, and in making their quinquennial allocations 'have consciously taken the view that undergraduate numbers are a genuine priority'. In this they have been strongly influenced by a growing school of thought among scientists typified in the Swann Committee's recent report. According to this, the effect of postgraduate study, and especially of the Ph.D. as it exists at present, is to direct too many of our best scientists and engineers to careers in research rather than in industrial production or school-teaching, where the greatest shortages exist. The evidence for this view is strong and we would not argue with it. But it seems quite doubtful whether the same line of argument applies in, for example, the social sciences. Postgraduate study is far less common in these subjects – only 14 per cent of students are postgraduates compared with over 20 per cent in science and technology, and the difference is even greater if overseas students are excluded. The demand for professionally competent social scientists is extremely high and it is increasingly difficult to be professionally competent without some postgraduate training. It will therefore be a pity if the limits on postgraduate expansion are applied indiscriminately.

While postgraduate numbers have grown faster than Robbins recommended, the proportion of overseas students, which Robbins recommended should remain constant, has fallen from 11·5 per cent in 1961–2 to 9·4 per cent in 1966–7.[1] Overseas students have come to represent a much smaller proportion of undergraduates, while remaining a fairly constant (or a slightly declining) proportion of postgraduates. This outcome is in line with the advice which the Chairman of the U.G.C. gave the universities in the letter which he wrote to Vice-Chancellors after the publication of the Robbins Report. In it he said: 'In the emergency period up to 1967–8 the Committee feel that the universities will not dissent from the view that priority should be given to the increase in the home demand, on which the Robbins figures now adopted were calculated; and that a corresponding proportionate increase in the intake of overseas students could not be expected.' The advice caused some despondency among the protagonists of the underdeveloped countries, but appears in fact to have been broadly followed. The absolute number of overseas undergraduates had already been stable since 1961–2 and has continued so. The number of overseas postgraduates has risen, but as a proportion of the total they have slightly declined – the decline occurring mainly in humanities and social studies. Further growth in the number of overseas students will now be less than it otherwise would have been, owing to the decision of Mr Crosland in December 1966 to press the universities to

[1] In further education too the proportion fell from 18·0 per cent in 1961–2 to 13·0 per cent in 1966–7.

raise their fees to overseas students to £250 a year as compared with the normal fee of £50.

Taken all in all, however, university development has followed fairly closely the lines proposed by Robbins. But the relationship between the universities and the rest of higher education has developed quite otherwise. As Table 4 showed, the universities provided 60 per cent of the places in higher education in 1962–3 and Robbins recommended the same proportion for 1967–8. But the actual proportion was 53 per cent. When the number of well-qualified school-leavers rose above the Robbins prediction, the Government abandoned the Robbins principle that a constant (1961) proportion should go to university and stuck to the Robbins number of places. The increased supply of students was channelled into the non-university sector. But behind this outcome lay a more fundamental divergence between the Government's and the Robbins Committee's view of the role of the universities in the system of higher education.

The binary system

This is not the place to dwell on the qualitative and administrative recommendations of the Robbins Report nor on the extent to which they have been implemented.[1] There is, however, the one issue of the 'binary system', which has major quantitative as well as administrative implications and must therefore be looked at.

As we said earlier, the quantitative aspects of the Robbins Report were accepted by the Government at the outset and have left a major impact on national history. A good number of the administrative recommendations were also accepted – for example the turning of the colleges of advanced technology into universities, the establishment of the Council for National Academic Awards, and the introduction of a B.Ed. in colleges of education.

But two of the most important administrative proposals were ultimately rejected. First, where Robbins had opted for two Ministries (one for universities and science, and another for the rest of education) the Conservative Government decided, after some months of deliberation and political infighting, to have a unified Department of Education and Science.[2] This decision must have affected the quantitative development of higher education, but it is impossible to tell whether it promoted or discouraged it.

1 For a discussion of such questions see Lord Robbins, *The University in the Modern World*. Macmillan, 1966, esp. Chapter 8.
2 This decision became effective on 1 April 1964.

The second major administrative decision going against the Robbins recommendations was left to the Labour Government and its Secretary of
State, Michael Stewart. The Robbins Committee had recommended that the
colleges of education should become parts of universities, being federated
into university schools of education. Each school would be financed through
its university and would be academically responsible to the senate. After
over a year's discussion the colleges and the universities (or nearly all of
them) came out in favour of the marriage, but the University Grants Committee raised an impediment and, on their recommendation, the Secretary
of State decided that 'for the present the colleges should continue to be
administered by the existing maintaining bodies'.[1] There were a number of
weighty practical, as well as the more philosophical, arguments in favour
of this decision – in particular the argument that in a period of acute shortage of primary (and especially of infant) schoolteachers, it could be
disastrous to remove the colleges from relatively direct Ministerial control.

But the period of acute shortage will pass and it was therefore encourag-
ing to note the phrase 'for the present' in the official announcement.
However, it was only months after this announcement that Mr Stewart's
successor, Anthony Crosland, enunciated in a speech at the Woolwich
Polytechnic a new principle to underline future Government policy, which
implied that the divorce between the universities and the rest of higher
education was to be regarded as permanent.[2]

This was the 'binary' principle, which said in essence that there should
be two systems of higher education at degree level, one in the autonomous
sector (the universities) and one in the publicly-controlled sector (the
technical colleges and the colleges of education); and the second should be
developed more rapidly than the first.

The issues involved here were, and remain, extremely complex, powerful
arguments existing for and against the policy. This is not the place to do
more than record them in summary form. The arguments in favour of the
policy include the following:

1. Universities are unwilling to develop applied studies at a high level
   on a large enough scale, and are correspondingly remote from industry
   and commerce.
2. Universities provide little part-time education and it is vital for part-
   time students that they can be taught in institutions which also provide
   high quality full-time education.

1 The decision was announced in the House of Commons on 11 December 1964.
2 The speech was given on 27 April 1965.

3. Bright young people from working class homes are either put off by universities or have qualifications (such as Ordinary National Certificates) which universities will not accept as satisfying entry requirements.
4. Universities are not sufficiently accessible to Government control for these evils to be remedied.
5. The unit cost of producing a comparably educated student is less in a technical college than a university.

Some of the arguments against the policy are:

1. Only the universities can give real status to applied studies.
2. Students will continue to put universities as their first choice; the binary policy by restricting university places will intensify the unhealthy competition for university entry.
3. A binary policy involves dispersion of resources on too many institutions and fails to reap the economies of placing large numbers of students in contact with the best brains, most of whom may want to work in universities.
4. There is no evidence that it is cheaper on average to produce graduates in technical colleges than in universities, even if we include the cost of university research in the cost of producing graduates; in terms of marginal costs it may be less sensible to expand relatively small colleges with staffs appointed for lesser responsibilities, than to create new universities.

Without elaborating on the debate we cannot help saying we are convinced that the binary philosophy is wrong and that, in so far as it is implemented, it will involve a greater waste of national resources than a policy in which the universities were given a larger role.[1]

Happily the policy has only been implemented in part. Its main concrete expression so far is the plan to create thirty polytechnics of ultimately around 2,000 full-time students each. These will be based on existing technical and other colleges and their staffs, though it seems likely that a considerable number of them will in fact involve a physical change of site.[2] However, on top of this, further education and teacher training have already expanded a great deal faster than the universities. It is time to look at the remarkable developments in these sectors.

1 For the Robbins Committee's arguments in favour of a central role for the universities see the *Report*, pp. 150–2 and 117–21.
2 See Department of Education and Science, *A Plan for Polytechnics and Other Colleges*, Cmnd. 3006. H.M.S.O., 1966.

Teacher training

The Robbins Committee recommended that teacher training should grow faster in the 1960s than any other sector: the shortage of school teachers (especially in primary schools) demanded nothing less. While the Committee were sitting the Government had announced a programme for about 80,000 places in England and Wales by 1970–1.[1] The Committee were told by the Ministry that, given the constraints of buildings, staff and the adaptive capacity of the colleges, it would be impossible to go above this plan in any year before 1969. However, from that year onwards the Committee recommended a further steep increase to 111,000 places by 1973–4.

In the event, the Robbins recommendations, and by the same token the 80,000 place programme, have been greatly exceeded – by about 26 per cent by 1967–8. This is mainly the result of the efforts of the Department to increase the productivity of the colleges and of the colleges' splendid response. The Department's interest in achieving increased productivity was long-standing, but the real drive for it stemmed from Mr Crosland's request to the colleges early in 1965 that they should, with minor modifications, use their buildings (already existing and planned) to house 20 per cent more students than originally envisaged.[2] Their recurrent finance was, however, adjusted so that the staff-student ratio was maintained. As a result the entry to colleges of education in England and Wales in 1967 was 35,000 compared with 26,400 in Robbins. Whether an increase of this order would have been possible if the output of qualified school leavers had been as projected by Robbins is uncertain. It probably would have been, with some reduction in the average qualifications of entrants. But the actual increase has been accompanied by no such reduction. This is due to the increased output of qualified school leavers. Since the rate of university expansion has not increased *pari passu*, a growing proportion of qualified school leavers have applied to colleges of education and a growing proportion of these have been admitted.

Plans for the future are still (at the time of writing) officially the 111,000 places in Robbins. However, this number of places will be nearly reached by 1969–70 with no further increase in entry over the present level. We can therefore be sure it will be exceeded.

1 The plan was for 80,000 places in 'general' and 'specialist' colleges. If all colleges are included (technical teacher training colleges as well) about 82,000 places were implied.
2 See College Letter No. 7/65 of 3 July 1965, following Mr Crosland's speech to the N.U.T. at Douglas in April 1965.

Further education

In further education too, the Robbins recommendations have been greatly exceeded, though by a quite different mechanism. This sector has always, since the war, acted as the safety valve for higher education, mopping up the demand not satisfied in the other sectors, and of course handling it in its own particular way. The Robbins Committee cast it in the same light in the future, and since it envisaged a constant (and, later, rising) entry rate to universities and a rising entry rate to colleges of education, it recommended a slightly falling entry rate to further education. In the event further education seems to have performed exactly the pre-assigned role, but the magnitudes have been different. The university entry rate has fallen since 1961 and the entry rate to further education has risen, bringing the number of entrants high above the Robbins target. This has happened less because buildings have been more intensively used (since in further education buildings can fairly easily be switched from non-advanced to advanced work) than because of increased student demand. It is because the demand can be absorbed in this way that the overall entry rate to higher education as a whole has remained relatively stable.

TABLE 6

Students on full-time advanced further education: by type of course. (England and Wales, 1961–2 to 1966–7)

| | *Thousands* | | *Percentage growth* |
	1961–2	*1966–7*	
London degrees	4·2	12·3	190
C.N.A.A. degrees and Dip. Tech.	1·3	6·9	438
H.N.D.	4·0	11·9	200
National Diploma in Design	5·8	6·4	10
Professional qualifications	8·5	17·0	100
Total	23·8	54·5	129

Which courses have expanded fastest? As we should expect, it is the degree courses. In 1961–2 there were 5,500 students on these courses, if we include for comparability the Diploma in Technology courses, most of which have now been converted to degree courses of the Council for National Academic Awards. Five years later, as Table 6 shows, the number had risen to over 19,000. Higher National Diploma courses have also grown rapidly while art courses have been more or less static.

Looking to the future, the plan for polytechnics will clearly encourage rapid expansion in further education. But, if we accept the safety-valve analogy, its expansion will also depend on the relation between the future growth in well-qualified leavers and the expansion of the universities.

The future

After a period of violent expansion, higher education is now moving into one of relative tranquillity, at least in terms of overall numbers. According to the latest projection by the Department of Education and Science the number of well-qualified leavers will be roughly static from 1967 to 1971, the continuance of the 'trend' being just sufficient to offset the declining numbers of eighteen-year-olds.

If this is correct, the present plans for universities will provide places roughly sufficient to maintain the entry rates of 1962 and after but not to revert to the 1961 rate, which would require a further 10 per cent or so of places. However, as we have seen, there seems to be a general mechanism which keeps the overall entry rate to higher education roughly constant. The Robbins Committee believed, moreover, that in a period when demographic pressures were suddenly relaxed there would be a tendency for the application rate to higher education as a whole to rise: the figure set on this was an overall rise of 10 per cent between 1967 and 1972; thus to keep the degree of competition constant would require an increase in entry rate of 10 per cent. The Robbins Committee envisaged that in the short-run this extra demand should be absorbed in teacher training and further education. It would certainly be consistent with present Government policy if this were to happen.

At present the new Planning Branch at the Department is undertaking the first comprehensive reappraisal of policy in higher education since the Robbins Report; and, particularly in the present uncertainties about public expenditure, it is not possible to predict what policy measures will emerge. But, granted the current expansionary momentum in teacher training and further education, it seems likely that the overall provision of higher education in 1971 will be as high as the Robbins approach would require, though its composition will be somewhat biased against the universities.

Changes of the kind we have already experienced would have been inconceivable even five years ago. Doubts abounded not only about the availability of suitable students ('more means worse'), but also about the ability of the institutions to adapt to expansion. The performance of each of the sectors, and most of all perhaps of the colleges of education, have confounded the doubters. Though a period of ease is now around the corner, rapid expansion will be needed again from the mid-1970s. This will only be daunting if the achievements of the last five years are forgotten.

A. H. Halsey and M. Trow

University teaching: the structure of a profession[1]

There are now over 25,000 university teachers in Great Britain apart
from some 2,000 part-timers. An understanding of the present problems,
discontents and conflicts within the British universities must involve a
study of the changing role of the don. This chapter constitutes a sketch
of the structure of the university teaching professions and their development in the recent past. It is a numerical outline covering the period from
the beginning of this century during which the role of the university
teacher has been transformed by expansion and specialization. This means
that the number of universities, colleges and departments has grown,
that the status structure of the professions has lengthened and that
specialisms have proliferated. These developments can be traced in public
statistics on the distribution of university teachers between universities,
grades or academic ranks and faculties or subjects. We deal with each
of these fundamental divisions in turn, tracing their development in this
century as far as available statistics allow.[2]

University groups

Among the forty-four university institutions[3] in Britain in 1968, eight
university groups may be distinguished, both academically and socially,

1 This chapter is a modified excerpt from A. H. Halsey and M. Trow *The British
  Academics* Faber and Faber, forthcoming.
2 The statistics, however, are unusually imperfect because of changes in administrative habits during the course of the century and especially because of the
  vagaries of Oxford and Cambridge records. The main source from 1919 is the
  U.G.C. in its Annual and Quinquennial Returns. Only for 1965–6 (Cmnd. 3586)
  is it possible, for the first time, to discover an exact count of the number of
  university teachers irrespective of the source of funds for their employment.
3 The University Grants Committee list for 1965–6 'covered 44 university institutions (including the former Colleges of Advanced Technology and the Heriot-
  Watt College). Of these institutions 35 were in England (Aston, Bath, Birmingham, Bradford, Bristol, Brunel, Cambridge, Chelsea, City, Durham, East Anglia,
  Essex, Exeter, Hull, Keele, Kent, Lancaster, Leeds, Leicester, Liverpool,

according to age and location. These groupings have significance for the life and career of the university teachers and for the pattern of relations between staff and students.

The largest group, accounting for more than a quarter of all university teachers, is made up of the universities in the great provincial industrial cities. They are Birmingham, Bristol, Durham, Leeds, Liverpool, Manchester, Newcastle and Sheffield. Most of the 'major redbrick' universities received their charters within a few years of the turn of the nineteenth and twentieth centuries. The second largest group, employing a fifth of the university teachers, is made up of constituent colleges of the University of London. London received its charter in 1836, mainly on the basis of the recently formed University and King's Colleges; it is now composed of thirty-three self-governing schools and thirteen institutes directly controlled by the university. Third in order, making up 14·9 per cent of the total are the seven Scottish university institutions: Aberdeen, Edinburgh, Glasgow, Heriot-Watt, St Andrews, Strathclyde and Stirling. Of these St Andrews is the oldest with a foundation in 1410 though with an additional college at Dundee founded in 1881. Aberdeen, Edinburgh and Glasgow are fifteenth- and sixteenth-century foundations. The Royal College of Science and Technology at Glasgow goes back to 1796, but received a charter as the University of Strathclyde in 1964. Stirling is new.

The other five groups each represent less than 10 per cent of the total. The fourth group in numerical order is a group of six 'minor redbrick' universities. Five of these were at one time provincial colleges preparing students for the examinations of the University of London. They received

3 (*cont.*)

    London, Loughborough, Manchester, Manchester Institute of Science and Technology (U.M.I.S.T.), Newcastle upon Tyne, Nottingham, Oxford, Reading, Salford, Sheffield, Southampton, Surrey, Sussex, Warwick and York); two in Wales (the University of Wales and the Welsh College of Advanced Technology) and seven in Scotland (Aberdeen, Edinburgh, Glasgow, Heriot-Watt, St Andrews, Strathclyde and Stirling). In addition grants were issued to the London Graduate School of Business Studies and the Manchester Business School. The University of Wales consisted of the four constituent Colleges at Aberystwyth, Bangor, Cardiff and Swansea and the Welsh National School of Medicine. In addition the University College of South Wales and Monmouthshire (Cardiff) received grants for St David's College, Lampeter. The University of St Andrews comprised colleges situated at St Andrews and Dundee. The University of London is a federal university which includes 33 self-governing Schools and 13 Institutes directly controlled by the University. Since, however, four of the Schools do not participate in the Exchequer grants issued to the University on the recommendation of the University Grants Committee, their staff and students are not included in the tables.' (University Grants Committee *Returns from Universities and University Colleges*, Academic Year 1965–6, Cmnd. 3586.)

their charters between 1948 and 1957. The other institution which is included in this group is the University of Reading which was founded in 1926. Between them they account for 9·3 per cent of all university teachers. The fifth group is that of the former Colleges of Advanced Technology. These are Aston, Bath, Bradford, Brunel, Chelsea, City, Loughborough, Salford and Surrey. Their incorporation during the past three or four years into the university system has pushed the ancient English colleges, the University of Wales and the new English universities into sixth, seventh and eighth place respectively. The ancient English foundations at Oxford and Cambridge, with their origins in the late twelfth and early thirteenth centuries make up 9 per cent of the total. The University of Wales comes next: it received its charter in 1893, though several of its constituent colleges have their origins earlier in the nineteenth century. Aberystwyth began in 1859, Bangor in 1885, Cardiff in 1884 and Swansea in the 1920s. St David's, Lampeter, also receives grants from the University Grants Committee under a scheme agreed in 1961 through the University College of South Wales, Cardiff. Finally, there are the English

TABLE I

British university groups

University group	Full-time staff, 1965–6 %
Major redbrick	26·7
London	20·0
Scotland	14·9
Minor redbrick	9·3
Ex-CATs	9·2
Ancient English	9·0
Wales	6·5
New English	4·4
Total Great Britain	100·0
(N)	25,294

'new universities' of East Anglia, Keele, Sussex, York, Lancaster, Kent, Essex and Warwick. Their staffs make up only 4·4 per cent of the British academics.

Current troubles in the universities are associated with large-scale organization. It is therefore appropriate to point to the most obvious and

significant characteristic of the institutional setting of the British university
teacher, which is its small-scale. Only London University is large by
modern standards and, quite apart from its modest size by comparison
with Berkeley or the Sorbonne, its staff of 5,058 is in fact divided among
forty-six more or less autonomous institutions into groups of teachers and
research workers numbering typically less than one hundred. Again,
Oxford and Cambridge, though of medium size in the range of universities
all over the world, each has its one thousand members divided into small
collegiate societies. The largest universities with unitary organization are
at Leeds, Manchester, Birmingham, Edinburgh and Glasgow. In 1965–6
their staff numbered 1,140, 1,077, 1,023, 1,070 and 1,015 respectively, and
it is precisely in these universities that there is some uneasiness about size,
especially as a factor in maintaining the traditionally peaceable relation
between staff and students in Britain.

The milieu in which the university teacher plays his role remains an
intimate one despite the relatively rapid expansion that has taken place
in the 1960s. The typical university department has no more than ten
academic members. The milieu, in other words, remains, in this respect
at least, perfectly compatible with the distinctive English idea of a university.[1] This traditional form of educational institution in Britain provides
for maximum solidarity between teachers and taught through the absence
of a separate administration and an emphasis on close personal relations,
achieved by means of tutorial teaching methods, high staff : student ratios,
and shared domestic life.

The second fundamental division of the university teaching professions
is by academic rank. The distribution in 1965–6 is shown in the last column
of Table 2.

The grade structure outside the ancient English universities is a
hierarchy with four levels. At the bottom, and for most recruits the
beginning, there is a nominally probationary grade of assistant lecturer.
Next comes the main career grade of lecturer which is subdivided by an
efficiency bar, reached after six or seven years' service in the grade, and
passed after review of the individual's competence and performance as
a university teacher and researcher. Third are posts of seniority but
without professorial rank – the reader and the senior lecturer. Promotion

1 For a discussion of the English idea of a university see 'British Universities',
European Journal of Sociology, Vol. III, No. 1, 1962, pp. 85–102: 'University
Expansion and the Collegiate Ideal', *Universities Quarterly*, December 1961: 'A
Pyramid of Prestige', *Universities Quarterly*, Vol. XV, No. 4, September 1961:
'The Academic Hierarchy', *Universities Quarterly*, Vol. XVIII, No. 2, March
1964: and 'British Student Politics', *Daedalus*, Winter 1967, pp. 116–36.

to this level is by individual selection and there is a restriction on numbers to two-ninths of the whole non-professorial staff,[1] though the medical faculties are exempted from this restriction. In some universities the distinction between readers and senior lecturers is a horizontal one: readers are recognized primarily for research and senior lecturers for teaching. In other universities the division constitutes a further elaboration of the

TABLE 2

Full-time academic staff in Great Britain, 1910–66

All Universities in Great Britain, except Oxford and Cambridge	1910–20	1919–20	1929–30	1938–9	1949–50	1959–60	1963–4	1965–6*
	%	%	%	%	%	%	%	%
Professors	31·4	31·4	21·8	19·6	13·4	12·0	11·5	9·8
Readers								
Assistant Professors	–	–	9·6	8·8	6·4	6·2	6·5	17·4
Independent Lecturers								
Senior Lecturers	68·6	68·6	–	–	9·5	12·0	12·8	–
Lecturers	–	–	36·2	40·4	40·4	48·6	46·0	50·4
Assistant Lecturers	–	–	24·6	22·4	19·6	11·6	10·5	16·8
Others	–	–	7·8	8·8	10·7	9·6	12·7	5·6
Total	100	100	100	100	100	100	100	100
(N)	1,478	2,277	3,049	3,819	7,682	11,483	14,927	25,294

* 1965–6 includes Oxford, Cambridge and ex-CATs and is based on all teaching and research staff irrespective of source of financial support.

hierarchy, the readers having higher rank. At the top are the professors, though here again the beginnings of further elongation of the pyramid are to be seen in distinctions between professorial heads of departments and other professors not adorned (or burdened) with this authority.

Moving down the ranks, the numerical proportions for all universities are professors 9·8 per cent, readers and senior lecturers 17·4 per cent, lecturers 50·4 per cent and assistant lecturers 16·8 per cent, leaving 5·6 per cent in posts of various kinds outside the main hierarchy.

These figures are national and so disguise many variations between universities and faculties. They include Oxford and Cambridge where the staff structure is made very different in reality by the existence of the colleges and where the proportion of professors and readers is relatively

1 The University Grants Committee has recently announced that henceforth professors as well as senior lecturers and readers are to be brought within the quota system and the overall maximum is to be 35 per cent of the total academic staff.

low. London has a high proportion of professors and readers, partly because of the strength of the medical faculty. The new English universities have a high proportion of professors as 'founder members'. Scotland and Wales have relatively few readerships though the former has a compensating high proportion of senior lectureships. The minor redbricks have fewer staff of senior rank than the major redbricks.

The chances of obtaining a senior post vary considerably between subjects or disciplines as well as between types of university. There is no space for the details here.[1] The outstanding point is that natural scientists gain promotion on average earlier and more often than men in other subjects.

The third main division of the university teaching profession is between subjects or faculties. It is important to notice here that, at the turning-point of British higher education which was marked by the Robbins Report, the traditional stereotype of the academic as an arts don had already become seriously inaccurate by 1963-4. At that point the arts faculties made up exactly a quarter of the total. The largest single faculty was pure science (28 per cent). The remainder, in descending order of size, were medicine (16 per cent), applied science (14 per cent), social studies (9 per cent), agriculture and forestry (4 per cent), dentistry (2 per cent) and veterinary science (2 per cent). Thus, even assuming that half the social scientists were 'pure', more than 40 per cent of academics worked in some kind of natural or social science based technology. The technologists, thus broadly defined, have the most plausible claim to be thought of as the typical university teacher. Subsequently, the colleges of advanced technology have been admitted to the university fold and the figures for 1965-6 show a consequent shift in the balance of staff between faculties. Arts men are now less than one-fifth of the total and almost equalled by the numbers in the social studies and education. The physical sciences constitute the largest single group (5,226) and the majority of university teachers are in some kind of applied studies in the social sciences, the social studies or medicine.

Apart from pauses imposed by war and economic depression the academic professions have grown continuously during the present century. The present number of upwards of 25,000 was something less than 2,000 in 1900. At the beginning of the century there were 471 members of congregation at Oxford (the resident M.A.s).[2] By 1964 there were 1,358.[3]

1 See A. H. Halsey and M. Trow, *op. cit.*, forthcoming.
2 *Oxford University Calendar*, 1900.
3 *University of Oxford: Report of the Commission of Enquiry*, Vol. II, p. 6.

TABLE 3

Fulltime staff 1965–6 arranged by grade and subject group

	Professors	Readers Senior Lecturers	Lecturers	Asst. Lecturers	Others	Total
	%	%	%	%	%	%
Arts	23·3	15·1	16·7	18·8	14·1	17·3
Social Sciences	17·4	14·9	19·0	16·1	12·2	17·3
Pure Science	23·8	25·3	25·8	30·8	37·6	27·1
Applied Science Technology Agriculture Forestry	15·6	20·0	24·2	15·8	21·0	20·9
Medicine Dentistry Veterinary Science	19·9	24·7	14·3	18·5	15·1	17·4
Total	100	100	100	100	100	100
(N)	(2,491)	(4,404)	(12,735)	(4,262)	(1,402)	(25,294)

Expansion since 1900

There were 525 full and part time teachers in the major redbrick universities in 1900:[1] by 1964 in these universities there were ten times as many full time staff alone (5,456);[2] the comparable figures for London were 248 and 3,750 – a fifteen-fold increase.

Though they have changed their relative numerical positions none of the eight university groups which we have distinguished has failed to increase its numbers during the course of the century. The ancient English universities are no exception, though they have been overtaken in size by all of the newer institutions except for the University of Wales and the post-second world war group of 'new English' universities. There were probably about 700 Oxford and Cambridge dons in 1900: in 1966 they numbered 1,287.

1 From *Reports from Universities and Colleges to Board of Education*, Cd. 845, 1901.
2 U.G.C. *Returns*, Table 9, Cmnd. 2778.

The pattern of expansion

The course of expansion has had three phases. The first began around the turn of the century with the foundation of the civic universities and continued after the first world war until the depression years of the 1930s. The second, more rapid, phase of expansion occurred after the second world war. Unlike its predecessor it did not fade out but instead has formed the basis for a third phase of 'Robbinsian' expansion in the 1960s and 1970s.

At the beginning of the first phase Oxford and Cambridge, quite apart from their overwhelming academic and social importance, were numerically the strongest group. But by the end of the first phase, just before the second world war, they had been surpassed by the major redbrick universities and overtaken by London. Our estimate is that academic staff at Oxford and Cambridge grew from 700 at the beginning of the century to something like 1,000 in the 1930s. In the major redbrick universities staff increased from 626 in 1910 to 1,349 in 1938-9 and in London from 202 to 1,057. In 1900 there were twelve colleges sending returns to the Board of Education. The civic universities at that time included Mason University College at Birmingham which had been incorporated from 1897, Bristol University College founded in 1876, the Yorkshire College at Leeds (1874), Liverpool University College (1881), Owen's College in Manchester which had been incorporated in 1885, Durham College of Science at Newcastle (1871) and Sheffield University College (1897). Within the first decade of the century Birmingham, Bristol, Leeds, Liverpool, Manchester and Sheffield all gained charters as universities. Then, together with Durham and its Newcastle constituent, these civic universities began to lead the expansion of the British university system and have continued to do so throughout the century.

The second phase of growth after the second war included the granting of independent charters to the former provincial university colleges which took London degrees at Nottingham, Southampton, Hull, Exeter and Leicester. The last-named became independent in 1957, bringing the total number of British universities to twenty-one. Meanwhile, the establishment of the University College of North Staffordshire at Keele without tutelage from London was the precursor of a much publicized movement at the end of the 1950s to found new universities with independence *ab initio*. The first of these, Sussex, admitted its first students in 1961. Subsequently, East Anglia, York, Essex, Kent, Warwick and Lancaster received charters and a new Scottish university, Strathclyde, was formed out of the Royal College of Science at Glasgow. No doubt these new foundations will add significant numerical strength to the staff of the post-Robbins system of higher education and so contribute to the third phase of expansion. But in the second phase they counted for little. The bulk of the expansion between 1947 and 1964 was borne by the established universities in the industrial provincial cities, by London and by the ancient universities in England and Wales. The new universities in England account only for 4 per cent of the total number of university teachers in Great Britain while the incorporation of the ex-Colleges of Advanced Technology has added a group slightly larger than that of the Oxford and Cambridge dons and slightly smaller than the staffs of the minor redbrick universities.

The changing hierarchy

In the foundation years of the civic universities the professors constituted the academic staff.[1] But in order to carry out their work they had to appoint assistants. These constituted a jumble of junior men and women with ill-defined status, salaries and conditions of work who usually had *ad hoc* contracts either with the institution or with the professor himself. Before the first war the assistants had come to outnumber the professors and it became apparent that, as a permanent feature of the academic structure, the titles, status and conditions of non-professorial staff had to be recognized and regulated. The subsequent trend has been towards an increasingly elaborate hierarchy. Between 1910 and 1964 the proportion of academics with professorial rank fell from 31·4 per cent to 11·5 per cent and has still further declined with the inclusion of the former colleges of advanced technology. Before 1920 the ranks below the professorship were neither equivalent from one university to another nor distinguished in the Board of Education statistics. Many of them carried low status and low pay but the proportion of assistant lecturers has declined, especially during the post-war period of expansion, and the proportion in the main career grade – the lectureship – has risen. Thus there have been two processes at work somewhat against each other. On the one hand the hierarchy has been lengthened with the creation of non-professorial staff and a corresponding decrease in the proportion of chairs. On the other hand, within the non-professorial ranks there has been a tendency towards

1 They often had to engage in struggles with local trustees to establish the elements of academic freedom and self-government which they held to be appropriate to their professional status and which many of them had brought to their new universities from the traditional academic guilds of Oxford and Cambridge. They quickly won academic democracy in practice if not in formal constitutions.

upgrading with a corresponding decrease in the proportion of assistant lecturers. In recent years there has been renewed pressure to increase the proportion of senior posts. The Association of University Teachers advocates the abolition of the assistant lecturer grade, to which in any case recruitment is more difficult in a period of expansion. The Association also supports, though it wishes to carry further, the announced revision of the quota system which has hitherto restricted readerships and senior lectureships in two-ninths of all non-professorial posts.

A second trend is also worth noting. There has been a decrease during the century of part-time university teaching. Thus, while the number of full-time academics has risen by over 20,000 in the past forty years, the number of part-timers has remained what it was in 1920 at about 2,000. This change to full-time university work has been especially important in medicine. The structure of the professions is distinctive at the older collegiate universities but, as may be seen from Table 4, they have experienced a similar development. As the number of dons has increased the professors have formed a decreasing proportion of the total, declining from one-sixth to one-tenth of the academic staff at Oxford since 1922.

TABLE 4

Full-time academic staff at Oxford and Cambridge (per cent)

	Oxford 1922†	Oxford and Cambridge 1961–2*	Oxford 1964–5‡
Professors	18	9	9
Readers	3	7	7
Lecturers	18	37	30
Assistant Lecturers (C)		2	
C.U.F. Lecturers (O)		15	
Demonstrators (C)		3	
Department Demonstrators (O)	60	2 } 40	45
University Research Staff		8	
College Research Fellows		5	
Other College Teachers		5	
Others	1	7	9
Total	100%	100%	100%
(N)	(357)	(1,993)	(1,127)

Sources:
* Robbins Report, Appendix III.
† and ‡ University of Oxford Report of Commission of Inquiry (the Franks Report) Vol. II, p. 39.

The changing balance of studies

University studies in the twentieth century have both widened in scope and shifted in the balance of the faculties. The first change, however, has been continuous and the second has fluctuated. Widening the scope of studies has meant that university teachers have specialized increasingly in particular branches of knowledge and a division of labour has emerged between research and teaching and between undergraduate and graduate supervision. One crude but dramatic illustration of the widening range of specialisms may be derived from the U.G.C. statistics on the branches of study of advanced students. In 1928, 123 subjects were distinguished: a quarter of a century later there were 382. In the meantime economics had been divided into economics, industrial economics, econometrics and economic history; the number of branches of engineering had risen from seven to twenty-two and such subjects as ethiopic, fruit nutrition, immunology, personnel management, medical jurisprudence and space science had appeared.

The arts faculties have declined steadily since the beginning of the 1930s when they accounted for half of all students. As we have noted, less than a fifth of the university teachers are now in the arts faculties. However, this decline was not a continuation of previous trends. On the contrary, the arts faculties had expanded rapidly from the end of the first war at the expense of medicine and applied science. These developments were remarked by the U.G.C. in their Report for 1928–9 and attributed to 'the attraction exercised during a period of bad trade and restricted opportunities in other professions, by the securer and greatly improved prospect of the profession of teaching; in Scotland, the general tendency (was) intensified by the official requirement that only graduates (could) now normally be admitted to the provincial centres for training as men teachers'.[1] Nevertheless, despite the continuation of 'bad trade' in the 1930s the trend was reversed and the medical faculties expanded rapidly.

After the second war, while the proportionate decline in arts continued, the pure sciences expanded to become the largest faculty, medicine fell back and the technologies and social studies increased their share to more than a half of the whole. The figures are shown in Table 3.[2] The recent rapid increase in the social studies faculties is especially deserving of note

1 U.G.C. *Report*, 1928–9, p. 6.
2 The percentage increase in social studies staff between 1961–62 and 1966–67 was 155·3 compared with 46·5 for all university teachers (U.G.C. *University Development 1962–67*, Cmnd. 3820, p. 26.)

TABLE 5

Median age of teachers, by grade and faculty, Great Britain, 1961–2

	Age in Years						
Grade	*Humanities*	*Social Studies*	*Science*	*Applied Science*	*Medical Subs.*	*All Teachers*	*Sample nos.*
Professors	53	50	49	51	53	51	381
Readers	48	47	48	39	47	47	187
Senior Lecturers	51	49	48	46	42	47	380
Lecturers	39	40	35	35	35	37	1,450
Assistant Lecturers	29	28	28	27	28	28	294
Other grades	29	38	29	29	32	31	314
All teachers	39	42	36	37	39	38	3,006
Sample numbers	753	432	898	405	518	3,006	

Source: A.U.T. Survey, 1962.

TABLE 6

Age distributions of staff, 1964–5

Age	Arts %		Science %		Technology %		Medicine %		All %	% (1962)
−25	306	8·4	205	7·7	76	4·4	58	3·4	645	6·6	(5·3)
26–30	775	21·2	731	27·4	343	19·7	285	16·6	2134	21·8	(17·2)
31–35	552	15·1	544	20·4	330	19·0	341	19·8	1767	18·1	(20·6)
36–40	574	15·7	456	17·1	402	23·1	360	20·9	1792	18·3	(20·7)
41–45	509	13·9	322	12·1	258	14·8	263	15·3	1352	13·8	(12·4)
46–50	351	9·6	146	5·5	117	6·7	176	10·2	790	8·1	(9·5)
51–55	294	8·1	105	3·9	96	5·5	115	6·7	610	6·2	(6·6)
56–60	178	4·9	94	3·5	61	3·5	74	4·3	407	4·2	(4·7)
61–65	98	2·7	58	2·2	53	3·0	44	2·6	253	2·6	(2·6)
66–	15	0·4	6	0·2	4	0·2	4	0·2	29	0·3	(0·4)
Total	3652		2667		1740		1720		9779		

Source: A.U.T. Survey, 1965.

The increased rate of expansion is reflected in a greater proportion of younger staff than in 1962 – the biggest increase in the groups under thirty years of age being in Arts. The over forties account for almost the same proportions as they did in 1962, so there has been a relative decline in the numbers between age thirty and forty. Just under 65 per cent of all university teachers are forty years old or younger.

given the widespread belief, whether true or false, that young university teachers and students in the social studies tend to be leaders in contemporary conflicts with university authority.

Age and sex

It would be instructive, though it is not possible from official statistics, to reconstruct the history of the age structure of the university professions. Presumably the celibacy rule in Oxford and Cambridge, which continued into the 1860s, must have distorted the age structure to produce a relatively old group of bachelor dons and a young group of unmarried fellows with comparatively few in their late thirties and forties. However this may be, it is certainly true that expansion is a disturbance to the age structure of any profession. At the end of the first quinquennium after the war the U.G.C. thought that, because of expansion, the average age had probably never been lower than it then was. However, the renewed rise in the rate of expansion in the 1960s still further reduced the average age of university

TABLE 7

Academic staff or Students by faculty, 1919–66*

	1919–20† %	1928–9 %	1938–9 %	1949–50 %	1959–60 %	1963–4 %	1965–6 %
Arts	38·7	53·3	44·8	43·6	27·3	25·1	17·3
Social Studies	–	–	–	–	6·8	9·4	17·3
Pure Science	18·3	16·7	15·5	19·8	25·7	27·9	27·1
Applied Science Technology Agriculture Forestry	16·4	11·1	12·6	16·0	19·3	18·1	20·9
Medicine Dentistry Veterinary Science	26·6	18·9	27·1	20·6	20·9	19·5	17·4
Total	(43,018)	(44,309)	(50,246)	(85,421)	(11,798)	(15,259)	(25,294)

* From U.G.C. Returns.

† Oxford and Cambridge student numbers were not included in U.G.C. returns for 1919–20. These numbers were taken from the returns for 1922–3, the first year they were included, and added to the numbers for other universities given in the 1919–20 returns.

Note: Student numbers are given for the years 1919–20, 1928–9, 1938–9 and 1949–50, and *include* Oxford and Cambridge. Staff numbers are given for the years 1959–60 and 1963–4 and *exclude* Oxford and Cambridge lecturers and below.

teachers. The median age of university teachers by grade and faculty in 1961–2 is shown in Table 5. By 1965 the age structure of the several faculties was as shown in Table 6. The increased rate of expansion is reflected in a greater proportion of younger staff than in 1962 – the biggest increases in the groups under thirty years of age being in arts. The over-forties account for almost the same proportion as they did in 1962 so there has been a relative decline in the numbers between age thirty and forty. Just under 65 per cent of all university teachers are forty years old or younger.

It may also be noted that the proportion of women academics has probably risen slightly during the century with the increased entry of women into the universities, but they still constitute a small minority of 10 per cent who tend to concentrate in the lower ranks and in the faculties of arts and social studies.

This arithmetic skeleton of the British university teaching professions is, of course, only the first step towards an analysis of the role of the university teacher in current redefinition of the nature of university life, its place in society and the relation between teacher and taught within it. The changing interests, attitudes and orientations which must be described in order to complete the picture of the don are left to other chapters in this book and to our forthcoming book on the *British Academics*.

Rowland Eustace

The government of scholars

The British Universities are autonomous institutions, under the formal control (outside Oxford and Cambridge) of people who are not themselves scholars. There has, over a long period, been a steadily increasing academic participation in this control, so that lay control appears to many to be giving way to scholarly self-government. This movement towards academic self-government has in recent years begun to face not only the lay governors, but also several other contenders for control. The most visible has been the student movement, which has been based partly on a call for a definition of the community of scholars that will include the students. The appearance of these contenders has naturally focused interest on self-government. This interest has strong links with traditional ideals of government at Oxbridge, but is in tune with, and probably strengthened by, a much wider interest throughout society in participation and consultation.

At the same time, the growth of the universities, and the increase in their importance and cost to society, have set up counter-pressures for control by non-scholars, inside and out. There is fear that control of the universities will be divided between the lay governors and, much more, the agencies of Government on the one hand, and the internal bureaucracy on the other. These fears are expressed widely, and with such authority, that it can be assumed that they are real and justified.

These two movements, one away from, and the other towards, control of the academic world by the community of scholars, each have long histories of their own. Until less than a decade ago this country was envied its skills in keeping any conflict between them outside the university; and in keeping the internal bureaucracy in place. Now there is less envy. Many scholars see the conflict as three-cornered, between laymen who are non-scholars 'representing' society, the internal bureaucracies, and themselves, the scholars. Others see it as four-cornered, with the students an extra contender for control.

Part of the conflict, the external part, is quite well documented. The internal part, the internal government, is much less so. There are few documents and the people concerned do not often write or reminisce about their work, which is highly subjective and of which views can differ as widely as those of a motor-accident. They will sometimes talk, and some impressions may be gathered which, with help from more official sources, may suggest useful approaches. In a short essay on a wide and little treated subject, approaches must be rather arbitrarily selected, and presented without much qualification. For the same reason, the generalizations are about the English universities founded after London, although, *mutatis mutandis*, the differences found elsewhere in the U.K. are probably not as great as they may appear.

Government is, reasonably, associated with the exercise of power. It is a general observation that power appears more concrete to those who do not think they have it: a truncheon of stated size and weight. To those who are thought to have it, it appears less substantial; at best like the flamingo given to Alice as a croquet-mallet. In universities the croquet is unusually dispersed and diffused, and the notion of force especially alien, so that the concept of power is confusing and unsafe. There have been attempts recently to force university authority to reveal its power, naked. The striking revelation, last session at least, was the slightness of what was then unveiled. Things do, however, happen, and in a short essay about who controls them, the word power may creep in as a convenient shorthand.

In writings about universities there is a clear, and usually fairly articulate, major premise that scholars should have a significant control of their own affairs; that there should be academic self-government. This has to be, as it is not always, distinguished from other sorts of 'academic freedom' such as the right to follow the argument where it leads and to teach the result; or the right of an academic institution to autonomy. Rather curiously, little sustained argument for self-government has been published; for instance, the matter is generally dealt with by implicit assumption in reports of Royal Commissions, and the papers circulated when a Charter is in draft seem remarkably deficient here. In the general literature, the argument is usually confined to asseveration, often as an aside backed only by the statement 'experience proves'.

Even the theoretical extent of academic self-government, however, is a surprisingly recent growth. When the modern university movement started, with the founding of what is now University College, London, academic staff were not expected to organize themselves in any way. By the end of the century an approach was being made towards self-government in purely academic affairs, although two important academic matters, the determination of curriculum and the award of degrees, were not usually included, because so few of the teaching institutions had degree-granting powers. The pattern, at the end of the last century, showed a sharp institutional distinction between teachers, examiners, and those who determine curricula, rather as is found on the Continent today in the State Examination systems. This was the pattern exported to Ireland and Wales and to India and New Zealand. More interesting, it was dominant enough for the Scottish Universities Act of 1889 to make provision for its extension to those ancient bodies, by permitting them to federate. In London, laymen retained a say in academic affairs even after the reorganization of 1930. The pattern was not broken until the chartering of Mason College as the University of Birmingham in 1900 with full powers. The 'purely' academic powers were reserved to the senior scholars, subject to the veto of the laymen. In the lifespan since that Charter, convention has so firmly ensured that in 'purely' academic matters the veto is not used, that it is generally agreed in the literature that its use would be unthinkable.

In general non-academic affairs, often referred to as 'financial', but including academic appointments, academic participation is theoretically much less well established, and the literature assigns an important place to the Council, with its majority of lay members. In the last century, the appearance of a few academic staff on Council (and the equivalent) was slow. In Scotland, the Acts of 1858 and 1889 actually introduced a lay element where, as at Glasgow, scholars had had virtual control. The pattern was sealed by the Charters granted to the new universities in the 1900s which placed responsibility for non-academic affairs firmly on Council, with a heavy lay majority. Considerable importance is still attached to this lay element; and in Ireland, T.C.D. asked the recent Commission for the appointment of laymen to its ancient Board. The pattern did not change much before the 1960s, but there was an observable trend to greater academic participation, first in increasing the actual size of the representation on Council, and second in increasing the 'democratic' element by introducing representatives of the non-professors. (The non-professors have also been gaining statutory representation on Senate, and even on its committees.)

In this decade, instruments of government began to show this trend more clearly. At Newcastle, there is power (not used), to reduce lay participation drastically, and elsewhere the powers of Council have been sharply curtailed, usually by giving rights of initiative to Senate, but at Lancaster by reducing them to the quite strictly financial (i.e. concerning investments, etc.).

Instruments like Charters may be expected to lag well behind actual practice. It is clear that lay activity has in practice been diminishing for some time: two decades ago the Council/Senate system could be exported to the Colonies, with the argument that the new local Councils must learn, and the belief that they easily would learn, the conventional restrictions on their apparent powers. A decade ago, authoritative advice was given that there was no need to trouble the Privy Council with innovations in the composition of Council: the risk of delay was greater than the difficulty of operating a modern convention under a traditional instrument. (Convention has become so powerful that it is noticeable today how few Registrars know their Statutes in detail.) The shift in emphasis visible in the newer instruments is thus strong evidence that the lay-dominated Council has not for a good many years exercised any initiative in university government. In fact, it is clear that Councils, as such, play very little part in what is usually thought of as governing at all, even though the academic element is generally in a majority at meetings. The recent case of overseas students fees, where Council and Senate decisions were actually at variance, is so unusual as to prove the rule, and even then, it was not always clear just how far the decisions to bow to the Government was a wholly lay one. Council operates almost entirely through its committees, which are generally technical in nature (and normally have a strong academic element). Budgets, for instance, have to be passed by a finance committee on which academic representation is generally least, but there is little evidence that the finance committee examines the policy behind the budget: its function is essentially that of the advisory accountant. Technical advice is thus the chief contribution of the layman. The usefulness of this advice may explain why so many (though not all) administrators value the services of their laymen so highly, and seem sometimes to forget the layman's legal role. They are sometimes a little puzzled by a reminder of the legal position – 'Oh yes, they are quite invaluable – oh, no, of course they don't control anything.' Laymen facilitate the desires of scholars; they do not themselves desire. There is quite enough in the implementation of policy in modern higher education that needs to be facilitated, to keep more laymen active than can be found. It is so difficult to recruit the minority of laymen who are willing, and able, to be active on committees, that there is in effect a systematic co-option of those who accept and support the autonomy of scholars, and who are proud to be asked to help. If indeed there are laymen with influence on policy in individual institutions, they are too rare for it to be possible to speak of lay influence on the system.

There has thus been a steady and cumulatively massive shift in the direction of academic self-government. At the same time, however, there has been a growth of internal administration which is more immediately apparent to the community, and is often seen as representing a shift away from self-government. The growth of administration has indeed been great (though not faster than that of the universities) so that a whole new profession is emerging, sustaining several national conferences a year. (Over 200 representatives attended the 1968 conference for junior non-financial administrators.) The academic who not so long ago was used to checking at coffee that the seminar-room was free at noon, now finds that he should have applied to a central office ten weeks ago; and he asks himself why all these intelligent graduates, many back from high respon-sibilities in the Colonies (where would universities be without the collapse of Empire?), why did they take up this career if it does not carry the satisfaction of power? It is easy to assume from this that we may read into our situation the problem of America. The American analogy is in fact useful, but in reverse, for it points up the very real differences both of form and of attitude between the systems, and may suggest that there is no inherent reason why our academic community need be overwhelmed by bureaucrats, or indeed why we should think that it is being so. There is a fundamental difference between American and British administration in that the American Vice-President or Dean is a member of the govern-ment, not a bureaucrat. He both chairs committees and executes their decisions: it is difficult to talk to, say, a Vice-President without first grasping that even if he knows about it, he is not familiar with our sharp division of responsibility between a chairman, who is normally a part-timer with the right to participate in decisions, and secretary who is a well-paid professional with no vote. The nearest equivalent that we have to the American administrator is our Vice-Chancellor, still normally a unique officer. Until the number of his full-time deputies increases greatly, our administrative dangers will differ from those of the Americans. A key characteristic of our administration is that its formal function is to record and carry out decisions of committees composed of non-administrators. It is a non-voting Civil Service. (It is interesting that the Irish Commission recommends the same for Ireland.) There is of course much scope for influence in that role, and there have been and still are immensely influential administrators. Their powers derive from their own excellence, and from their uniqueness: especially so in a small institution, for when the affairs of an institution can be carried in one head, it is difficult to argue with its owner. But one result of increasing size may be that that advantage to the administrator diminishes.

It is not merely the restricted function of the administrator that is important: attitudes are equally so. Here again is a vast difference from America, where the climate of opinion is not warm to academic control: over here it is. Some of the younger recruits to administration are apt to be impatient of the perversities and delays no doubt inseparable from endless consultation and committee government, but they are not encouraged by their elders. Even those senior administrators still wielding real influence through their unique knowledge, believe sincerely and deeply, and to the outsider almost contradictorily, in the supremacy of the academic will. It may surprise how rapidly the ex-colonial officer, though probably a little surprised at what he may have been accustomed to regard as inefficiency, absorbs the academic ethos and accepts the need for collective decision-making. This is not something that shows up from outside; and it is noticeable that as academics move further into the decision-making process, they drop their stereotyped dislike of a stereotyped bureaucrat. They begin to appreciate, with surprise, the bureaucrats' ready acceptance of the role of midwife, not progenitor. Moreover, the university bureaucracy differs from the Civil Service in that it works much closer to its master. Its characteristic job is to service committees on which serve, as it were, Members of Parliament. As a result, the administrator seems frequently to identify with his committee rather than with his profession; and to tend to put the committee's interests first. He may even be instructed by its chairman (an academic) not to consult his administrative superiors. This can be an issue of some importance, as when Dean and Registrar compete for jurisdiction over the Secretary of the Faculty. University administration is made to look like a hierarchy, but it is a pyramid on which, as with jars for growing strawberries, production takes place at the sides as well as at the apex. It is a great pity that all this is not better appreciated: administrations could help themselves notably by making the position clearer. Universities tend to get plastered with prohibitions signed by the Registrar. In Glasgow, it is 'No smoking. By order of the Senate.'

Where in the balance of self-government does the Vice-Chancellor stand? He is formally the 'Chief Academic Officer'; he has a vote and his activity therefore can be said to be part of self-government. As compared with an American President, this is probably fair, though as compared with a German Rector, less so. He is also the 'Chief Administrative Officer', and he is very reasonably seen as an administrator rather than as a scholar.

Traditionally, his office has been of great importance, and the fortunes of universities have depended on him. Though in the larger institutions of today he may be less visible (even the new universities are rapidly approaching the size of a major university twenty years ago) the office clearly remains by far the most important in the government of the university. It may be seen, therefore, as a limitation on self-government, but for our purpose, the most striking fact about a Vice-Chancellor is that he has no formal power. His unique position, at the cross-roads of all information, gives him great leverage. But at every turn, and notably on Senate and Council, he can be outvoted: he can do little that his dons really don't want: and there are indeed whole areas, mostly academic, into which he would not venture. If he has a policy, he has therefore to use the, extensive, abilities of a chairman and to exercise persuasion. He may not always have to persuade great numbers and he is always protected by the advantages of position and knowledge, but, if the representatives of the community of scholars want to they can defeat the most assiduous, the most skilful Vice-Chancellor. Occasionally they do so in open conflict. But normally, this very important fact is thickly concealed, because it has to become a prime object of administration to avoid such a defeat. Administration becomes the preparation of acceptable initiatives. Partly for this reason, but no doubt also because of the nature in the academic enterprise, government becomes intensely consultative: the proliferation of committees and informal conferences becomes formidable. Within this web of communications it will be difficult to say whether the impulses of initiative flow up or down; for our purposes it does not greatly matter which – they have to go through the web.

This power to insist on consultation is, certainly, a form of self-government. But it is essentially negative, the *liberum veto* of the self-government of Oxbridge. Positive action requires work, and above all knowledge, in its preparation: it is difficult to discuss an initiative unless it is known to be viable. Hence of course the Vice-Chancellor's (and the bureaucrats') leverage. Senate has in the past been able to take action. But in general it has long been too large a body; and recent growth has made it a body usually able to act only through committees. This may represent a decline in self-government, because even though the committees are academic, policy involves co-ordination. What is beginning to appear, however, is the small Senate committee determined to master the facts and to exercise a direct positive influence on the development of policy. There are some signs that this was coming in any event, for reasons perhaps connected with the Vice-Chancellor's realization that he could

no longer carry the place in his head and with the scholars' realization that
Senate was losing control. The strongest cause seems, however, to be the
end to expansion. For ten years universities grew by the attraction of
excellence. The new resources could be applied at the growing-points and
there was often (as seen in retrospect, anyway) enough for all. The check
to expansion means that resources can now be obtained only by actual
cutting back at some point. Largely because they are consultative communities universities are exceptionally ill-adapted to that painful process. It
is one in which the Vice-Chancellor may need a far deeper consensus. This
deeper consensus may require the widening of the group in possession of
knowledge and the award to it of more direct responsibility. One method is
the creation of more effective, and representative, development committees
of Senate, concerned not only with broad policy, but also with the annual
budget, otherwise often the Vice-Chancellor's own province. This process
appears to be showing up a need for more sophisticated information about
the operation of the university, and there is some evidence the administrations are being strengthened with statistical officers and the like just
because the development committees see a need for information beyond
that hitherto required by Vice-Chancellors. Such information is having in
any case to be produced to satisfy external questioners. If a Vice-
Chancellor's sources of administrative leverage rest heavily on his command of information, then the more sophisticated techniques now being
introduced may be beginning to transfer some of this leverage to committees of Senate which have access to the results.

So far, the discussion has not distinguished between academic self-
government and academic democracy. But since professors form a majority
on Senate, and have wider responsibility at subject level, self-government
may still mean little more than professorial participation. It is, however,
possible to trace a long-term movement towards greater non-professorial
participation, visible, again, in the formal instruments of government.
Except at L.S.E. we are still far from full participation, but there is now a
significant representation, normally elected, of the non-professors on
Council, mostly around 5 per cent but sometimes over 10 per cent. The
figure is greater on Senate, commonly 30–40 per cent. On Faculties (not
very important) it is commonly a majority. It is still unusual for any
professor to be excluded from Senate, but there are signs that the trend is
towards eliminating the special governmental position of professors,
notably in the composition of the Senate at Newcastle. Without such
elimination, the effect of democratizing is to increase still further the size
of Senates and this is generally thought to reduce their effectiveness. In

any case, the increased size of the university has driven the main locus of academic life towards the subject level, to Departments and 'Schools'. For this reason there has been a sustained move to increase participation at these lower levels, and especially at the subject level. This movement is sometimes impelled from above – it is often a Vice-Chancellor's solution to the problem of participation – but also from the level. It is made easier when, as is now common, there is more than one Chair to a Department because the position of a professor becomes less special, particularly if the headship of the Department then rotates. Formal participation has been made more necessary as size increases, for some Departments are now of a size reached by established Universities before the First War. Its essence has to be the formalization of consultation (which may or may not have existed informally) and must therefore involve the creation of departmental committees. Sometimes this is on a vast scale, up to a score.

This long-standing movement towards wider self-government in universities has certainly not run its natural course, and is in tune with the wider demand for consultation and participation in society as a whole. It has, in effect, been taken up by the student movement for participation, which has used many of the assumptions and ideals represented by the A.U.T., somewhat to its dismay and even confusion. The non-professorial groups (who are important in the A.U.T.) fear, naturally enough, that they will inevitably be worse off. But it can be assumed that the movement for participation will grow, that formal participation by non-professors will not diminish, and that that by students will grow considerably or very considerably.

Whether the numbers that will be involved will permit the real participation to grow as much, or force an actual contraction, is the question of the moment. But it would be likely, and it is usually assumed, that the movement has not kept up with the expansion, and there can be no doubt that there are substantial numbers of teachers who know very little of what is going on. No doubt many of them do not wish to know. It has always been so to some extent and it would only be the emergence of a large class of such teachers that would indicate the breakdown of community and the impossibility of democratic self-government. Fears that such a class is now forming have led to the search for other ways of involvement in the community; such as general information-sheets, and assemblies for the discussion of general policy. These of course interest only those who want to be involved, but there seems to be evidence that they do in fact also increase both the sense of community, and make representative systems more effective. In so far as universities have any success in widening participation and consultation they run, naturally, into the mathematical division of influence: the more who share, the less has any individual. One of the present difficulties is that where no one person has any power, because all decisions have to be accommodations of many views consulted, it becomes hard to say who is responsible. The more complete the self-government, the harder to press the levers that will produce action. The newcomer to active university government continually supposes that the arena of decision is over the next hill, and learns slowly that it is around him, too indistinct to be immediately tangible. The need to gain the consent, or more likely, to avoid the dissent, of the main groups of opinion must inevitably give an advantage to those who know the ground best. The students, with less time to learn, or to acquire a collective understanding of the atmosphere of the system and seeking action before the end of term, may merely think that procedure has been used as a device to rebuff them. Not always, no doubt, quite without justification. It is, moreover, an inherent disadvantage of participatory government that it is generally easier to block action than to take it: the point of participation, as far as most people are concerned, is no disturbance without consultation. Students, present for a maximum of five or six years, may grudge the time and effort needed to persuade, or again think they are being systematically cheated. (It seems to me, however, on very limited evidence, that student leaders may understand the realities of human relations rather better than some junior staff leaders.)

Consultative government is inevitably 'inefficient' in certain ways, notably in its lack of speed. This 'inefficiency' has traditionally been defended as a price of academic excellence; hence the willingness of universities to attempt to extend it. They have been able to consult extensively, and have been able at the same time both to acquire a very reasonable scholastic reputation in the world, and to produce graduates at a very reasonable cost. In other words, they are 'efficient' in other, and much more important, senses. It is arguable that their 'efficiency' in these latter senses will fall if universities cannot ensure that the community of scholars believes itself to have adequate opportunity for participation and consultation. Despite fears, it looks as if they are succeeding in ensuring that; and that they will be able to extend effective participation still further, especially at the departmental level. Such evidence as there is suggests, further, that they are succeeding in their attempts to include students in decision-making. Most universities already have long lists of committees on which students are represented, some of them important committees, and the number is steadily increasing. This suggests that universities could extend the process without damage to themselves; though whether this will ensure that students come to believe that they have adequate opportunities will have to wait on more experience.

It seems fair then to say that, at least by comparison with the turn of the century, or with overseas systems, the universities have a very large measure of self-government, and are maintaining a significant degree of 'democracy'. If so, the universities are in tune with one of the two movements discussed above, that towards participation in decisions affecting one's environment. What of the other movement, that towards 'social' control?

In its present form, the movement for 'social' control is recent. It has a good many sources leading back to both political parties; and, perhaps, also to official circles and to some of the Foundations – certainly to journalists. The chief source of actual pressure is from government and its agencies. Two main objectives are sought – first, some sort of 'efficiency' in the use of resources, and second, some sort of social relevance.

The first objective, efficient use of resources, involves administrative techniques which tend to make the internal bureaucracy more visible by insisting on centralization or by introducing unfamiliar methods into decision-making: 'efficiency' is often taken, by writers defending academic freedom, as the natural opposite of independence. This arises partly in reaction to the belief of some outsiders that a clear chain of command, and clear commands, produce efficiency. In a discussion with a consultant, who had recently advised a university about how officials would establish what should be commanded in some small matter, he made a lengthening list of those who would have to be consulted: finally, he was taken aback to be asked whether he was not now describing a Senate meeting? But there is more to 'efficiency' than that. For one thing, it is more than desirable that universities should know about themselves. This may lead to simple savings – the results of space-utilization surveys are already clear evidence of that – but there is the much more important result that decisions can then be taken in the light of the facts. There is a powerful movement amongst both academics and officials, to find criteria of decision which do not rely wholly on judgement or influence. One exponent of more sophisticated information remarked, 'We are eliminating hunch and bargaining.' A university which enables itself to use its resources better increases its efficiency, but also its autonomy; and by making the improved knowledge available to decision-making bodies, some universities are, as we have seen, increasing the degree of self-government by their academics as well as by their autonomy.

The problem is that the demands of efficiency may not stop there, and that, especially, financial uniformity may be insisted upon. Uniformity of salaries has long been imposed, after a bitter dispute by Cambridge: and is generally acquiesced in. Uniformity is also being imposed on buildings: tiresome when applied to student accommodation; more serious as it introduces more norms in specialist buildings, like laboratories. Even this intrusion may not really touch more than the fringes of autonomy: for one thing, the variety that can be achieved within the norms by a good architect is considerable. (Some people even benefit, because a maximum standard comes to be taken as a minimum.) Much more important is an apparent move towards standardization of teaching costs. The U.G.C. has now made a sharp advance into that area, and has actually provided for official publication some – rather doubtful – comparative faculty costs. It is known that its grants are related closely to that entity known as the weighted student and the fear is that it is only the crudity of the methods of loading this alienated figure that prevent the grants from being related to him, exactly. Even here, many administrators, academic and official, seem quietly confident. And, indeed, until the student movement became prominent, it looked as if the most significant development in university government might be a growth of a more 'professional' attitude to decision-making, using methods which, coincidentally, were being imposed from outside. The proponents of this development, some very highly placed, saw (and see) this as a move away from traditional 'literacy' to something they described (and describe) as 'numeracy'. By the use of improved information, some Senate committees were being enabled to re-evaluate and gain control of their development. These committees may now be well placed to deal with the outside pressure.

The demand for social relevance cuts very much closer to self-government than that for efficiency. Here again, there is nothing new in the idea that universities should be kept up with the times, even by Government. During the heyday of the U.G.C., apart from the Earmarked Grants, there was little direct official pressure. Partly, as successive Chancellors of the Exchequer emphasized, because Governments believed that the universities should be trusted to respond themselves; partly no doubt because new developments could be introduced outside the system, as with the growth of the C.A.Ts. It was thought for a time that one benefit of the Binary System would be a deflection in this way of public enthusiasm away from the universities. But the amount of resources required by the universities, especially when public expenditure is being cut, has begun to raise questions that strike directly at areas excluded from even the purview of the university's Council, such as the need for so many research students, for small departments, or for changed teaching methods.

The Research Councils have, through a control over a high proportion of research studentships, and through their ability to evaluate postgraduate courses, a potentially important leverage. The U.G.C. has taken to writing what amount to open directives; and there is pressure from the Schools Council to revise entrance requirements. From the point of view of autonomy, it does not so much matter if the pressure comes from government or in the form of an agreement reached by the Vice-Chancellor's Committee. (Some of the pressure against, e.g., small departments, comes from high up the Vice-Chancellorial range.) In either case the result will not, by definition, be what the community would have decided for itself. Of course, the universities, acquainted with the facts, should want to act in the national interest, even against their own, but that is an argument, much used, for leaving the universities alone. It does not, however, seem to be any longer an article of faith in the Ministries, or indeed, to judge by the tone of their talk to gatherings of administrators, among officials of the U.G.C., who are now being recruited from the D.E.S. rather than from the Treasury.

This new pressure on the universities is, however, at an early stage, and some of it comes from a government not noted for its administrative successes or for its prospects. Even if there may be a permanent change in the climate of opinion, it is not clear yet how far the encroachment will be pressed. A Minister remarked not long ago to a private meeting that if a Minister thinks he can tell the universities what to do, he will find he is wrong almost before he has finished speaking. More important, it is not clear yet what resistance it will provoke. The drive to increased self-government and participation within the university will strengthen resistance, especially if intervention takes the form of pruning. Those writers, mostly students, whose analysis reveals the university as a mere arm of productive society, a machine to turn out the establishment cadres, are still far ahead of reality. The system is certainly not yet a mere machine; it has immense reserves of traditional prejudice against the official and the competitive worlds. Industry still complains that it does *not* produce the cadres; Appointments Officers still seek for new openings for graduates trained on profoundly anti-commercial, non-vocational, assumptions. The pressures are not, in fact, primarily from the productive world. The call is as much for more doctors, teachers, social workers; and simply for more higher education.

The issue is not yet decided. It is perhaps early (though, as Professor

Beloff has pointed out, not unreasonable) to mourn academic freedom.
While the decision is being taken, the government of universities is becoming an attempt to satisfy the disparate demands for control made by
society, by staff and by students. Over the next few years, it should provide
interesting material for study.

Ernest Rudd

The troubles of graduate students

The growth of graduate study

Within the rapidly expanding field of research into higher education, the problems of graduate students have remained a relatively neglected area. This is not altogether surprising as in most British universities and many American universities graduate students have only relatively recently become a substantial part of the student body. In Britain in 1938–9 there were 3,000 full-time graduate students, apart from those following courses of professional training in school teaching, and they were 6 per cent of the 50,000 students. By 1968–9 they are likely to be over 15 per cent of students, having increased tenfold while the total student body has increased fourfold. In the U.S.A. in 1939–40 masters degrees and doctorates amounted to 14 per cent of the 217,000 degrees awarded. By 1965–6 they were 21 per cent out of a total of 680,000 degrees.

There is no single factor that explains adequately this growth of graduate education. In Britain it springs in part from a growing belief in the value of graduate study as a preparation for university teaching, coupled with an increased need for entrants to university teaching during a period of rapid expansion of the universities; but the scale of the growth far exceeds the needs of university teaching. In part it reflects the provision of grants on a more generous scale – few in earlier generations even considered the possibility of staying on in the universities for further study after graduation because there was little point in considering what was financially impractical. The more generous provision of grants in many countries has itself been the result of two influences – the desire of governments to increase the amount of research in their countries in the belief that this will lead to faster scientific or economic growth, and pressure from universities which increasingly see themselves as research institutions rather than institutions for the teaching of undergraduates. Academics are anxious to have graduate students under their supervision, partly because they find teaching at the frontiers of knowledge intellectually more satisfying, but also because they know that their careers are more dependent on their reputations as researchers than on their teaching. Last, but by no means least, the expansion of knowledge has not been matched by a pruning of equivalent amounts of older material from undergraduate syllabuses, so that there has been a tendency for a spill-over into the post-graduate years of material that cannot be accommodated in the undergraduate syllabus.

Amongst the few studies of graduate education that are available, Berelsen's, *Graduate Education in the United States*,[1] has the defect that it collected data from recent recipients of the doctorate whose memories of their trials and tribulations can be expected to have softened a little with time, but did not cover those students who had dropped out, often as a result of their inability to surmount the difficulties in their path. I shall therefore rely heavily for data on the problems of graduate students in the U.S.A. on two studies that have been given only limited publication – a very timely study of doctoral students at Berkeley carried out by Dr Ann Heiss in 1963[2] and a study of wastage by Tucker, Gottlieb and Pease.[3] For data on British students, I shall use the results of a study made by my own research group at the University of Essex, which covered both past graduate students at all British universities (all those who began their graduate studies in 1957–8) and current students at eleven British university institutions. Some of our results are published;[4] others are being prepared for publication.[5]

A typology of research students

The undergraduate may well regard himself as a product of mass production, a can on a conveyor belt being filled by machinery. Each research

1 Berelsen, B., *Graduate Education in the United States* (New York: McGraw Hill, 1960).
2 Heiss, Ann M., *Berkeley doctoral students appraise their academic programs* (Mimeo. Center for the Study of Higher Education, University of California, Berkeley; 1964).
3 Tucker, A., Gottlieb, D., and Pease, J., *Attrition of graduate students at the Ph.D. level in the traditional arts and sciences* (Mimeo. Office of Research Development and the Graduate School, Michigan State University, East Lansing, Michigan; 1964).
4 a. Rudd, E., and Hatch, S., *Graduate Study and After* (London: Weidenfeld and Nicolson, 1968).
   b. Rudd, E., 'The rate of economic growth, technology and the Ph.D.', *Minerva*, Spring, 1968, pp. 366–87.
   c. Rudd, E., 'Postgraduate research in the humanities', *Research into Higher Education 1967* (London: Society for Research into Higher Education, 1968) pp. 27–42.
5 This research was carried out in the Unit for Research into Higher Education, which from 1964 to 1967 was financed by the Calouste Gulbenkian Foundation.

student, by contrast, has very individual problems arising from his own research, which, because research is the pursuit of new knowledge, must be as different as possible from that of any other student. In spite of this basic individuality it is possible to group research students into a broad typology; indeed it is necessary to do so in order to understand what kind of people they are and the causes of their discontents. As with all typologies it makes broad generalizations – a few individuals may not fit snugly into any one box, or may go equally well into either of two.

First there are two rather similar categories, the dedicated scholar and the would-be academic. The dedicated scholar is there primarily because of his interest in a particular field of study and his wish to do research. He probably also wants to become a university teacher because this is likely to be the career that will give him most freedom in research, but he may well have given little thought to a career. Rather over a third of British students and about the same proportion of those in American universities have given answers in surveys that would put them into this category. In both countries they make up half of the humanities students, but markedly less in other fields.

The would-be academic has much clearer ideas on his future career. He may be attracted to a university career by the opportunities for scholarship, but other aspects of university life are likely to be in his mind too. He takes a less expressive and more instrumental view of his studies, seeing them as a means to an end. Such students form about one-eighth of British research students, but in America are a rather higher proportion, perhaps as much as one-third, reflecting the fact that a Ph.D. is a ticket to academic jobs to a far greater extent in America than here.

Third come those who see their graduate studies as giving them an advantage in a career that seems likely to lie outside the university world. They may see a masters degree or doctorate leading specifically to a career that they definitely want, or, in more general terms, simply as a qualification that will bring quicker promotion and a higher salary in most careers that draw in university graduates. About 20 per cent of British research students overall, but 30 per cent of the technologists, come into this category. It takes in fewer Americans however, probably not more than a sixth.

Next come the drifters, those who have stayed in the university for graduate studies not because of any positive attraction of the graduate work or the university, or as a conscious decision for a career, but because there is nothing else that attracts them, there is nothing else they want to do elsewhere. By staying a little longer in the university they can defer a decision for a while. It is not surprising that in Britain the drifters are to be found especially in science – the expansion in the number of grants available for graduate study in science has enabled teachers to dangle them before potential research students. Amongst the scientists there are more drifters amongst those with first class honours degrees than amongst those with second class and other degrees. Altogether the drifters make up about 12 per cent of British research students, and a similar proportion in America, but about 20 per cent in science in Britain.

Two more groups remain to be described, the Peter Pans and the students who are covering up their first degrees. The Peter Pans differ from the drifters in that they are kept in the university not so much by the lack of any attractive alternative outside as by the positive attraction of being a student, an unwillingness to grow up and leave the university. They form only a small percentage of the graduate students in Britain and America – some 3 or 4 per cent of students gave answers which would put them in this category, but this may well be an understatement. In countries where there is little pressure on students to complete their undergraduate studies, such students sometimes became perpetual undergraduates.

Lastly there are those who are trying, by gaining a higher degree, to cover up the poor quality of their first degree. Only a few British students (1 per cent) gave a main reason for becoming graduate students that put them in this category, but our survey of students who began their graduate studies in 1957 found that about 20 per cent of them had lower second or third class degrees or pass degrees, and so on balance it seems likely that this category ought to include rather more than 1 per cent of students.

Graduate students can be expected to react differently to the current unrest in universities according to where they fit into this typology. But before considering the part that graduate students are playing in our unrestful universities we must look at their own reasons for discontent.

Relations with other students

The first reaction of many British research students to starting their graduate studies is one of elation that now they no longer have to study subjects merely to pass exams in them. They have only to do work that is relevant to their research. They are not working for any outside boss or large impersonal organization, but only for themselves, in their own chosen field of study. But with this often comes an acute anxiety that for the first time they are working on their own without external controls and without even the ability to pace themselves against their fellow students.

In various forms this feeling of unhappiness at the extent to which they are on their own stays with many of them throughout their research and for some it becomes in various ways their predominant problem. Two related aspects of it were recurrent themes that came up spontaneously at various points in our interviews. These were social loneliness and intellectual isolation. In part they both spring from the inevitably solitary nature of much research. In a few fields of science students often work together, helping one another with their experiments. This is the case especially where large machines, manned by teams, are used for research, as in nuclear physics. But such team work cuts across the normal condition for the award of a doctorate, that it should be for the recipient's own research. It is therefore the exception rather than the rule even in the sciences. When we defined team work so widely that it would include a group working on separate but related problems within the same general field, only 36 per cent even of the scientists we interviewed said they were part of a team. Those who have to do field-work, such as the geologists and some biologists, may spend many solitary months each year tramping mountains and moorlands.

For the student in the humanities team work is virtually unknown. They cannot even make the contacts that arise when students are working in the same laboratories, sharing the same equipment. Much of their work must inevitably be done in libraries, which are places of silence. Also in the British universities they are unlikely to have any study-room or similar work-place provided, which they can share with their fellow research students. Only one in nine of the humanities students whom we interviewed were provided by their universities with any working place outside the library. For most of the remainder their normal place of work, when they were not in the library, was their home, often a solitary bed-sitting-room or a room in lodgings.

The British students most afflicted by loneliness, at least at the beginning of their research, are those who change universities, but many of those who stay on find that most of their friends have left. It might be expected that they would make new friends amongst the graduate students, and this happens to a certain extent; but the British universities, which still generally launch a student directly into his research without any preparatory postgraduate courses, often provide no focal point to bring him into contact with those of his peers with whom he has most in common. Only the Peter Pans are likely to want to make new friends amongst the undergraduates. The other graduate students feel themselves to have

less and less in common with the undergraduates – they have noticed the
well-known phenomenon that the undergraduates are getting younger all
the time.

It might be expected that American students would be less affected by
loneliness, for they start their graduate work by attending a series of
courses, so that the new graduate student is likely to meet in classes those
of his contemporaries who are working in the same or related fields. In
other ways, however, he may find it more difficult to make friends. It is
more customary to change universities on starting graduate studies in
America. Only 29 per cent of our sample and 26 per cent of the Robbins
sample[1] of British graduate students had changed universities on starting
graduate studies. By contrast 83 per cent of those recipients of doctorates
in the U.S.A. in 1966 who had gained their baccalaureates in the U.S.A.
had done so at a different institution.[2] Also the larger and more anonymous
the university, the more difficult it probably is to make friends. D.
Mechanic's study, *Students under Stress*[3] showed that most of the group
of graduate students he was studying had a close network of interrelation-
ships, being brought together by the proximity of their offices and work
within the same area of their subject, but there were a few social isolates in
other buildings and other areas.

Heiss comments, however, on the problems of loneliness of the unmarried students, quoting a student who said, 'To date this problem has
caused me more stress than academic problems.' British students made
very similar comments to us. When we asked our students if in their view
a postgraduate student's life is lonely, in humanities and social studies only
one British research student in five, but in science subjects 55 per cent,
said that it was not lonely. Few universities in Britain or America provide
the kind of really attractive social centre for graduate students that could
help to break down the barrier of loneliness.

Graduate students' loneliness shades into their intellectual isolation,
because the kind of problems of everyday life that the students want to
talk about to their friends tend to be those that arise in connection with
their research. As one of them said to us, 'You can meet people but are
lonely as there is no one with the same interests.' Therefore those students
who commented to us on their loneliness also commented on the lack of

---

1 'Committee on Higher Education (Robbins Committee) Report', Appendix 2B
   Cmnd. 2154 11–1 (London: H.M.S.O., 1964), p. 65.
2 'Doctorate Recipients from United States universities' (Washington D.C.:
   National Academy of Sciences, 1967), *Publication 1489*, p. 53.
3 Mechanic, D., *Students Under Stress* (New York: Free Press of Glencoe, 1962).

intellectual contacts with fellow students. This seems to be less of a problem in American universities; 36 per cent of Heiss's respondents belonged to informal graduate study groups, while Berelsen found that a substantial proportion of recent doctorates thought they had learnt as much from their fellow students as from the faculty.

One of the reasons for the greater degree of intellectual isolation in British universities is the relatively small numbers of graduate students in certain fields in many universities. The number needed for fruitful interchange of ideas is small – perhaps only two – but in some fields at some universities even that number is not achieved. The number needed for an effective seminar group is substantially larger, and the result of having too few students in a given area of study is that they feel the lack of seminars in their own field while complaining that most of the seminars provided are too remote from their topics and often unintelligible to them.

Relations with staff

A lack of satisfactory seminars is only one aspect of students' intellectual isolation. Many students also feel strongly about the remoteness of the staff. This is a matter on which students' views vary considerably. Two students in the same department may give diametrically opposed accounts of the attitudes of the staff towards the graduate students, which suggests that the failure to make contact may be found as much in the student as in the staff. It seems clear not only from our own study but also from the surveys of Heiss and Tucker *et al.* that the student who finds it easy to take the initiative in making contacts with the staff generally meets with every encouragement. The question that has to be asked is whether these contacts should so universally be left to the initiative of the students.

The majority of students both here and in America are satisfied with their contacts with staff. Similarly the majority of students are satisfied with the quality of their supervision. There is, however, a substantial volume of dissent. This concerns especially the early stages of research. When we asked British students if they were satisfied with the closeness of supervision, 38 per cent thought that it was not close enough in the early stages of research. This is a period which students often compare with being taught to swim by being thrown into a swimming bath, which may be a good way to teach swimming, if we ignore the number who drown, but is rarely a happy experience. At the later stages the number who thought it was not close enough dropped to 24 per cent. At each stage it was the students in social studies who were least satisfied. The percentage of Heiss's respondents who thought their major professor should give them more direction in the thesis programme varied from 34 in humanities and social sciences to 46 in professional schools. Similarly Tucker *et al.* found that 49 per cent of respondents rated the teaching faculty as 'fair' or 'poor' on sensitivity to students' needs, though only 17 per cent gave these ratings for the faculty's research skills, and 5 per cent for their knowledge of the field.

In our interviews with graduate students we were acutely aware of the plight of the minority whose supervision was defective, ranging from merely not being as good as it might be to being outrightly negligent. The student is often extremely dependent on his supervisor's aid and guidance at every stage, from the choice of a soluble problem of the right size for a thesis, onwards. One of the most common defects is that the supervisor knows too little of the area in which the student is working. If he is a senior member of staff he can spare too little time for the student, but if he is more junior the student suffers for the supervisor's inexperience.

Fortunately for the students' peace of mind, they were often unaware of incompetence on the part of the supervisor of which I sometimes became very conscious when interviewing them.

In Britain, inadequate contact with the supervisor is most common in the humanities or social studies, though by no means unknown in the sciences – it was a scientist who told us that her supervisor did not ask her about her progress for nearly a year. A few scientists have the opposite complaint – they are used merely as pairs of hands to carry out their supervisors' research; it was a science professor who defined Ph.D. work as 'Research carried out by a supervisor under more than usually trying circumstances'. We did not ask students a specific question here and so the number who mentioned this may not be a good measure of its frequency. In Tucker's survey 30 per cent of students marked as valid the criticism of doctoral study that it exploited its students by using them as cheap labour. Where this occurs it is a reflection of the increasing pressure in the universities towards research.

The facilities for graduate studies

Libraries are for most students of the humanities or the social sciences what both equipment and laboratories are for science students – both tools of research and place of work. For all research students the adequacy of their tools of research is of such importance that it is often more important than adequate instruction and supervision. We heard many complaints about the equipment and libraries, but it was not always easy to know how to evaluate these. The equipment needed for scientific research is constantly becoming more expensive, and at constant prices the cost per scientist for major equipment seems to be rising by some 10 or 20 per cent per annum.[1] Clearly a student does not have an absolute right to use any equipment he may want for his research, regardless of its price. He does, however, have the right not to be put on to research on a problem for which the equipment is not available and either cannot be made available or cannot be obtained without very long delays – it is almost always the supervisor who chooses the detailed topic in science. But 36 per cent of our research students in pure science and 40 per cent in applied science complained of difficulties with the supply of equipment.

Similarly scholars will always complain about their libraries, as did 40 per cent of our students in humanities and social studies – there will always be some rare book or manuscript that the library cannot provide, or some special arrangement of the catalogue needed for a specific piece of research. The important question is how reasonable are the complaints. Most of those we heard were extremely reasonable, in that they concerned considerable difficulties that students were meeting in getting the basic books for their researches. Our findings on this have been confirmed by the report of the Parry Committee on university libraries.[2] The inadequacies of many university libraries reported to us by our respondents have made me come to the conclusion that, in Britain, adequate library facilities for most research students are available only in those few towns that house the older copyright libraries, where there are large historic collections and where the privilege of acquiring free all copyright books gives them large numbers of current acquisitions.

It may be asked why, so often, universities take on research students when they cannot hope to have enough to make a viable group within a given field, when they cannot provide them with efficient supervision, with adequate facilities for their work and with the equipment and libraries they need. Sometimes the answer is that the student needs to go to the expert in his chosen field. Not every university can have an expert on the church in eleventh-century Spain, or the parasites of the intestinal worms of fishes. Sometimes, however, the answer is that the student is there

---

1 Cohen, A. V., and Ivins, L. N., 'The Sophistication Factor in Science Expenditure', *Science Policy Studies No. 1* (London: H.M.S.O., 1967).
2 *University Grants Committee, Report of the Committee on Libraries (Parry Report)* (London: H.M.S.O., 1967).

because, on the one hand, he did not know in advance of the inadequacies of his chosen institution, while, on the other, the university takes him on regardless of its inadequacies because its own internal pressures towards research produce a need for research students. Also the pressure towards research produces a wish to offload the teaching of undergraduates, and to a considerable extent in America, but to a far lesser extent in Britain, this teaching is done by the graduate students.

Examinations and courses

There is another students' stress that is specific to America – the need to pass a number of formal hurdles in addition to the satisfactory completion of research and the passing of an oral examination on it. Before an American student can be allowed to submit his dissertation he must successfully pass a number of courses, generally over a period of two years, he must pass examinations in, generally, two foreign languages, and he must pass a qualifying examination, often with both written papers and an oral examination. The provision of the courses gives the research student in the better American universities a broad understanding of his subject combined with a preparation for research that his British counterpart too often lacks; but some of the courses seem to the students too remote from their field of interest, and there would probably be widespread agreement in both Britain and America that, whereas the British student receives too little preparation for his research, the American receives, in some ways, too much. They tend to regard the successive hurdles which they have to pass as initiation rites. Also failure at these hurdles, which may often be completely unrelated to ability at research, is one of the reasons for the higher drop-out rate of American students.

Married students

The current trend towards lower average ages on marriage is producing an increasing proportion of married graduate students. Their financial position can be better or worse than that of the unmarried, depending on whether their wives are at work and they get by on the sweat of their fraus, or whether they have children and extra mouths to feed but no extra money from which to feed them.

They generally avoid the loneliness of the unmarried, but at some cost. The student is likely to work erratic hours, depending on the flow of ideas, the progress of the work, the need to carry out experiments that cannot be left off in the middle, or, in America, the imminence of the Ph.D. qualifying exam and other hurdles. At times most of the student's thoughts throughout his waking hours will be on his research. As one of them said to us, 'The big problem is the shortage of hours in the day.' At the one extreme, a spouse who is a fellow student is likely to work similar hours, and in a similar way. At the other extreme, a student may find that a spouse whose education finished at a much earlier stage is unable even to begin to understand the problems that are uppermost in his mind, while a wife who is left alone with small children all day may resent spending solitary evenings too, especially when her husband's student status gives them a much lower standard of living than they would otherwise have. Under these circumstances any marriage that is not very firmly based may not survive.

Graduates and revolts

It may be wondered why, when a substantial proportion of graduate students are working under the difficulties I have described, they are not in a constant state of revolt. So far it seems clear that the majority of them have taken relatively little active part in student unrest, though, when they do take part, their greater maturity tends to bring them into leading positions, so that it is easy to get an exaggerated impression of the extent of their role. In the extent of graduate participation there are some differences between Britain and America, due, I believe, to two factors. First, much of the support for recent student revolts seems to have come from social studies students, especially sociologists, with the scientists and technologists playing a far smaller part. In the U.S.A. in 1963-4, 24·7 per cent of the higher degrees awarded in fields other than education were in the social sciences (excluding law).[1] The comparable figure for Britain was 7·2 per cent.[2] The recent rapid rise in the proportion of graduate students in the social sciences, if it continues, may have interesting implications for the future.

Secondly the American graduates' greater participation in under-graduate teaching brings them into closer contact with the centres of

[1] Business and commerce, geography, psychology, basic and applied social sciences (excluding history). Source: analysis of data given in Wright, Patricia. Earned degrees conferred 1963-4 (Washington U.S. Dept. of Health, Education and Welfare: U.S. Government Printing Office, 1966).
[2] Data from: U.G.C. *First Employment of University Graduates 1963-4* (London: H.M.S.O., 1965). Preliminary analyses for 1966-7 shows that this figure had risen to 11·7.

student discontent and makes them as Jenks and Riesman[1] have pointed out, the shop stewards.

In Britain, however, only the scientists and engineers, who generally take a relatively minor part in student politics, do much undergraduate teaching. On the other hand most of the circumstances I have been describing tend to isolate graduate students from dissident undergraduates. A student who spends his days and nights working in a library away from his university, or in his lodgings, may not even know what is happening in his university. Even if he generally works in the university, when he has few social contacts, or, being married, centres his social life outside the university, he is unlikely to become highly involved in student protest. But, most important of all, the characteristics of most graduate students, and the impact on them of research, are likely to turn them away from undergraduate protest. The dedicated scholar and the would-be academic are likely, as they get deeper into their researches, to become so immersed in them that they give little time or thought to anything else. It takes a great deal to prise the really dedicated scholar from his work. It is only the most fundamental and all embracing episodes – those in which most of the undergraduates are involved and many of the faculty side with the students – that will draw in any graduate students other than the Peter Pans; though, as I have said, once they are drawn in they are likely to play a prominent role.

Graduate students do rebel against their working conditions, but they do it in a different way – they drop out. At undergraduate level about 15 per cent of students leave the university without gaining a degree (though some gain one elsewhere later). At higher degree level we found that in humanities and social studies 50 per cent and in science and technology 24 per cent of the students who entered graduate study in 1957–8 had not by the summer of 1966 achieved the degree at which they were aiming. Tucker's study makes it clear that if there were comparable figures for the U.S.A. they would show substantially higher drop-out rates than the British figures. The high drop-out rates more than any other fact make it clear that all is not well with graduate education in Britain and North America.

1 Jenks, C., and Riesman, D., 'The War Between Generations', *The Record*, October 1967, 69 (1), 1–21.

Robert Chester

Role conflict and the junior academic

Daily experience of university life makes it clear that among more junior academic staff there exists a measure of disaffection, amounting in extreme cases to social and political alienation from the university and its arrangements. This point has been emphasized at those universities which have recently experienced militant student action, where some members of the academic staff have been heavily engaged in the confrontation on the student side. Such overt demonstrations of estrangement, however, are not the only, and probably not the most important, problems relating to the commitment of younger academic staff to the university institution and its values. For one thing, it might be noted that not all those who have involved themselves in militant protests have been either young or junior; one significant group consists of disillusioned 'old rebels', who in a sense are seeing their own past relived in different terms, and whose hearts are clearly with the demonstrators although they know that failure is much more likely than success. The major point argued here, however, is that open and extreme alienation of this kind, often based on political affiliation, is less dangerous to the universities than is their own failure to incorporate fully into their value-structure and institutional arrangements the most recent cohorts of academic recruits. Conceivably, the understanding and resolution of the problem of engaging commitment from staff may be strategically more important to the universities than the issues posed by student unrest. What follows is an attempt to sketch some possible causes of the current situation, and some clues to what needs to be done.

Conventionally the work of an academic is said to fall into three parts, teaching, research and administration. This rough analysis, however, oversimplifies the tasks in which academics engage, and a more exact specification is needed to give clear definition to the academic role. An academic, then, is likely to engage in the following activities, either concurrently or at different phases of his career:

1. Initiating undergraduates into a cultural and academic tradition.
2. Teaching undergraduates in fields which are directly related to subsequent vocation.
3. Teaching undergraduates in fields which are not directly related to subsequent vocation.
4. Training students to enter a profession.
5. Supervising the education of graduate students in advanced areas of specialized disciplines. Such students provide the pool of future academics, and this work is very closely linked with the research activities which follow later.
6. Assessment of students by the media of essays, tutorial performance, written examinations and theses.
7. Pastoral guidance of students in social and personal matters, especially where these have relevance to academic performance.
8. Research in the sense of original work on the frontiers of a discipline.
9. Research in the sense of problem-solving commissions.
10. Research in the sense of any original or critical thinking in an academic form.
11. Superintendence of research assistants and other research staff.
12. Administration at various levels, via committees, formal office or informal responsibilities.
13. Participation in the deliberative structure of the university.

Many of these items are of course interconnected, but they compete within the allocation of personal resources and they call for diverse aptitudes. More importantly, such tasks call both for training, and for socialization into a set of academic values, and these are matters which tend to be non-existent or neglected in contemporary universities. Universities invest a beginning academic with a professional role without there being formal arrangements to impart the skills necessary for major areas of his work, to foster the internalization of appropriate values, or to ensure incorporation into the public life of the institution. Induction into most major professional roles is marked by processes which impart both skills and values in an integrated fashion, and certainly in every other branch of the teaching profession it is deemed desirable, if not necessary, for there to be training in pedagogic skills. For historical reasons such processes may have been less necessary in universities, but developments in the post-war period, accelerating in recent years, have led to an increasingly problematic situation, and it is necessary to examine these developments further.

In the past universities were relatively small, new staff were recruited in small numbers, and recruited from a student body which by and large was not of a temper to challenge the university *status quo*. Processes of induction were informal, and most recruits were prepared to accept educational procedures which were legitimated by their venerability. There was little recognition of the fact that teaching, assessment, selection, administration, etc., have an expertise of their own, based on research the results of which, although often less than certain, are many times more valuable than personal guesses or traditional modes. In much of what they did (and do) academics of all levels of seniority were (and are) amateurs, much like the recently-castigated administrative branch of the Civil Service. The student body was an acquiescent clientele, the state took relatively little interest in university matters, and the public at large were not much concerned with institutions of high education. These kinds of conditions meant that the universities needed to give little thought to matters of professional socialization or the engagement of loyalty to the institution, but the radical and rapid expansion of higher education in recent years has rendered such lack of attention not only obsolete but dangerous.

Expansion has led to a changed demographic pattern in the academic profession. There has been a great influx of staff at the level of assistant-lecturer or just above, and a redistribution of existing academics for promotion elsewhere, with the consequence that in many departments there is a gap in the middle range of seniority. The induction of large numbers of inexperienced young staff without there being constitutional and social arrangements to secure their incorporation into the existing university community has led to a tendency for the newcomers to form an age-specific sub-culture, one function of which is to form a bridge between the roles of student and professional academic. A situation has arisen where many younger academics no more feel part of 'the university' than do most students, and in extreme cases this has resulted in continued identification with student cultures or aspirations.

Further, it seems likely that expansion has led to the appointment of individuals who might not earlier have been appointed. Selection committees (which in any case lack clear definitions of what they are seeking and objective procedures for finding it) have tended to apply narrower criteria of selection, thus bringing into the academic ranks many who lack commitment to teaching or to learning outside of a specialized field. Such individuals tend to be humanistically impoverished, committed to their professional specialism rather than to academic life, energetic and market-oriented, and thus migratory and underassimilated in terms of loyalty to particular universities or to an educational mission. Tendencies of this kind are reinforced by certain features of the promotion system which are to be discussed.

It must be noted also that recent incomers to the academic profession have been recruited from the student generation of the 1960s. That is to say, they are part of the generation nurtured in the post-war world of relative welfare and affluence, in which their future comfort and status is assured, and in which higher education is increasingly viewed as a right rather than a privilege (with corresponding diminution of emphasis on responsibilities). Their world also has been one in which many major orthodoxies have been overturned, in which a specific youth-culture has developed and in which many previously docile or subject groups have become self-consciously assertive. Such a generation is disinclined to accept existing practices simply because they are traditional; rather the reverse – that which is traditional is examined closely and with suspicion. Increasingly students are seeking effective participation in university life and decision-making, and this must be reflected in the attitudes of new staff. Pitched into his role of teacher with few guide-lines or directives, the newcomer is likely to be aware of defects in existing methods of teaching and assessment, and sensitive to his own amateurism. Further, his experiences in the department give him a new and sometimes disturbing perspective on the academic process, particularly as he becomes privy to the attitudes and concerns of senior staff and, occasionally, to their lack of response to contemporary ideas and lack of concern for expertise. Too commonly senior academics seem unable to disentangle cherished and important values from the particular institutional forms in which they first encountered them, and this leads to a generational gulf in perceptions not only of what is desirable but of what is possible.

New staff also enter institutions whose structure is at best imperfectly adapted to current conditions and needs. The constitutions of most civic universities have located power firmly in the hands of what is now only a small minority of the academic staff, the professoriate. Furthermore, many events have conspired to concentrate power even more at the centre than previously, or to locate it outside the university altogether. Factors which have had such centrifugal or centripetal effects may be desirable in themselves, but undoubtedly they have led to a situation where younger academics feel cut off from decisions which affect them. The need for large grants for research purposes has meant that outside bodies decide what projects should be undertaken, and where, and the awarding of such grants creates an obligation within the university to place responsibility, and therefore authority, with a particular (and usually senior) individual. In many fields therefore the idea of a university as a circle of academic peers practising a craft comes to be replaced by the idea of a set of research bureaucracies, with attendant division of labour and hierarchy. The migratory pattern amongst staff leads to the vesting of decisive influence with more permanent and established figures, particularly older professors, and the expanded size of Senates has meant a decrease in collective effectiveness and increase in the tendency for business to be controlled by a minority. Competition between departments for development funds, buildings, staff and other resources creates political conditions which lead to the need for centralized control, and inter-disciplinary departments or centres create problems which tend to be resolved by their boards reporting to high levels than do departments, e.g. to Senate rather than to Faculty Boards. Dependence on public finance, and the massive state investment in higher education means that crucial decisions are taken either outside the university altogether, or inside but under considerable pressures to act in a particular way. These, and other factors which could be listed, have reinforced the hierarchic and authoritarian features which were already implicit in the organization of most universities, and have also increased the size and influence of administrative staff, and the potency of administrative considerations. Thus the conception of what constitutes 'the university' comes to be narrowed to its administrative organs and officers, and it is not uncommon to hear academic staff referring to 'the university' as though it were something which stood over *against* themselves, rather than *consisting* of themselves, their students, and their graduates. Furthermore, tension between academic and administrator often arises because the administrator is implementing policy decisions in the shaping of which the academic played no part and of whose existence he may have been unaware until a specific implementation occurred. Undoubtedly, impersonalization of relationships, exclusion from deliberation, and the priorities of administrative rationality can foster the self-conception of being merely an employee of the university rather than a member of a community, thus leading to a weakening of moral commitment and of sense of professional identity. Qualitative and quantitative developments, then, have created problems for universities related to the engagement of staff loyalty and commitment to central values, and this has occurred at a time when in any case universities are far from clear in their self-understanding. What a university is, or should be, is the subject of much debate, and what younger staff rapidly learn is that ritual claims to be a community of scholars are in most cases simple cant. Further, the newcomer finds himself faced with certain role-conflicts or dilemmas. It has already been noted that he is defined as a professional without there being any training in (or testing of) certain areas of his work, and that as a teacher he is left to find his own way. Immediately he begins he becomes aware of the problem of what *sort* of teacher he is to be, whether an instructor, a sage, or a Socratic mentor. Many students seek to press upon him a combination of instructor and sage, and this is likely either to clash with his academic ideals or to reinforce any tendency he may have to regard his teaching as a mechanical chore to be dealt with in minimal fashion. In the case of the former possibility there may result either a corruption of the ideals, or the development of intolerance towards the general run of undergraduates for their failure to live up to unrealistic expectations.

This matter is closely related to promotion practices and career prospects. Although teaching, research and administrative contributions are all allegedly considered in promotion decisions it is difficult to find academics who believe that this is really the case. There tends to be a subtle discounting of undergraduate teaching, and there are indeed difficulties in objectively measuring teaching skill. Further, it is not so much *research* as *publication* which is rewarded, and this is an incitement not only to concentrate personal resources on the research side of the role (for which anyway the academic has been more adequately trained), but possibly also to concentrate on short-term research projects which lead to early publication. Again, the rewards of publication are national, whereas those of teaching and administration are local. Thus, migratory, discipline-oriented staff are confirmed in their attitudes, and those committed to the local institution and to an educational mission may find themselves disadvantaged in career prospects. It might be noted that such factors are likely to be exacerbated in due course when the recent influx of assistant lecturers leads to promotion blocks and heavier competition.

Also related here is the question of autonomy. In many cases the need for research grants leads to dependence on the patronage of senior colleagues who have more developed relationships with grant-giving bodies. Additionally, career advancement is very dependent on the recommendation of an individual's head of department. These situations create pressures to conformity which clash with the ideal of the autonomous scholar and may generate resentful quiescence. Undoubtedly some feel that there are penalties attached to independence of thought and action, and to the allocation of more than minimal resources to teaching and counselling. Such feelings doubtless do injustice to senior colleagues, and the penalties may be more apparent than real, but since it is what men think to be true which guides their actions some are led to play safe and to leave affairs of importance to others.

It is not the contention here that the universities are filled with younger staff who are universally uncommitted, disaffected or perplexed. Rather it is claimed that such features have increased, are increasing, and ought to be diminished. Undoubtedly there are many younger academics who are under-assimilated or insecurely-motivated, some small number who feel extremely alienated, and a larger number who experience frustrations and discontents. New entrants to the profession need arrangements to facilitate the role-change which they have made and to equip them with the knowledge and instruments which they need for their development as professional men. Because of the changed demography of the profession, and because of the changed internal and external context of higher education, the university needs to attend much more explicitly than hitherto to its modes of incorporating younger staff into its value system, deliberative structure and community life. The question of training is clearly raised, not only at the introductory stage, but as a firmly institutionalized feature on an on-going, in-service basis, with provision for making widely available the results of research into relevant educational matters. Universities have been curiously reluctant to investigate their own methods of teaching and assessment or how best to promote fruitful research. Continuous critical review of methods and agencies would mesh well with a training system, and do much to ensure the acquisition of a professional skill in teaching, besides restoring proper weight to the teaching aspect of the professional role.

Even more important than training, however, is the acquisition of an appropriate academic stance. From the point of view of the institution it is clear that while there is room for great diversity of styles among academics there is also need for commitment to a core of university values and for some feeling of involvement in the affairs of the particular university. From the point of view of the academic, the arrangements made for his freedom, consultation and representation have crucial importance for the ways in which they symbolize the underlying value-structure and influence his capacity to internalize and transmit scholarly ways. If he is to be an intellectual craftsman, and to effectively initiate others into the craft, then he needs to operate within a context of arrangements and relationships which support rather than subvert the major academic values. The most fruitful approach to meeting the needs of both institution and individual would be to ensure that academics are drawn early into the complexities and responsibilities of decision-making, most specially at

the departmental level. An individual's commitment to policies is undoubtedly greater if he has shared in the shaping of them, but more
importantly, such responsible participation is an imperative of the kind
of work which academics do and the kind of values which inform it. Even
without constitutional changes it is possible to develop arrangements
which are more collegiate than those commonly found, and collegiate
arrangements are more likely than others to draw newcomers into social
and political relationships with established members of the university.
Since the seniority gap is also a generational gap, the ensuing dialogue is
likely to have beneficial consequences for both parties, and also for the
policies and ambience of the institution. If there is to be rational and
informed decision-making, if there is to be organized scepticism within a
communality of knowledge, and if discourse is to be dispassionate, open-
ended, critical and continuous, then the university must devise relationships which foster the necessary qualities and mobilize the energies and
talents of all its members. Only in this way can an institution which is both
scholarly *and* a community develop.

The most recent few years have been a tumultuous period in the development of the universities, and there has been preoccupation with the sheer
mechanics and logistics of expansion. Undoubtedly strains have developed
which have resulted in student unrest and staff disquiet, and the time has
now come for an examination of the meanings and latent consequences of
existing procedures and relationships. As they become larger, more
diversified and difficult in their complexity for anyone to know fully,
universities must develop a more self-conscious approach to the problem
of engaging value-commitment and institutional loyalty from academics.
Otherwise they may find that individual modes of adaptation arise which
not only threaten attenuation of purpose and dilution of values, but lead
to corrective action imposed from without in ways which threaten the
foundations of academic freedom and university autonomy. As centres of
critical rationality and engines of change the universities have a duty to
attend to their own motes, as well as to the beams of others.

Geoffrey Martin

Organizational forms and styles of protest

For the vast majority of students today, including the moderates and the revolutionaries, society by its very structure forbids popular involvement in change. There is little argument between us about racial issues, social security and the tightly knit hierarchy of social structures including Government, because for all of us, radical change must come. Equality of educational opportunity, economic planning and peaceful coexistence are the targets to which we all aspire. To all of us Britain seems to be wallowing in a deep depression of self analysis and there is little sign of moving ahead. Many students abhor a technological society which ignores the need to preserve the dignity of people by offering them a choice, but instead, dictates the areas and strata in which they are compelled to remain for the rest of their lives. A bus conductor in Liverpool has little opportunity to become anything other than a bus conductor. A scientist in Unilever will in most cases remain a prisoner of the vast industrial mono-lith. A bureaucrat will remain a bureaucrat because he is compelled to absorb the dictates of bureaucracy and become a victim of the system. The student himself, who at least has three years to look around and evaluate his future, is forced in the end to choose between relatively few alternatives, all of which reduce his eventual freedom of movement. Even if he avoids becoming a slave of the Establishment machine, he has little real opportunity to influence decisions or appeal to the decision makers. Above him are the small group of leaders – the politicians, the industrialists, who, between them, present a virtually impervious stratum to all who dis-agree with their policies. Only the few students who accept the old order are allowed to take over.

To almost all students this is the image of Britain today. It is unpleasant, frustrating, but it has to be accepted or rejected. It is corrupt, unfair, unequal, and by its very nature must remain so. Students have recently undergone a visible change in their attitudes towards society in general. Very few indeed, are prepared to accept the traditions which have been established down through the years. This change of heart is the result of

GAC

many factors. The ever increasing size of the student population has meant that a wider cross-section of society become students and naturally corporate interests inevitably arise as a result. Students are a recognizable social grouping and are seldom content to abide by the dictum 'a student is a student is a student'. Why should youth be compelled to remain silent when the Government and the country are facing new challenges – economic and racial and social. Student pressure is here to stay but the students themselves have not so far agreed how far their influence can extend and how best it can be effected. It is the role of students which divides them more than any other factor. Arguments about their influence, propaganda and organizational strength have resulted in a deeply divided student community and so far only those who advance the most revolutionary ideas have hit the headlines.

Much nonsense has been written about ways of dealing with the so-called student revolt without any real understanding of why they are rebelling and what they want to achieve. Many students who agree that society is unpleasant are utterly at a loss when deciding ways and means of rectifying the problem. How to implement one's policies has for several years been a more important problem for students than agreeing on a particular policy. In educational reform, virtually no differences of opinion exist between students about the areas in which reform is necessary. The real problem arises about how to achieve success and the way in which their ideas and policies must be pushed. Most students agree that their representatives should participate in university government. Some argue that this participation should not be achieved through democratically elected representatives but instead they want large numbers of delegates under strict mandate from the student population at large – a situation that logically leads to student power.

In order to understand the student problem properly one must accept that the basic conflict is between those who have decided to reform within the present structure of society or the university structure because they see no other effective means of achieving anything, and those who want to remove the social structure itself.

Throughout the 1950s and early 60s many causes were espoused by students and others, but the futility of public demonstrations traditionally used to influence Government policy drove students into despair and paved the way for the recent extreme emotional outburst leading to violence and mass uncontrolled demonstrations.

It might be worth some short analysis of the background to these frustrations. Usually it has been the case that a considerable degree of idealism has characterized youth. Before the war it was fighting in Spain. Immediately after the war the United Nations provided a goal worth supporting, and the principles annunciated in the U.N. Charter appeared to many young people to be the answer to a new and healthy World Order.

The advent of the Bomb and the ensuing Campaign for Nuclear Disarmament represented to many student activists in the 50s an important crusade towards a better way of life and the eventual establishment of World Peace. Anti-apartheid was yet another cause widely supported by young people who believed that men were born equal no matter the colour of their skin, their religion or class. But significantly, of all the causes and campaigns mounted by students, which followed each other with ever increasing frustration on the part of the participants, the evils were allowed to remain, the Government turned a blind eye and many young people turned away revolted, confused or reactivated in their desire to try again. Despite the loss of public support, the increased maturity of those who grew older, and the cynicism of those who rationalized furiously, the message was passed from student generation to generation that more effort was required. Leaving aside the Hungarian bloodshed of 1956 which merely disillusioned those who were members of the Communist Party – a small minority by any standards – and reinforced the non-Communist beliefs of those who were not, the late 50s and early 60s brought forth even greater perplexity for the marching idealists. The Vietnam war, at one time a relatively minor trouble spot in South-East Asia, grew rapidly into a sordid blood bath, which few could defend and even fewer justify. It was to become the single most important subject for anti-U.S. propaganda the world over, and the issue upon which many student tacticians fastened their hopes for the first popularly based overthrow of established Government policy. Demonstration followed demonstration until the whole leftist propaganda machine fed on itself and created a massive and increasingly popular movement against the United States, its allies and capitalism in general.

When in 1964 a Labour Government was elected, the vast majority of imaginative youth watched eagerly for a fresh lead from the British political scene. The Vietnam debates were eagerly followed in the House of Commons but, in the end, although the Government refused to send troops, it continued to lend enough support to U.S. policy to disgust many who genuinely believed that Labour meant the Socialism that it preached. Later an economic crisis laid bare the dependence of Britain on the U.S. for its economic survival, and this chastening fact, quickly followed by the C.I.A. student scandal, which exposed a network of treachery across the world, was more than most radicals could stand. It had been conclusively proved, particularly to the most ardent revolutionary, that democracy, government, and our society, would pay virtually no attention whatever to anything that they had campaigned for through recent years. The gap between Parliament and people was widening continually. The Government was under attack, the political parties in Parliament were attacked, and the Communist Party, the one-time haven of the Left was angrily dismissed as nothing more than neo-Stalinist. There was little or nothing left to cling to or support. Militarism on the right, Stalinism on the left and hypocrisy in the democratic socialist centre. The radicals were completely fenced in on all sides. There was no ideology or non-disruptive strategy that had not been tried. There were few politicians who escaped the rising tide of dissent and personal aggression. The only way out for the frustrated radicals was to attack with all the pent up emotion they could muster. But among them were a few who intelligently succeeded in harnessing the latent frustration into an extremely broadly based attack on the organizational structure of British society itself.

There may be many interpretations of the course of events over the last ten years which has led to the present state of student unrest. The variety of interpretations is not so important as the fact that a difficult situation now exists. The public and, most important of all, the decision makers must learn to understand fully the cause of the trouble. Apart from extremist activists the present situation greatly affects the student moderates. They want to work within the system but this does not mean that they necessarily believe that the system is satisfactory. They do not, and moreover they recognize the dangers of becoming absorbed within it. But by and large they have decided that with careful planning their policies can be effected, and the system itself changed, without undue sacrifice to efficiency and order. The extremist elements have become so dissatisfied with constant failure to make an impression by normal methods that they have recently decided the social structure itself must be removed as a precondition for any lasting changes whatever. This is essentially a step towards anarchy but it is no good saying that by moving close to anarchy if not by supporting it these groups should be discarded and destroyed. There is too much confusion to distinguish the true anarchist from the supporter of his methods and anyway he seldom uses anarchy as an incentive. Often the most able and articulate spokesmen among the revolutionaries will shy away from charges of promoting anarchy. They do not seriously believe that it is anarchy that they effectively preach and its methods they use and their supporters are more interested in the policy than in a description of the means used to achieve it.

Obviously, among the advocates of social revolution there are the tacticians, the political planners. Whether they rely on theorists like Marcuse for an instructive approach to their mass activities, or whether they themselves have worked out a plan of political strategy is not as important as the fact that one exists. On British University campuses, in student organizations of all kinds, there is information upon which an almost identical strategy for action can be planned. The press have accused a dangerous minority of American and overseas students. Communists have been blamed, but the techniques now in use have seldom been understood. They are simple, and provided a good theoretical base has been agreed, any students with common sense could conduct the entire operation.

Success depends on obvious facilities being at hand: the creation of a suitable atmosphere of mistrust between students and the authorities. This can easily be achieved by propaganda – anonymous leaflets levelling false accusations or articulate spokemen prepared to become martyrs; the establishment of negotiating objectives which are unattainable and which easily result in popular loss of confidence in democratically elected student leaders; the manipulation of mass ignorance and the need to act always under mandate from the mass; the antipathy to compromise solutions; the total emphasis placed on complete and uncompromising success immediately. These and other simple techniques are used time and time again by extremists to create initial confusion and later on mass involvement.

Not a very obvious but an important technique is the practice of using already established democratic student unions at a local level as a target for attack so that self styled extremist leaders can exploit the situation to their own advantage. When a suitable issue arises on which it is planned to base an extended campaign against authority and upon which little or no support is forthcoming from the democratically elected student union leaders, inevitably an unofficial group will be established. The leaders of such a group will not be elected but will profess to reflect the mass of student feeling. Informal so-called open mass meetings will be held where spokesmen demand outrageous concessions, and in the end widespread support will be enlisted for what seems a popular move amongst an emotional and confused audience. The student union, the official body, is thus deemed irrelevant to the issue and subsequently ignored. The Essex University situation in 1968 was in many respects a classic example of the revolutionary approach to mass action and unrest. The student union was pathetically weak and several months before the crisis the revolutionaries succeeded in disaffiliating it from the National Union of Students. This simple manœuvre prevented any other body of students from interfering in the subsequent turmoil. A controversial issue was chosen to exploit germ warfare. A meeting to discuss it was broken up in chaos by extremists, and the speaker from Porton Down roughed up in the corridors of the building. Publicity followed in the national press, questions were asked in Parliament, the activists were suspended by the Vice Chancellor acting under duress, and immediately grievances were raised on the nature of the disciplinary procedures. Victimization was alleged and ensuing sympathy attracted large numbers of supporters. The attack was broadened to cover not only discipline but the whole of the university system and the way it was run. Teach-ins were quickly organized and the students refused to negotiate in committees on any matter.

In the end the university was completely at a standstill. Many ordinary students who joined in what seemed a popular issue failed even to understand the tactics of which they were so necessary a part, whilst giving lusty support to the few willing martyrs who appeared to have been victimized. In commenting on Essex and the possible need for reform within it, one should not forget that it is one of the most forward looking institutions in Britain. The demands made during the crisis were impossible to meet on any reasonable basis and were therefore ideal when used as impossible negotiating platforms by those who wished to reject negotiation in favour of nationwide publicity and the spread of unrest. The Essex student had followed L.S.E. with honours, and in subsequent months more and more colleges and universities used similar techniques to disrupt work and extract concessions under duress. The important point is, that in almost all places where this technique was used, concessions were granted where moderation had previously failed.

However, the case at Essex was one in which the student union locally was weak and ineffectual. In places where that is not the case and in particular at a national level, several attempts at structural change of a very basic nature within some organizations has begun. All of these have been launched during the last two years and are interesting indications of how the very nature of our democratic system itself is now under attack. They are designed to prove the futility of negotiating with authority and the necessity to effect change by mass action of a militant type. A small but important example may illustrate the point.

From large delegate conferences down to small local meetings the role of the chairman is important. He is required to be non-partisan, to protect the right to dissent, to prevent disorder and to act with discretion concerning the time taken to conduct business and the number of speakers on each side of an argument. A good chairman will perform these functions to the satisfaction of most delegates provided they accept that he must be given responsibility to exercise his judgement. He is respected if the result is impartial and the business proceeds. In conferences of the N.U.S. in which a very large number of interest groups are present the chairman is traditionally limited by regulation in what he may or may not do. But in the past he has always been seen to bear heavy responsibilities. Recently this has altered radically and it has been extremists who have taken initiatives to bind the chairman to such a degree with regulations and rules that it has become exceedingly difficult to steer such conferences without being compelled to resort to lengthy procedures which bore, confuse and often anger the average delegate. To revolutionaries the chairman represents authority and it too must be removed.

The result is obvious. One regulation to control a chairman's action means that other regulations become necessary in order to control or limit other actions he may take, and if one is not prepared to allow the chairman discretion and sometimes authority then logically the chair must be subject to regulations providing for every type of situation which arises. The tactic is that chairmanship becomes a legally directed technical operation. It requires regulations to resolve each different situation. A chairman ceases to be able to exercise human judgement but instead must respond automatically according to the rule book. The resultant effect is chaos. The revolutionaries, who reject the need for the normal chairman at all, favour someone who is a spokesman for their united voice, or a 'megaphone', used to communicate agreement on mass policy. The virtual strangulation of chairmanship with intricate rules is a necessary means of discrediting popular direction of meetings through the chair in the eyes of modern anarchists. Not unnaturally in student meetings where the platform party has usually more continuity than the transient members of each delegation, the platform, not the revolutionaries, is blamed for perpetuating rules and bureaucracy when in fact it opposed their initial introduction. Thus because the chairman is required to follow rules and exercise his authority to impose them he is attacked more often because they exist. Few chairmen can survive such a situation and therefore the need for a chairman at all is more easily resolved.

This example is only one of many where anarchist student pressures are breaking up or bringing to a standstill the normal democratic functioning of conferences and organizations of all kinds. The N.U.S. holds the largest conferences of students in Britain and provides an interesting case study of the means by which democratic bodies can be slowly brought to their knees if attention is not drawn to the methods used to inhibit their operation.

The need to maintain majority rule to ensure the democracy of organizations is also being questioned by the extreme left. Whilst attempts will continue to be made in order to elect extremists to the Executive bodies of all kinds of useful and effective organizations, the views of minorities are now being used as the vehicle for current manœuvres designed to disrupt the organizations themselves. Whilst in a healthy organization, accountability to the electorate necessitates certain concessions being made towards minority views, but eventually insists upon obedience to the decisions of the majority, currently it is minorities that are used to launch attacks on structures which extremists mean to destroy. If the minority point of view is not provided for by the Executive body responsible, then despite the prior interests of the majority, which must exist in a democratic framework, the minority alleges neglect against the Executive organs responsible. Following such accusations *ad hoc* bodies professing knowledge of minority problems and possessing minority support set themselves up as parasites whose existence depends on criticism of the original decision or efforts to implement it, and invariably centres on the competence of those leaders required to produce the results. The effects of persistent martyrdom by such groups is to polarize a given situation, and in cases where continuity is lacking they can successfully cause an acute division of loyalty, particularly on the part of young, inexperienced people who wish to appear fair. When the structure, not the policy, is used as the reason for exploitation of loyalty, organizational difficulties become much more acute. Refusal to accept the decision of the majority in student organizations has become a real source of irritation and is more and more often used to confuse. Over a period of time such tactics can obviously weaken the influence of the organization concerned. If no agreement on a framework can emerge it is difficult to agree on how the framework can be used.

To the public at large the best known example is undoubtedly the young Liberals' attitude and behaviour within the policy-making bodies of that Party. They have changed it in a relatively short space of time from a parliamentary political Party in which dissenting voices on policy could be voiced within an orderly structure, into an organization in which the real debate is the structure itself and whether its leaders should operate within Parliament or instead become an anti-parliamentary mass opposition group.

Perhaps it is unusual to have dwelt so much on the details of how organizations are run and the impact of the current revolutionary philosophy upon them. The picture which is now emerging in the student world generally shows conclusively that original frustration over a wide field has resulted almost naturally in an involuntary attack on the nature of organizations of all kinds. Very few people will ever think about the importance of the role of a chairman because until recently parliamentary procedures in all kinds of organizations have worked to the satisfaction of the members. British parliamentary democracy has until now been held up as an ideal in itself. Now it is under heavy attack. People in authority have ignored or underestimated the feelings of emotion behind the dissenting groups or alternatively have hoped that the problem would just go away in the course of time. They have made a serious error of judgement. Those like the Vice Chancellors who are now attempting to understand the students and trying to change the Establishment approach to the student problems should be supported. Unfortunately the legacy of the 'wait and see' policy has resulted in a deep pool of bitterness and mistrust, which will take time to relieve.

We are now witnessing only the beginning of real change. Current student unrest will certainly move out of the colleges and into the Trade Unions and industry. Whilst it broadens its appeal, more trouble will arise. The technical colleges under the control of local authorities are a virtual time bomb waiting to be exploded. If there is legitimate grievance in the universities there is even more cause for attention to be paid to the public sector of education, where the facilities and the attitudes of the authorities are very much worse.

Moderate elements among students who prefer to work within a system must be supported and their plans for reform carried out. It would be politically disastrous if moderation was allowed to flounder, while a smouldering battle was mounted between revolutionaries and those who want to smash them. There is only one way in which to save the situation – speedy reform of existing institutions including Government and the House of Commons, the universities and colleges, the trade unions and industry. The onus must fall upon those in positions of influence, because it is only they who can prevent a continuation of confusion, and in doing so, protect the interests of the country generally.

Alan Shelston

Students and the Press

In the *Daily Telegraph* of 21 November 1966 the following leading article appeared, under the heading 'Student Impertinence':

Today's projected demonstration by students of the London School of Economics over the disciplinary action contemplated against the president of their union is an outrageous piece of impertinence. The young man who is at the centre of the trouble is not being accused, as he might well be, of holding ridiculous and ill-informed opinions about the past conduct of Dr Adams, the new Director of the L.S.E., but of having published those opinions in the Press when expressly ordered not to do so by his academic superiors. As it is, the erring pupil is to have a full chance of stating his case before the school's board of discipline and, surprisingly, the National Union of Students is also to be represented. To demand in addition to these concessions all the rights of a grown-up on trial before a court of law is no more defensible than it would be if demanded by a schoolboy about to be beaten.

Underlying this absurd row is the claim, restated in today's report by the N.U.S., for a large measure of direct participation by undergraduates in the university government, including its disciplinary functions. Some of the new redbrick universities have gone some way to conceding this claim and, provided blatant abuses do not result, should not be censured by outsiders for having done so. It is not, however, for the young people themselves to lay down the conditions under which they should be taught and cared for at lavish public expense. The state could find some ethical case for prescribing to the universities the code of discipline they should apply: parents have an even stronger case for insisting that their views should not be neglected. Naturally, what a great many undergraduates want is a total suspension of discipline – at least in all matters affecting personal morality. Most parents have no wish to extend this licence to their offspring. Happily, only a small minority of pretentious adolescents, generally of small intellectual ability, want to waste the best years of their life in organized agitation and in administering affairs which they lack the capacity and time to handle properly. In the interest of education they should be firmly resisted.

The occasion of this article was the disciplinary action being applied at the London School of Economics against the student leader David

Adelstein for his part in the extensive protest against the behaviour of the School itself in its handling of the Adams appointment and it can be said to have some historic significance as one of the first newspaper editorials to be devoted to the protest phenomenon as such. It is worth quoting in full, not merely because it raises so many of the false assumptions that were rapidly to become commonplaces of the kind of arguments that it puts forward – the points about 'lavish public expense', 'personal morality' and 'small intellectual ability' recur again and again in what might be called the literature of the period – but because of the way in which the splendid complacency of its paternalistic tone dates it as an historical document. Nothing could define more clearly the growth of the student protest movement than the light in which the analogy drawn here between Adelstein and a recalcitrant schoolboy awaiting well-deserved retribution, or the automatic recourse to the *in loco parentis* argument, now appear. Moreover, the grudging acknowledgement of the radical trends of 'some of the new redbrick universities' ('new' *or* 'redbrick', incidentally?) together with the outright rejection of the suggestion that students should 'lay down the conditions under which they should be taught and cared for' have a genuinely archaic ring when one considers the current tendencies, even in the more conservative sections of the Press, to accept the claims of students for a considerable degree of control as reasonable and, almost, just.[1] One might indeed say of the arguments deployed here that now they would only be heard in the more remote corners of Senior Common Rooms: certainly the Press has learnt to express itself more diplomatically.

The Adams affair at L.S.E. was the first of a series of incidents to make a dramatic impact through the mass media on the general public, and to reinforce a popular image of the student as an outspoken and often unkempt anti-social element, suspect in matters of personal morality and social aspiration and certainly unreliable in his political allegiances. The phenomenon undoubtedly has its origins in the civil disobedience associated with C.N.D.; until the late 50s the popular idea of a student – or rather 'undergraduate' – was best represented by the kind of tweedy and unintellectual buffoon, sowing his conformist wild oats, who appeared in films like *Doctor in the House*. But the change brought about by C.N.D. and reinforced by the pornographic interest, in some sections of the Press, in the behavioural attitudes of a supposedly permissive generation – 'Student Lovers – New Scare' said a headline in the *People* at the time

---

1 Thus the *Daily Express*, 14 March 1968, exhorts students to 'campaign more vigorously for more student participation in university affairs. Where this exists – there is very little trouble.'

of the Profumo affair[1] – was a gradual one of which the public were perhaps only half-aware; hence the rather surprised reactions in some quarters to student activism over the Adams affair. The decisive factor in bringing the radical student to public notice was undoubtedly the increasing coverage given to his activities by television. When C.N.D. was at its height television was only in the early stages of its influence as a formulator of priorities amongst the communications media, furthermore a visual medium has its limitations in charting a rake's progress. The events at L.S.E. in late 1966 and early 1967 were ideal material for news bulletins, however, and they were brought into everyone's living-room twice nightly and over a period of some months. When they were followed by demonstrations against the increase in foreign students' fees, and by such visually dramatic occurrences as the disturbances in Berlin at Easter 1968, the Grosvenor Square demonstrations and finally the street fighting in Paris last summer, protest became, for the general public, the representative student activity.

Any discussion of the way in which the Press has handled the issue of student protest must keep in mind this determining influence of television. It is not merely that television, by its capacity to act as a kind of instant moving tabloid, has an inevitable superiority of dramatic impact over the traditional media, it has completely altered the basic function and thus the techniques of the Press itself. Deprived of first claim on the news of the day, its straightforward reporting function is greatly diminished: its scoops are restricted to events which occur between ten in the evening and the early hours of the morning. Otherwise it is limited to covering, and perhaps extending and diversifying, items towards which television has already dictated basic attitudes. McLuhan's dictum that 'The first item in the Press to which all men turn is the one which they already know about'[2] is thus unavoidably true for we know the morning's headlines before the paper comes through the door. As a consequence of this virtual impotence in the field of its traditional function the Press has to rely increasingly on its capacity as a medium of commentary and interpretation rather than reportage: all newspapers now constantly aspire to the conditions of the Sunday Press, which itself acknowledged and reinforced these conditions by the introduction of the supplements. Features and articles,

1 Examples are many and various, e.g. the *Daily Mirror*, 1 May 1964: 'The vicar was taking his dog for a walk in the early hours. . . . He casually glanced into the backs of one or two cars. . . . And what he saw led him to demand a curfew for university students.' As a Jamesian character observes, 'Nothing exceeds the licence occasionally taken by the imagination of very rigid people'.
2 *Understanding Media*, Routledge, 1964, p. 211.

falling largely into two kinds, the immediate follow-up of an individual item of news and the extended analysis in depth, have thus assumed increased importance. It can be argued that this can provide for greater objectivity and I think evidence could be found to support such a case. Equally obviously though it can provide for greater selectivity of approach. Thus an analysis in, for example, *The Times*, will present a student world solely concerned with Che Guevara, Debray, Marcuse and the early Marx, while the *Sunday Express* will head an article on student unrest with a vivid photograph of a girl student struggling with the police and captioned, 'Britain 1968. A day in the life of a student'.[1] Criticism of the Press has always had a weakness for conspiratorial theories; in fact the impression gained from hours spent over newspaper files is primarily one of the ephemeral quality of their content rather than of any hard-bitten Machiavellianism on the part of their editors. Inevitably though, assumptions about reader demand are the controlling factor in deciding priorities of presentation and this is as true of the *Guardian* as it is of the *Daily Mirror* or, as in the instances quoted, of *The Times* as of the *Sunday Express*.[2]

The evolutionary processes which I have defined are an aid to the understanding of the current student image as it appears in the Press. The modification of its traditional reporting role is very clear in the way in which events concerning students are handled. In the first place many student disturbances, in that they tend to take place at late evening meetings, do provide the press with an opportunity to anticipate its electronic rival and such events will tend to receive coverage that is probably

---

1 *The Times*, 28 May 1968; the *Sunday Express*, 2 June 1968. Professor Max Beloff has argued, in the *Sunday Telegraph*, 9 June 1968, that 'in the elevation of the ill-digested compound of primitive Marxism, anarchism, Maoism, etc., to the dignity of a philosophy they (i.e. the students) have been aided and abetted by the quality Press of the Left.' The categorization is a vague one, but as my examples will show the distinction cannot be made in terms of definable political sympathies on the part of the newspapers concerned.

2 It should not be too readily assumed that attitudes towards reader demand differ very widely amongst various sections of the press. There are obvious exceptions, but one can find some striking examples of common ground. Thus the *Daily Mirror*, 17 June 1967, announces: 'A "swinging" time for students. More than 1,000 students from Britain's new universities will meet this weekend – to talk about drugs and sex. The students, from eight universities set up since world war two will also discuss the Middle East situation and take part in plays, dances, folk singing, jazz concerts and a revue. The occasion: the fourth New Universities festival, which is sponsored by the *Daily Mirror*. The place: the University of East Anglia, Norwich. Star attractions at the three-day festival include novelist Brigid Brophy, master jail-escaper Alfie Hinds, varsity dons, M.P.s and the Yardbirds pop-group.' Could any of the supplements have done better?

disproportionate to its actual news value. Thus the *Daily Mail* of 9 March 1968 gave its main front-page news space to an account of disruption at a meeting which Denis Healey had addressed at Cambridge the night before; the actual report was fairly brief, in terms of column-inches, but it was surmounted by an enormous headline: 'RIOT STUDENTS FIGHT POLICE'.[1] A similar disturbance at a lecture given, or in the event not given, by Patrick Gordon Walker at the University of Manchester on 1 March 1968 again received extensive national coverage. Treatment of items such as these will vary extensively from paper to paper and for fairly obvious reasons. The *Guardian*, with its Manchester interests, gave more attention to the Gordon Walker incident than its rivals, while a day of demonstrations at Oxford which television had ignored and which was reported at the foot of the *Guardian*'s front page, achieved main headline status in the *Daily Telegraph* on the same day: 'OXFORD PROCTORS STORMED – Undergraduates fight University "Bulldogs"'.[2] The traditional priorities still receive acknowledgement. The events themselves, however, although scoops over television, still take their tone from the dominant medium and this is true also of the day-to-day items which appear in what I have suggested is the secondary reporting role of the press, the extension and diversification of themes already popularized by a television lead story. This function is probably most extensively performed by the *Daily Telegraph* and the *Guardian*, newspapers whose attitudes to television are, one suspects, still governed by conservative presuppositions about class and literacy. On some days in recent months the inner pages of these two dailies have seemed to consist of a series of reports from the battle-fronts of England's provincial universities which, to change the analogy, appear with the predictable and wearisome familiarity of assault cases in the *News of the World*.

One can, however, detect positive advantages in this process of diversification. If news reportage rarely reaches the informative comprehensiveness of, for example, the *Guardian*'s coverage of the original L.S.E. affair, or its presentation of more recent events at Hull and at the Colleges of Art, it has at least led to an increase of interest in the universities and perhaps in higher education generally and one should not be too ready to assume that this interest could be more honestly described as prejudice. Interest in activism can lead to interest in student conditions generally and perhaps more specifically to interest in courses, teaching methods and

1 The *Daily Mail*'s secondary front-page feature on this occasion was an article reprinted from *Varsity*: 'This is *my* Cambridge – by Prince Charles.'
2 *Daily Telegraph*, 4 June 1968.

residential matters. Above all, the assumption that all higher education adopts the life-style of Oxbridge has been destroyed. The *Daily Telegraph* may tend to imply that the Rubicon has only finally been crossed when 'undergraduates' fight 'university bulldogs', but in fact examination of its coverage of university affairs over the past few months shows extensive and far from merely critical attention being paid to, for example, the National Union of Students. The Radical Students Alliance will not be slow to suggest a motivation here of course, and in fact the N.U.S. has clearly tended to get an increasingly good press for what now appear to be moderate demands, but when one considers the leading article with which I opened this discussion the process can be seen as one of enlightenment, albeit of a sometimes qualified and reluctant kind.

When one turns to the flood of features, commentary and analysis that student protest has engendered the same conclusions can initially be drawn but the reservations are, I feel, more necessary. From news items the reader is largely free to draw his own conclusions: even where Pavlovian references to, for example, students' personal appearance colour the story itself I suspect that the reader is preconditioned to expect and ignore them.[1] As I have suggested though, this kind of material has ambivalent qualities, above all in its capacity for appearing objective while leaving enormous scope for manipulation of the evidence.

At its crudest this manipulation is instantly recognizable and thus, as in the case of loaded reporting, of limited influence. Populist commentators like Robert Pitman in the *Daily Express*, John Gordon in its Sunday counterpart and 'Peter Simple' in the *Daily Telegraph* have long carried on a dialogue of the converted with their readership on a predictable range of subject-matter: the mirror-images of their utterances can be seen in the correspondence columns of the papers for which they perform. I suspect that their kind of commentary cannot really be said to be affecting the way in which people think so much as giving expression to attitudes which already form part of a public consciousness which is not as extensive as persecuted liberals would like to believe. For all John Gordon's efforts the law no longer actively persecutes homosexuals. Far more serious, in terms of the influence they have on the public image of the university world, than the columnists' opportunist sniping are those articles and features which pretend to examine in some detail either individual events, or the protest phenomenon in general, and in doing so present an image of

---

1 e.g. the *Daily Express*, 14 March 1968: 'Seventy-five mini-skirted girls and long-haired bearded agitators' and 11 June 1968: '300 bearded and mini-skirted students.' The latter example at least provides opportunities for the imagination.

the university world which may satisfy the curiosity of the outsider but which has only limited relevance to that world as known to teachers and students.

Again, the crudest examples of this kind of distortion are undoubtedly the least harmful. For example, Colm Brogan, in the *Sunday Express* of 2 March 1968, castigates university teachers who show sympathy with student protest in terms which would imply that the very university system itself is threatened by the infiltration of a group of political and moral degenerates. Under a banner headline: 'WHY DON'T WE SACK THESE TEACHERS ?' he writes:

> Far more outrageous than the antics and the anarchy of the students themselves is the behaviour of those members of the teaching staff who condone the lawlessness and even take part in it . . . they are supposed to be responsible people.
>
> Can that be said of Dr David Craig of Lancaster University, who proposed that men and women students who wanted to sleep together should have accommodation provided for the purpose ?

Here there is no attempt at all to distinguish between totally different issues, and no attempt to put the issues themselves into the context in which they arose – the article is in fact an ugly and extended tirade. If it is unpleasant, one can perhaps reflect that its influence is probably limited: the *Sunday Express* claims a readership with Class A incomes not lively minds. The article does pretend to be well-informed, however, and public knowledge of what goes on at universities is not so extensive that it can be relied upon to supply the necessary correctives. It must be stressed that not all features that appear in the popular press are as unbalanced as this example – student representatives are in fact often given an opportunity to state the student case, although again one would want to question motivation in some instances.[1] When Tariq Ali features in the *Daily Mirror* one doubts whether the objective is to make him more popular.[2] But whatever the tone or bias of such material the real problem lies in its concentration on specific issues which, to a public with little awareness of the perspectives

---

1 It has to be said that as one examines newspaper files the impression that the Beaverbrook Press stands apart from the rest of its contemporaries in the consistent emotionalism of its appeal is a very strong one and a separate article might be written on its techniques. See, e.g. its coverage of the Grosvenor Square incidents, 18, 19 March 1968 and the persistent references of the *Daily Express* educational correspondent, Bruce Kemble, to the red menace amongst student militants, an element which most commentators take care to place in perspective.
2 'The First Voice of Protest' (19 April 1968).

against which such issues must be seen, come to represent university life as a whole.

Essays by individual hands always carry an implication of bias: this is less obviously the case with those surveys and analyses, often carried out by teams of reporters, which have the apparent objectivity of a genuine research project. Usually supported by a certain amount of statistical evidence and purporting to cover a wide range of comment and opinion they ostensibly aim to discover the realities behind the protest phenomenon. The limits of their objectivity are immediately apparent when one considers the way in which they invariably accept without question the student evaluation of the university as an institution consisting solely of the total sum of its student population. Research, if mentioned at all, is usually dismissed as a distracting irrelevance, responsible in itself for a great deal of student alienation, while the wider role of the university within the community is never considered. It is inevitable of course that an analysis of student protest will concern itself largely with students: what I think one has a right to expect is that student claims about the universities, about their priorities, their syllabuses and the effectiveness of teaching, should be seen in the context of the university as a whole and not simply in the light of the student idea of a university.

For surveys such as these the students themselves are the main source of information, as indeed they often are in news stories as well. In fact Mahomet need not approach the mountain: a Manchester journalist of some standing assured me recently that during the University term his news editor has constantly to be protected from the journalistic enthusiasms of the city's student population. There can be no doubt at all that an important factor in student activism is its successful exploitation of the press. Such a situation at least promises to assert more useful priorities than have sometimes appertained in the past, but the problem for the universities is that an analysis of student behaviour by reporters 'sent to twelve universities' will tend to accept without question statements by individual students on the 'petty restrictions of resident university life' or to the effect that 'communication with the staff is extremely bad'[1] and the statements themselves thus become truisms in the light of which action is expected from the universities. Even if our house were in order we would have to be constantly moving the furniture. Indeed, since a popular line of approach is to accept some aspects of student protest in order more effectively to isolate its extremist elements there is a positive motivation towards accepting criticism of the internal affairs of the universities

1 *Daily Express*, 12–14 March 1968.

themselves as ground on which the students can be met. The process can be seen to be as much a matter of habit as deliberate intention. When the *Sunday Times* reports of the University of Essex students that,

Their contact with the staff is continuous because, whether they like it or not (and most of the staff do like it), there is no way of escape [19 May 1968]

or the *Guardian* complains in a leading article of examinations that

Their unfairness is notorious. They favour the student with a good memory, or a persuasive pen, or merely calm nerves [3 June 1968]

the implication is that there is really no dispute about such matters: universities, and their teachers, who fail to share such attitudes are dragging their feet. In fact, issues like those of staff-student relationships and methods of assessment are open and complex and to question student claims which have become journalistic truisms is by no means an expression of reaction.

Concern with issues such as these must inevitably seem parochial against a background in which, as *The Times* said in its six-day feature, 'Students in Revolt' (27 May to 1 June 1968)

it is possible to follow a fairly coherent trail from the American Civil Rights movement to Berkeley, and then to Berlin and the Sorbonne, with branches leading off to Turin, the London School of Economics and Essex.

The development of an international perspective to student protest has been the aspect most eagerly seized upon by what is usually called the quality press, and particularly by the larger Sunday papers. The intellectually fashionable has always been their stock-in-trade and they can handle with seeming confidence the wider perspectives of a movement

aimed at all fountainheads of bourgeois authority, whether they be represented by their vice-chancellor or the consensus politics which have allowed Britain to support the Vietnam war. [*Sunday Times*, 19 May 1968]

In the enthusiasm for these international and political perspectives it is impossible not to feel that an image of the university is being created in which the part looms considerably larger than the whole. This is not to underestimate the force, or indeed the value, of student activism in an attempt to evade its implications, but on reading the series in *The Times*, for example, I felt inescapably that coherent, well-documented, informative and sympathetic as it was, within its own terms of reference, it offered a very limited and restricted picture, above all in that in all of its six sections it made no attempt at serious discussion of the role and structure of the higher educational system which is the localized environment of the student protest movement. Instead I felt myself involved in a world which the communications media, with the help of the articulate student, had made: in this sense the medium had indeed become the message. There may well be some justice in *The Times*'s argument that 'National frontiers mean less than generation frontiers nowadays' but to simplify issues in this way is of little use if only one side of the frontier is to be seen and this, I suspect, is a fairly common factor in the presentation of university affairs, even in those newspapers whose predispositions towards authority are usually undiscriminating in their sympathy.

In a discussion as brief as this it is impossible to do more than suggest certain trends of Press behaviour and even as one attempts this limited objective one is aware of the qualifications and reservations that have had to remain unexpressed. When institutions as diverse as the universities and the Press interact the variables are limitless and to draw conclusions from individual examples is inevitably misleading. One effect of student protest has undoubtedly been to force the universities into the world at large: the academic can no longer grumble at, or delight in, his obscurity. As I have indicated, this seems to me desirable; much academic suspicion of the Press in the past has been, I suspect, automatic rather than considered. The state of affairs by which the universities were represented in one section of the Press by lists of Oxbridge examination results and accounts of the Boat Race, and in another by accounts of alleged moral degeneracy on the part of their students, was hardly a satisfactory one and student protest has at least directed public interest to more relevant areas. Furthermore, if a great deal of comment is implicitly hostile to the students themselves this hostility, with obvious exceptions, has a way of trimming its sails to the wind. Undoubtedly the presence of a taxpayers backlash is detectable, and it is encouraged from time to time by what it reads in its newspapers and sees on its television screens; the effect though, I suspect, is a limited one and students cannot seriously claim to be an underprivileged minority group in terms of a comprehensive social perspective. Of more serious concern is the tendency of the Press to embrace the students with one arm while rejecting them with the other and in doing so to formulate an image of the university, and indeed of students themselves, to which both university and students, now publicly exposed, may feel under pressure to conform. It is right that the universities should no longer have automatic recourse to tradition to justify their activities; the extent to which the communications media should determine their development seems rather more questionable.

Paul Rock and Frances Heidensohn
New reflections on violence

Preface[1]

We propose to discuss only two facets of student violence. The first is the
manner in which the popular image of the student has changed from that
of a person who is prone to healthy excess into that of a dangerous subversive. The second is the new ideology which justifies and prescribes
violent solutions to political dilemmas. Changes in the public definition of
students are almost as important as changes in student behaviour itself.
This definition sustains and guides a whole range of actions affecting
students. It influences informal and formal relations, university, police,
local authority and government policy. The reactions of these others to the
new violence are of great significance in forecasting the possible shape of
student behaviour. They determine whether confrontations between
students and authority increase in hostility, or lead to compromise or to
capitulation. In turn, these confrontations will have an impact on the perspectives of the groups involved. Student violence is part of a dialectic
which can only be understood in these terms. The second section of this
chapter describes the ideology against which the reaction has occurred.
There is some disparity between the 'public's' conception of the student
militant and his own self-conception, but there is a great disparity between
these conceptions and his actual performance. To this extent, the response
of the Press has not been entirely inappropriate. It seems that journalists
have been reasonably aware of the considerable shift in ideas and beliefs
held by a significant minority of students.

Our examination is limited in another way. The violence which we shall
describe is *physical* violence entailing assault, injury and the illegal use of
force. This violence is not an isolated part of the militant's armoury. He
classifies it as a tool which is intimately connected with other gestures of
protest and believes that the difference between a prolonged 'sit-in' and

1 We are grateful for the help and comments which we have received from Earl
Hopper, David Martin, Terence Morris and Andrew Moss.

physical attack is slight. Both are illicit styles of action which symbolize disenchantment with conventional political behaviour. The writings of the militant left define violence very generously as exploitation, as abrasive relations and as affronts to the dignity of man. We will, nevertheless, employ the term in its stricter sense.

Students have become popularly associated with violence, although the *amount* and *degree* of student violence in this country seem to have remained fairly constant. What *have* changed are the style and quality of violence and the manner of its presentation in the mass media.

In the past, violence has frequently been used as a political weapon by those receiving instruction – the London apprentices had a turbulent history of violent demonstrations, and revolts in the public schools were common in the late eighteenth and early nineteenth centuries. There are, of course, marked dissimilarities between these earlier 'student disorders' and recent events in British universities. The student body now has a different membership, social position, and function. Educational procedures and institutions have changed. Nevertheless, it is interesting that there is little novelty in the fact that objections to educational and political phenomena are pursued with violence. Pupils at Winchester held their college for two days in 1793 as a sympathetic response to the French Revolution. Harrow students staged a rebellion which lasted for three weeks. The headmaster of Rugby's door was blown up with gunpowder in 1797, and, in 1818, Eton students responded to the regime of their headmaster with 'a period of rioting. Detonating balls were thrown about in school. Masters' windows were smashed. Part of the Long Wall was knocked down.'[1] The headmaster was a target for rotten eggs and his desk was destroyed. In 1818 again, 'another rising at Winchester had to be put down by two companies of soldiers with fixed bayonets.'[2] This rising had a curiously familiar quality. Tremenheere, who was a pupil at the time, remarked that 'the fact that the boys (nearly two hundred) of one of the most renowned Schools in the kingdom rose against the Authorities, took possession of the College, barricaded it unassailably, disregarded remonstrances, solicitations and threats of physical force, and only yielded when their demands were granted, bears, to the present generation, an aspect of romance.'[3] What seemed slightly incredible in 1892 (when Tremenheere

1 C. Hollis: *Eton: A History,* Hollis and Carter, London, 1960, p. 203.
2 H. C. Barnard: *A History of English Education,* University of London Press, London, 1947, p. 18. (This account is somewhat in conflict with Tremenheere's description.)
3 E. L. and O. P. Edmonds (eds): *I was there: The Memoirs of H. S. Tremenheere,* Shakespeare Head Press, Eton, Windsor, 1965, p. 2.

wrote), now appears plausible after the recent demonstrations at the Hornsey College of Art and the Guildford School of Art. These earlier acts were
political because they were directed at changing the distribution and
exercise of power in educational institutions. It is arguable, then, that the
events of 1967 and 1968 are merely a renaissance of an established tradition
of student political protest.

Between 1851 (when there was a rebellion at Marlborough) and the
1960s a radically different style of violence was adopted by English
students. Sporadic outbursts of deviance were safely confined to socially
approved occasions – Guy Fawkes' Night, Election Night, New Year's Eve,
Boat Race Night and the Student Rag. These occasions were the means
whereby violence was accommodated and institutionalized. Students and
the authorities who were trying to control them appear to have arrived at
an understanding which defined the limits of 'acceptable' behaviour and
the ways in which the limits could be extended at these ritual times. Periods
of sanctioned licence became recognized events in a university's social
calendar in much the same way as similar events had been incorporated in
the lives of other groups – the Saturnalia, the Dionusia, All Fools' Day, the
Mardi Gras, the Fasching, Carnival and so on. The successful functioning
of many institutions and societies requires organized periods of release
from restraint and the universities conformed to this model.[1] Release was
never total – it was circumscribed in many ways. An instance of the
unwritten emphasis on permissible behaviour was provided by what
happened on the night of 5 November 1934. Actions then were clearly
thought to have exceeded the bounds of acceptable conduct.

Eight undergraduates were before the magistrates, charged with assaulting
the police. The cases were a sequel to rowdy scenes in Oxford on the night of
Nov. 5th. . . . Mr Fox (the Chief Constable) said a large part of the sport of
the crowd was baiting the police. 'Many of the undergraduates,' he continued,
'vied with the unattached hooligans in the honours of the game. The conduct
of the crowd was inane, offensive, and the *reverse of gentlemanly. There was
no goodhumoured fun, which the police can tolerate as well as anybody else.*'
[*Daily Telegraph*, 14.11.1934] [Emphasis added]

Dissenting factions in the universities sometimes clashed at these times.
Relations between the 'aesthetes' and the 'hearties' were not always pacific.
'At Oxford on Election Night, 1923,' for example, 'a prominent aesthete in
evening dress . . . was mobbed by a crowd of drunken hearties; in self-
defence he felled a Rugger Blue with a loaded stick. Hitherto aesthetes had

1 Erving Goffman makes much the same point in his discussion of institutional
ceremonies in *Asylums*, Anchor, New York, 1961, pp. 93–9.

been expected to undergo debagging and having their rooms wrecked without protest or compensation.'[1] Violence, then, was perfectly proper if it could be defined as 'good-humoured fun'. Although there was an intense preoccupation with politics in the universities, and unemployment, Bolshevism, Fascism and the Spanish Civil War loomed large in the lives of many undergraduates, violence was not a legitimate way of pursuing political ends. There were, of course, incidents which were not restricted to these special occasions and physical conflict sometimes arose between political groups. In the main, however, violence was a manifestation of a kind of Junker joviality and the divorce between student politics and student violence remained complete until the 1960s.

Students themselves recognize their new status as a corporate group and the importance of their 'violent image'. This is partly a result of their response to the newly refined public image, but it is also a reflection of a significant and largely autonomous shift in 'student consciousness'. The processes underlying this 'shift' are extremely complex, but certain factors in the political history of the post-war years have been of critical importance in mobilizing the student body as an 'action group' and in making violence a meaningful weapon for them. First of all, the Campaign for Nuclear Disarmament, by mobilizing interest in and commitment to its cause from a mass of young people, appears to have 'politicized' them, making them aware of issues and of the powers who enforce decisions and maintain policy. The Campaign eventually also introduced styles and techniques, such as the sit-down, which student protesters now adopt. Sensitized as they have thus been to political issues,[2] students in the 60s have faced two forms of political reality which have been vital in forming their consciousness. At home, there has been disillusionment with existing political parties, especially those on the left, and by extension, with the traditional political processes of a 'democratic' society. But abroad, above all in the Third World, students have observed the success of national liberation movements and social and cultural revolutions. The leaders and philosophers of these movements have become their heroes, as their disenchantment with the policies of their own rulers, particularly over the war in Vietnam, the focal point of much discontent, has increased. Above all, the old national power blocs have been challenged by new viable political models. Against this background, then, the change in student consciousness

1 R. Graves and A. Hodge: *The Long Week-End*, Faber and Faber, London, 1941, p. 124.
2 The Civil Rights Movement in the U.S.A., at least in its earlier white-dominated days, seems to have fulfilled a similar role for young Americans.

and self-perception has been gradually taking place. Public attitudes towards students have altered more abruptly, apparently as a result of immediate events.

In 1968 there was a sudden redefinition of the student as a problematic and menacing figure. Forty-eight per cent of the people interviewed in the *Evening Standard* Opinion Research Centre Poll of 21 June 1968 thought it likely that 'we could have violence and trouble, such as France has recently experienced, in this country', and 60 per cent believed that 'young people today are generally . . . not understood by middle-aged and elderly people'. It is this redefinition which is interesting because recent violence has, in fact, been rather slight and may not have increased substantially. Newspapers have been eager both to encourage and to question this new response. An editorial in the *Daily Sketch* (11.3.1968) proclaimed that:

'Britain has been traditionally tolerant of students and their healthy excess of political zest from High Tory to Low Trotskyite.

But violence is another matter.

STUDENT VANDALS DESERVE NO MORE SYMPATHY THAN SOCCER VANDALS.

The police should not hesitate to charge them; nor magistrates to punish them. The universities should have no compunction in sending them down; nor local authorities in cutting off their grants. . . .

Nevertheless, Worsthorne in the *Sunday Telegraph* (10.3.1968) said that 'the general adult reaction . . . is one of almost vindictive hostility to the student population', and an editorial in the *Sunday Times* (10.3.1968) spoke of 'anti-student hysteria'. The 'Anti-Students', argued the editorial, generalize 'their way through an instant diatribe: the waste of public money, the insult to the name of education, the ingratitude, the cheek, the damnable distraction of all this politics.'

We believe that this response has added a new figure to popular mythology – the violent student vandal who is irresponsible, unpredictable and dangerous. Complex societies depend upon mythologies which contain symbolic representations of social processes and developments. These representations take the form of highly stylized social types who personify the 'essences' of crucial phenomena. People do not seem able to deal with very much ambiguity and cannot devote much time to examining issues. The Teddy Boy, The Hippy, The Bureaucrat and The Student are all puppet figures which caricature 'reality'. These figures are grouped into 'goodies' and 'baddies' into 'folk devils' and saints, into 'Heroes, Villains and Fools'.[1] They exist to simplify and structure the world. When a

1 Cf. O. E. Klapp: *Heroes, Villains and Fools*, Prentice-Hall, New Jersey, 1962, and *Symbolic Leaders*, Aldine Press, Chicago, 1964.

student clashes with a policeman, one immediately knows what has taken place and which protagonist one should sympathize with. Similarly, 'sex crimes' are invariably committed by maniacs or 'sexual psychopaths'.[1] These mythological figures are typically clustered together. The Teddy Boy evolved from the Spiv and the Cosh Boy and was identified with vandals, hooligans and thugs. Social types rarely emerge without pedigrees and families. Once a type is established, therefore, it is highly resistant to change and public attitudes require substantial jarring before it is reclassified.

Until recently, students were unproblematically familiar. They receive a high status in British society because they tend to be middle-class by birth and successful by the 'objective' standards of competitive selection. Moreover, they have been traditionally granted a licence to be violent. Reclassification of the safe, boisterous student into a vicious hooligan entailed difficulties which were only overcome when 'incontrovertible' evidence compelled a change of definition. A novel and challenging situation made old ideas untenable. This jarring situation occurred in March 1968, when the Minister of Defence visited Cambridge University.

A number of incidents before March acted as a dramatic prologue to the Healey demonstration. In March 1967, students 'sat in' at the London School of Economics and a demonstration at Cambridge resulted in the denting of the Prime Minister's car and the injury of a police sergeant. In January 1968, Aston University Council members forced their way through a group of protesting students. In February, a brick was thrown at Enoch Powell's car when he was at Essex University and red paint was thrown at an American Embassy official at Sussex University. In March, Patrick Gordon Walker was harangued at Manchester University and at King's College, London.

These were not very violent events. Indeed, the violence was often suffered by students rather than inflicted by them. At Aston University, for example, 'umbrellas and briefcases were handed out as the council members stumbled over students blocking the entrance to their room. Students tried to stop some from leaving by holding on to their legs and one student was struck before he let go' (*Daily Express*, 16.1.1968). Threats to conventional ideas were also countered by dividing up students into a conforming majority and a deviant minority. The actions of the few did not challenge conceptions about the many. The Member of Parliament for Colchester, who had accompanied Enoch Powell, observed that 'some of

1 Cf. E. H. Sutherland: 'The Diffusion of Sexual Psychopath Laws', *American Journal of Sociology*, Vol. 56, pp. 142–8.

the remarks and obscenity hurled at Mr Powell were quite outrageous, but, in fairness to the university, the abuse came from a noisy minority'. Similarly, Mr Gordon Walker said that 'if the repute of the majority is in fact besmirched – as I believe – by the actions or posturings of a minority, the majority must be ready to stand up and be counted'.

The word 'student' still evoked favourable connotations at that time, but these incidents promoted uncertainty and a preparedness for further change. They also ensured that Mr Healey's visit to Cambridge of 8 March was well attended by newspaper reporters and television and film cameramen. Accounts of what actually took place differ, but it is clear that the people responsible for informing the public were impressed by the sheer numbers of participating students. The *Daily Telegraph* (9.3.1968) mentioned 'vicious rioting' and referred to '1,000 yelling demonstrators'. The *Daily Express* (9.3.1968) stated:

Hundreds of slogan yelling students trapped Defence Minister Mr Denis Healey in a taxi in Cambridge last night. They rocked it violently, beat on the windows, and tried to force open doors. Volley after volley of eggs spattered the cab. . . . A senior police official said: 'I have never seen anything so violent in my police life.'

This demonstration was presented and received in an extremely dramatic manner. The public was told that 'utter violence broke loose' (*Daily Telegraph*, 9.3.1968) and that 'the scenes of disorder . . . were unpardonable' (*Sunday Telegraph*, 10.3.1968). Not only was the violence 'utter' and 'unpardonable', it was also treated as thoroughly novel and surprising. *The Times* (11.3.1968) observed that 'the public is sitting up and taking notice, for the origins of these disorders and the form they take are new to English academic life'.

Coupled with this misleading ascription of novelty, a 'thin end of the wedge' argument was advanced to lend a sinister dimension to the *potential* shape of domestic disorders. People reacted, or were advised to react, not so much as to what *was* but what *might* be. Mrs Shirley Williams, Joint Minister of Education, informed the House of Commons on 16 March that 'violence could be used by those who want to destroy the very system which students enjoy'. On 12 March, Mr Healey announced that violent demonstrations 'are a threat to the British people and the whole system we honour'. The nature of student politics abroad was used to strongly colour the Cambridge demonstration. References were routinely made in the Press to violence in Japan, France, America and Germany and the attack on Mr Healey was shown to be a precursor of more uncontrolled and disruptive agitation. Quintin Hogg, for example, remarked on 11 March that:

Last year, if three Cabinet Ministers had been jostled and pelted ... I should have been at best indifferent, at worst contemptuous. This year I am openly alarmed at the contempt for authority and respect, if not for the persons, at least for the office of our national leaders, the growing move away from democracy and parliamentary government the cynicism of public life. These may be the consequences of a Government clinging to office without moral authority. But they are the marks of the Weimar Republic in Germany, the Third Republic in France. They are the marks of a sick society on the verge of a dictatorship, not of a healthy democracy.

The reaction to the Cambridge demonstration was thus fairly immediate. Questions were asked in the House of Commons by Kenneth Lewis and Philip Goodhart. Mr Lewis expressed his discomfort about the politicization of student deviance. He stated that 'we have in the past been used to having student protests that were nonviolent, we enjoyed them, and hope the students did too. We are not enjoying them any more. They are getting a little out of hand.' 'Good humoured fun' had been usurped.

On 20 March the Police Federation *Newsletter* attacked the tolerance displayed by academic staff and magistrates to the 'mob violence which now goes unchecked at our universities'. Education committees at Norfolk and Wolverhampton debated whether they should cancel the grants of students who were involved in demonstrations. Wolverhampton Education Committee adopted this policy and its former chairman declared that the town was 'giving a lead to the country' (*Daily Express*, 29.3.1968).

The emergence of a new form of deviance is often heralded by a period of intense discussion and evaluation in the newspapers. Erikson argues that 'an enormous amount of modern "news is devoted to reports about deviant behaviour and its punishment. . . . (Newspapers) constitute the main source of information about the normative contours of society. In a figurative sense, at least, morality and immorality meet at the public scaffold and it is during this meeting that the Community decides where the line between them should be drawn.'[1] Throughout March, the Press discussed and presented student violence as an important issue. Editorials praised or deplored the growth of public hostility towards students. The *Daily Express* for example, published a special series of articles which analysed what had taken place. One such article, entitled 'The Student Revolt – Bloodless but it's Civil War', stated that 'students in Britain are in revolt

1 Kai T. Erikson: 'Notes on the Sociology of Deviance', in Howard S. Becker (ed.): *The Other Side: Perspective on Deviance*, Free Press, New York, 1964, p. 14.

... students, – short of money, tired of being treated like children and disillusioned with their National Union – are being urged to violence by Left-wing militants' (12.3.1968).

Authoritative figures attempted to explain the confluence of violence and politics. In their effort to impose a meaning on what had taken place, they often resorted to theories of conspiracy and organization. Just as delinquency is explained in terms of 'gangs',[1] and observers make descriptions of groups manageable by referring to the 'King of the Junkies', the 'Queen of the Hippies', and the 'King of the Teddy Boys', so were patterns of student action simplified into conspiracies, cells and subversion. Sir William Alexander, Secretary of the Association of Education Committees, stated in the March edition of *Education* that 'there is little doubt that there is deliberate organization seeking to cause disruption and provoke displays of bad manners by university undergraduates. . . . One hears of people who seem to spend most of their time going from university to university to try to do a bit of rabble rousing.' Lord Leatherhead, in a House of Lords debate, spoke of student violence 'by organized cells of subversives' (*Daily Express*, 14.3.1968).

The Cambridge demonstration was apparently important enough to lead to a total reformulation of the popular image of students. Within a few days, violence became an expected component of student protests. When a large number of students lobbied the House of Commons, the *Evening Standard* (13.3.1968) thought it necessary to point out that 'it was a quiet demonstration with no violence'. Similarly, the *Sun*'s predictions about a demonstration implied that violence had become routine:

Sunday will be another one of those days when policemen link arms to stop surging crowds getting into Downing Street, and young protestors get carried away in both senses of the word. Another big protest against the Vietnam war is planned. Inevitably, some of the protesters will be students. Indeed, I am told that the lads from one provincial university are planning to bring with them a telegraph pole to batter down the door of No. 10. . . . Anyway, pole or no pole, Sunday's goings on will surely bring another cry from those who think our students are going Too Far. [*Sun*, 12.3.1968]

The response to the Healey affair had been impressive, yet there had been little threat to social control at Cambridge, there had been few injuries and only five charges were preferred against students. The university itself did not appear to share the feelings of outrage expressed by others. It took no action against the demonstrators and refused to ban future

1 Cf. David M. Downes: 'The Gang Myth' in the *Listener*, 14.4.1966.

protests. The police forces mustered to protect Healey were extremely adequate. The *Sunday Times* reported that:

. . . the proctors and police had been drawing up their defence plans. The police, remembering the demonstration against the Prime Minister at Cambridge last October, decided to pull in more than 100 men from all over the mid-Anglian region. And, although there were only five arrests on the actual night, one policeman told a demonstrator that there were enough police vans 'to accomodate the lot of you one at a time or altogether'.

Mr Healey was not hurt, but his car was dented and blood (presumably student blood) had spattered it. Apart from the attacks on the car, the only instances of violence described by the newspapers were those suffered by undergraduates. The *Daily Express* (9.3.1968), for example, stated that 'men and women students threw themselves in front of the taxi. A strong posse of police in turn hurled the troublemakers into the gutter.' A *Daily Telegraph* (9.3.1968) reporter said that 'I saw several undergraduates lying crumpled at the roadside'. It seems that violence was not planned by the students (*Sunday Times*, 10.3.1968) and, when it did occur, it was anything but 'utter' and 'unpardonable'.

Turner and Surace[1] have suggested that 'overt hostile . . . behaviour is usually preceded by a period in which the key symbol (representing the unpopular object against which hostility is directed) is stripped of its favourable connotations until it comes to evoke unambiguously unfavorable feelings'. 'Student violence' is as much a creature of a change in symbols as a change in student behaviour. Students are observed through perspectives provided by newspapers, television, authors and the radio. It was not the event but the authoritative definition of that event which structured the public response. The Cambridge demonstration received a great deal of prior publicity and it could hardly have been treated as insignificant whatever form it took.

Students themselves recognize their new status and the importance of their 'violent image'. Violence appears to have become *purposive* and desirable for only a militant minority (in a recent poll only 5 per cent approved of its use in demonstrations); yet in the same poll (*Daily Telegraph Magazine*, 28 June 1968, by Social Surveys (Gallup Poll Ltd.)) the majority of students at two universities (69 per cent) thought that there would be *more* demonstrations over the next two or three years and that these would become *more violent*.

1 R. Turner and S. J. Surace, 'Zoot-suiters and Mexicans: symbols in crowd behaviour', *Amer. J. of Sociol.* 62 (1), July 1956, pp. 14–20.

This activist minority seems to have gained an extraordinary degree of public attention and to have impressed their own colleagues by their force. They are the clearest exponents of the revived and political student violence and we shall focus our discussion on them although we realize they are atypical. We have been interested by the unanimity of opinion of both students and public on the image of the violent student and the contrast that this presents with the comparatively unspectacular events which have so far occurred in this country. This contrast is all the more notable in recent months because the amount of student protest *activity* has enormously increased, with a fresh 'sit in' being announced almost daily. The explanatory scheme which we offer below is far from exhaustive. It reduces an extremely complex ideological position to a simplicity which is probably misleading. No one student perspective contains all the elements we enumerate. Nevertheless, with the increasing politicization of deviance, this catalogue of newly acquired functions of violence may be a useful framework for understanding recent events.

First of all, and perhaps of primary importance, is (1) *Dramatic presentation* of events and complaints which results from the use of violence. This symbolic dramaturgical feature of violence is exemplified in an article called 'Red Paint' by Adrian Mitchell in *Black Dwarf* (1 June 1968, Vol. 13, No. 1), a student revolutionary journal. The article advocates the daubing of red paint on the 'murder machine' of firms, embassies and bases involved in the U.S. Vietnam war effort, 'Because Red Paint is a symbol of blood and fire. Because Red Paint illustrates destruction but does not destroy.' In a comparatively peaceful Britain, where the police go largely unarmed and the annual murder rate is between three and four per million inhabitants, a country once described by Professor Radzinowicz as almost 'pathologically crimeless', symbolic violence may be very significant and rapidly arrest public attention. The violence which does exist is 'well orchestrated' and institutionalized, very much confined to the home where children can be beaten, or to rowdy sessions in 'pubs' on Saturday nights. Even the slightest disturbance of this equilibrium may be seen as threatening – as in the case of the 'Mods' and 'Rockers' riots at seaside towns.

Violence can dramatize and exemplify the militant student's situation and draw attention to the phenomena which he wants to destroy. This manipulation of violence seems to be closer to modern theatrical 'happenings' or the arbitrary confrontation filming techniques of M. Jean-Luc Godard, than the pragmatic approach of urban guerillas. After the Grosvenor Square demonstration of 17 March Mr Tariq Ali was quoted as having said, 'It was not planned as a violent demonstration. *It never is.*'

(Our italics.) At an earlier Grosvenor Square demonstration in October, it was noted by observers that the crowd leaders *avoided* entering an unguarded U.S. embassy doorway and preferred to confront the police who were guarding another entrance.

The confrontation of students with police, those symbols of law, order and the British 'way of life' (*or* of 'bourgeois capitalist repressive tolerance'), may be profoundly significant to the 'militant'. It causes a polarization of 'them', the oppressors, and 'us', the revolutionaries, which may lead to a restoration of man to himself.

(2) This *instrumental polarization* through violence, has important functions for group solidarity – perhaps a rare instance of a classical Marxist pattern in the growth of student revolutionary consciousness. As Rudi Dutschke, a prominent member of the militant German S.D.S. put it (in an interview in *Konkret*, March 1968):

> The pitch of our counterviolence is set by the violently repressive methods of our rulers. We accept the activities of underground groups because they are a continuous learning process for those who take part. Only by practice . . . can clear and effective forms of opposition be evolved . . . this means nothing less than a revolutionary struggle for a free society.

In Britain much so called 'student violence' appears to have been unplanned. Militant leaders have been criticized by their fellows for their lack of an appropriate strategy. John Hopkins, in an open letter to Tariq Ali, the leader of an anti-Springer demonstration, said,

> 'you've got to start training/briefing your demonstrators in the necessary arts (i) self defence, (ii) military tactics. It is just insane to pit a band of potentially violent but helpless people against the organised army of the State – the police. [*International Times*, April 19]

Nevertheless, even such unstructured violence is seen as purposive, because the 'revolutionary situation' will only be produced by (3) *precipitating 'revolutionary' events*. That is, there is always a necessity to stimulate and encourage revolution although a patently revolutionary situation may not have presented itself. Within 'traditional' Trotskyist terms it was vital to work for, and await the rising of the socialist working class. However, two separate but converging ideological currents make this no longer necessary. The first is the 'message from the Third World', especially Latin America, and Cuba, with its stress on local guerilla warfare and the need only for, in Régis Debray's term, the emergence of the 'historic vanguard' to lead it.

Who will make the revolution in Latin America? Who? The people, the revolutionaries, with or without a party. [Fidel Castro]

This perspective is liberally interpreted as justifying in Britain, as well as in the colonized Third World, the usefulness of the statement that 'The duty of every revolutionary is to make revolution'. (A popular Havana street slogan.) A second force which springs from revered and ancient European academic traditions, rather than from the warfare of the Third World, are the ideas of the neo-Marxist philosopher, Herbert Marcuse, who synthesizes Marxist and Freudian critiques of society in an attempt to show that modern society is so unavailingly corrupt and repressive, so much a perverter of man's true nature, so much a *violator* of mankind that any defiant gesture towards it is appropriate.

Activist students in this country have studied the texts of Marcuse, the works of Fanon and the guerilla manuals of Che Guevara. Vital events have also occurred elsewhere – in Berkeley, Berlin, Paris and Prague. Participation in a violent demonstration has almost become as essential a status symbol to the modern militant as duelling scars were to the members of a 'schlagende Verbindung'. (4) *experience-in-itself* seems to have become of great importance, a very different kind of euphoria from that obtained by smoking marijuana or taking an LSD 'trip', but exciting in a parallel way. Roger Smith, describing the student revolt in Paris, states that:

A revolution is gathering momentum. . . . You feel it in the air, the tension, the exuberance, the sense of history. What was only dreamt of is becoming possible here . . . the power is with the people . . . the students are more important than Parliament . . . solidarity, a united purpose are worth more [where] the student and worker are one. [*Black Dwarf*]

We have suggested earlier that one of the apparent virtues of violence is that it strips naked the hideous body politic of capitalist society and reveals its 'true' nature as an evil and authoritarian system where 'freedom' and 'free speech' are only hypocritically permitted within the confines of consensus politics. Again it is the symbolic function of violence in (5) *The stripping capitalism of its fig leaf* which seems to be an end in itself rather than have an ultimate or practical purpose.

In this sense, violence may be seen almost as if it were a public relations or educative enterprise, designed to demonstrate to the public the truth about the repressive society whose excesses they condone. In the same way, techniques of violence, or at least the adherence to a theory advocating use of violence, may be used as a means of convincing society that protesters have *rejected the conventional processes of social democracy* and are challenging the whole system. Students seem to have been much misunderstood on this issue. The Press and other commentators have urged them to use the 'normal' channels of protest, but most students have insisted that they regard the Parliamentary system as 'farcical' and 'hypocritical'. Violence is a clear way of making this explicit, just as the peaceful demonstrations of the C.N.D. in the late 1950s and early 60s were a serious endeavour to convince majority and conservative opinion by 'responsible' behaviour. Convincing demonstrations in Britain are difficult: our architecture and our town-planning do not form good bases for protest; we lack the broad avenues and vast plazas of Paris or Berlin, which were built to impress and sustain authoritarian regimes and were ideal for large marches and mass meetings. Even our public buildings and monuments lack a sense of occasion and symbolic value.

A seventh aspect of violence, and one where public and student attitudes are in most marked conflict must be emphasized. Students are criticized for not being more explicit about the future they foresee as resulting from the upheaval of the revolution (this occurred recently on a B.B.C. television production, *Students at Large*, from the South and West). But a central feature of the student viewpoint is that one cannot predict, that the very experience of violence will precipitate changes in *consciousness* and *perception* which will enable significant changes to occur. In a sense this is an argument about the sociological basis of knowledge and has some proven basis in experience. Violence is undertaken, not merely to destroy the old order in a material sense, but to bring about qualitative changes in the participants. Almost a pentecostal enlightenment is being sought.

The eighth virtue of violence for student protesters today, we would suggest, is that it can, through the phenomenon of shared experience mentioned above, (8) *bring about the international unity and brotherhood of all students*. As Dick Atkinson, a sociology graduate student at L.S.E., said in an interview with David Jenkins of the *Evening Standard* (8.4.1968) 'students are beginning to identify common enemies . . . they look to Third World heroes, Fanon, Che and Carmichael'. Jenkins summarized the interview:

An increasingly cohesive international force has emerged in the last year on the political scene – students of the world are rearing up at systems they say are designed to isolate, repress or silence them.

This solidarity with movements abroad has become increasingly vital to the self image of the student power movement in this country as foreign students have blooded themselves further in the struggle for freedom while

IAC

the British situation has remained relatively quiet. As long as student
violence exists in token form at least in this country, or the theory of its use
is being discussed, activists can place themselves on a continuum of world-
wide violent revolutionary protest with the Japanese Zengakuren at one
extreme and themselves at the other.

Foreign models are vital to militant students in this country. Although
Mr O. H. Parsons writing to *The Times* (27.3.1968) points out that 'the
whole history of the fight for British freedom is littered with dehelmeted
policemen and batoned demonstrators' and cites the Peterloo Massacre,
John Wilkes and the suffragettes as examples, British students seem to
ignore this heritage and look elsewhere for inspiration. Clearly they have
absorbed the post-war lesson of the decline of Imperialism, that guerilla
warfare and sabotage may be rewarding and that most governments of
capitalist societies will withdraw rather than fight a bitter struggle or that,
when they do, as in Vietnam, their gargantuan power can be outwitted by
a much punier enemy. The significance of incidents in American ghettoes
has also been vital: it suggests that effective guerilla tactics are possible
even in the urban areas of industrial society. Finally, the examples of
Prague and Berlin, but above all of Paris, have shown that 'students
rebelled and forced the government to retreat, and the workers followed
their example' (Eric Hobsbawm), and he adds: 'What France proves is
that when someone demonstrates that people are not powerless, they may
begin to act again.' Within the framework of events there are also the cult
heroes of the movement: Castro, Che Guevara, Stokely Carmichael, who
have contributed both examples of successful action in the field and
theories of the strategy of violence in the revolution.

The public image of students has now changed and students are themselves involved in redefining their own role and self perception. What these
two conceptions have in common is the stress laid in them on violence, the
disturbance of equilibrium, orderly life and the stimulus of social disorder.
What is of sociological interest in this process is the way in which, as the
new stereotype develops, public attitudes to, and even policy towards,
students may alter. The 'student' seems, almost, on the verge of being
labelled a socially deviant type with all that that may imply in terms of loss
of social prestige and privileges. The image of his social antithesis, the
'angry taxpayer, threatening to cut off resources', has already been con-
jured up (by Mr P. Gordon Walker). The advent of student protest has
produced a redefinition of the student body into the 'good' students, the
majority, and the militant and 'bad' minority who constitute a threat. The
reaction to the demonstration in Grosvenor Square on 17 March which was

almost universally hostile to the student demonstrators and gave great prominence to the bravery and restraint of the police and the 'gallant' police horses, indicated that students were *generally* regarded now as deviant and difficult and associated with violence. It is very difficult for any social scientists to predict, least of all in such a volatile, though fast-hardening, situation. Students might participate, or indeed lead, a social revolution. The repressive organs of capitalist society might suppress student militancy which has taunted its powers. (A recent joint statement by university vice-chancellors indicated that a 'firmer line' might be taken with militants.) It seems more likely to us that the dialogue already begun will continue, but with increasing polarization of attitudes on both sides. Public relationships *with* students and relations *among* students are likely to be based on unambiguous assumptions about the nature of students as violent.

Two possible alternatives which will result from this crystallization of attitudes and positions are:

1. That the price to be paid for student violence, social stigmatization and rejection, may be seen as too high by many young people who basically seek qualifications and the passport to a middle-class career through a university education. There might thus be a de-escalation of protest, perhaps even a right-wing reaction. These are all at least possibilities.

2. If student militancy does continue (and there seems every likelihood that it will, August 1968) a considerable cleavage of opinion based on social class lines may appear. On the whole the middle-class reaction to student activities has been comparatively favourable; the 'quality' Press have linked these episodes with events in the past and claimed to see a familiar, even a reassuring style in the protests. Some politicians have also insisted that there is 'nothing to concern ourselves about'. For the working class, the student is a much less familiar and acceptable figure and student protest is more likely to be attacked and condemned by this source. But it is, after all, the professional middle classes who, as academics and administrators, control the universities and hence they will be able to use positions of power both to check the protest movement and to limit attempts to suppress it. But this process would lead inevitably to further class polarization. As we have said, prediction in this situation is not possible. We have simply tried to describe the situation as we see it and suggest directions it might take.

Stephen Hatch
From C.N.D. to newest Left

One day in December 1955 in Montgomery, Alabama, Mrs Rosa Parkes refused to give up her seat in a bus to a white man, for which offence she was arrested. One might think that this incident could have no possible connection with the unrest in British universities in 1968, and with the quite new direction taken by the student left since 1966. But in fact it touched off a train of events which has proved one of the main strands in the development of the present university crisis. The immediate consequences was the lengthy and eventually successful Montgomery bus boycott, and this in turn helped to kindle the then quiescent Civil Rights Movement. The struggles of the Civil Rights Movement need no elaboration here: their significance in the present context lies in the techniques of protest and the spirit of militancy they engendered. Many American students, and a few British also, took part in Civil Rights activities, and some of them subsequently applied the same techniques (i.e. demonstrations, boycotts and especially sit-ins) within the universities, notably during the course of the Free Speech Movement at Berkeley in 1964 and 1965. The example provided by the events in Sproul Hall, together with the ferment generated by America's increasing involvement in Vietnam, are what precipitated the great wave of protests in American universities.

In Britain too the events in Sproul Hall made their impression on radical students, while one or two of those who participated in them later came to Britain as graduate students. And it was not long before the example of the FSM was followed in Britain: during the Adams affair at the London School of Economics in 1966 and 1967 events exhibited a pattern with many parallels to that at Berkeley – an initial protest succeeded by a clumsy attempt to discipline a few of the more prominent protesting students, leading to a sit-in which was successful in protecting the students threatened with disciplinary action, but which has not yet led to radical changes of the kind demanded during the course of the protest. And as with Berkeley in America, so the L.S.E. affair has had a seminal, precipitating influence in Britain.

To return to Mrs Rosa Parkes, the importance of her primitive and unpremeditated form of protest resides not only in the ensuing chain of events, but also at a more general level in the possibilities it opened up for militant action by minorities demanding rights and seeking liberation from oppression. In Britain strike action has long been familiar in industry, but outside industry there has tended to be a dichotomy between on the one hand legitimate political activity consisting of peaceful demonstrations or conventional propaganda aimed at altering public opinion and so modifying the behaviour of public elected bodies, and on the other hand revolutionary activity aimed at overthrowing the existing system. This dichotomy was intensified during the last World War and the Cold War that followed it when the survival of parliamentary democracy was felt to be a crucial issue. Hence the tradition of direct action in Britain has hitherto been a weak one: during the campaign against nuclear weapons there were attempts at direct action, but they achieved little except publicity. Now, with the aid of the American example, direct action has been given a quite new vitality and effectiveness by students.

In America the emphasis in current protests has moved away from insistence on the strict Gandhian non-violence initially exemplified by Martin Luther King. The tempo is now more violent, but there remains a body of techniques and a tradition of action intermediate between conventional, legitimate political activity and violent attempts at revolution. For minorities acting in a specific milieu with specific grievances these intermediate techniques can be particularly effective, while at the same time not involving the kind of outright threat to the whole system that invites immediate repression. Hence the left now has a new set of weapons with which to pursue its objectives: these greatly facilitate militant action and the recruitment of individuals to participate in it. Indeed action has been facilitated to the extent that the possibilities of action seem to have outrun the development of a programme, so that whereas in the past it could be said that the left had goals but not the power to achieve them, now in Britain the student left has the means of action and a vocabulary of protest derived from America, while remaining a little indefinite about its objectives.

The diffusion of ideas from abroad helps to explain the form and direction taken by student protest in this country: but it does not tell us why these ideas fell on fertile ground, why there were students in Britain ready to put them into effect. Much of the answer to this question lies in changes in society, in the universities and in the relationship between the two, affecting particularly the role of the student. These are outside the terms of reference of this essay, which is concerned simply with the radical movements themselves: to appreciate how these have developed it is necessary to go back a few years.

Since the war one can distinguish two completed phases of left-wing politics, and a third phase which has just opened. The first began with the high hopes of the 1945 Labour Government and faded out in the sterile conflict arising from the Cold War. During the early 50s the major division among the student left, as in the left as a whole, was between Communists and anti-Communists, and it was a time of conservatism, either of the Stalinist kind or of the Labour orthodoxy kind, with its counterpart at the national level in the predominance of the Conservative Party.

All this was changed quite dramatically by Hungary and Suez. The former produced a strong reaction against Communism: party membership declined almost to nothing in the universities, and ever since that time the possibility of Communist takeovers in student organisations has been virtually non-existent, though it may have lingered on in the minds of professional anti-Communists. Indeed in recent years the threat to the social democratic left has come not from Communists but from Trotskyites or quasi-Trotskyites: thus both the Labour Party's youth organisations – the National Association of Labour Student Organizations (NALSO) and the Young Socialists – were disbanded after they were captured by elements completely opposed to the party leadership, many of whom had Trotskyite leanings. From the opposite direction Suez gave a powerful jolt to the widespread complacency about British society.

The first development on the British left arising from the new situation was the appearance of two journals, the *Universities and Left Review*, primarily the creation of a group of Oxford graduate students, and the *New Reasoner*, founded by a number of staff from Northern universities who had recently left the Communist Party. In 1960 these merged to form the *New Left Review*, and in the meantime there had been a rapid but short lived growth of New Left Clubs all over the country. Although there were significant disagreements within the New Left of those days three broad trends can be detected in its thinking; a neo-Marxist counter-attack of a not particularly fruitful kind on revisionism in the Labour Party, Crosland and Gaitskell being the main targets; an attempt to widen the scope of politics through concern with a broad range of cultural, 'quality of life' issues, focusing particularly on the mass media; and a challenge to the system of international relations left over from the Cold War, favouring non-alignment, hostile to NATO and nuclear weapons, and very much in sympathy with the Campaign for Nuclear Disarmament.

C.N.D. was itself the slightly younger offspring of the same political conditions, but its initial impetus came from a rather different set of people. Its progenitors were the 'left establishment', notably Kingsley Martin and the *New Statesman*, and throughout its period in the public eye its chairman remained Canon Collins. But its main support in numerical terms immediately became the younger generation. Soon it overtook and rather submerged the New Left, which failed to coalesce round any kind of common programme and after 1960 subsided from being a movement into simply an intellectual journal, while at the same time taking on a more tough-minded Marxist line. The decline of the New Left was related to that of C.N.D. C.N.D. reached its apogee with the victory of the unilateralist motion at the Labour Party Conference of 1960. Its decline sprang from a number of factors: Gaitskell's ability to reverse the Scarborough decision, his subsequent death which dissipated the left/right polarization within the Labour Party, Kennedy's successful resolution of the Cuban missile crisis, and finally the rallying to the Labour flag occasioned by the 1964 and 1966 general elections. So ended the second post-war phase of left politics: like the first it had lasted ten years.

Before turning to the third phase, it may be worth commenting upon some of the more salient features of the second phase. During these years the New Left was the main intellectual focus for radical students, while the C.N.D. constituted their main channel of political action. Both were run by young middle-class radicals, and students formed a large but far from exclusive section of the participants in each organization. Finally, though often contemptuous of the activities of Labour politicians both thought that what the British government did was of some significance, while the New Left was interested not only in international relations and the Third World, but also in the issues and problems of British society (though not particularly in higher education).

In terms of the British political situation the immediate background to the present phase of left politics is disillusionment with the Labour Party. Many radical students gave their support to the Labour Party in the 1964 and 1966 elections, and felt that under a Labour Government some of their ideals might find expression. But the collapse of a large part of the Government's home policies with the July measures of 1966 and the failure to adopt a sufficiently left stance over Vietnam, Rhodesia and immigration control dissipated student support for the Labour Party. At the same time the leadership of the National Union of Students had entered a very cautious and respectable phase, being inclined to value the status associated with its position more than the pursuit of radical objectives. Consequently

growing dissatisfaction inside the N.U.S. coincided with a profound disenchantment with parliamentary politics.

One of the responses to all this was the formation of the Radical Students
Alliance in November 1966. Some of the founders, who embraced a wide
spectrum of political views from Young Liberals to Communists, saw it
primarily as a challenge to the leadership inside the N.U.S., others as a
militant body with a much wider frame of reference than the N.U.S.; but
broadly speaking it was aiming to present more radical demands on university issues with the emphasis on student power, to press them with
greater militancy, and to involve the N.U.S. and students as a whole in a
much wider range of political issues. It was not possible in the view of the
R.S.A. to treat educational matters in isolation, as the N.U.S. traditionally aimed to do. An all-embracing student political consciousness was
needed.

The R.S.A. was never an organization of great power and influence, and
its achievements have been limited. It received a considerable impetus from
the L.S.E. affair, and helped to generate a militant response to the increase in overseas students fees early in 1967. But now the N.U.S. has
itself moved to the left, and during 1968 little was heard from the R.S.A.,
apart from the publication of two pamphlets.[1] Its membership was never
large, and in accordance with its opposition to bureaucracy it maintained
only the most tenuous organization. As a focal point for student militancy
the R.S.A. coexisted with the Vietnam Solidarity Committee (V.S.C.) and
has effectively been supplanted by the Revolutionary Socialist Students
Federation established in the summer of 1968; though in Britain no
organization has yet reached the position of the Students for a Democratic
Society in the U.S.A. Hence the series of protests that began at the L.S.E.
late in 1966 and affected so many universities in the summer term of 1968,
when the French and German students were setting such a heady example,
are not linked by any strong organizational threads, though these could
develop in the future.

What then does the student left have in common? So far very little
evidence has been collected, or at any rate published, about the characteristics of the protesting students in Britain. In America, however, there is
quite a lot of evidence from which certain broad conclusions can be drawn:
the radical students tend, it appears, to come from liberal, permissive,
professional, well-educated families, to be above average in intellectual
ability, and to be studying social science or arts subjects. General impres-

1 *Education or Examination* by Tom Fawthrop. *Teach Yourself Student Power*, ed.
David Adelstein.

sions from Britain and the evidence collected by Parkin[1] about a slightly earlier generation, the younger participants in C.N.D., suggest that the student left in Britain is not dissimilar to that in the U.S.A. Of course radical students vary greatly among themselves but it seems they are more likely to be trying to give expression to liberal ideals inherited from their parents, than to be reacting against repressive home circumstances or the strains of upward social mobility. Likewise, within the universities the rebels are not the failures of the system, nor are they philistines rejecting all academic and intellectual ideals. Rather they adopt some of the values pursued at least nominally by the educational system – concern with ideas, the development of the critical intelligence and so on: their criticisms are then directed at the universities for failing to live up to these ideals, for compromising themselves by liaisons with industry or the military or the government. Hence it seems that the rebels with whom we are concerned are not people whom the universities have failed to wean away from limited home backgrounds or from a narrowly vocational view of their university careers: rather they are people whom the universities have all too successfully detached from and made critical of society.

Many different adjectives are used to describe the political stances of the militant students. Some of them represent an ideological position – Maoist, phenomenologist, liberatarian Marxist, anarchist, anarcho-syndicalist, Trotskyite and so on. Others betoken a more specific organizational affiliation: thus some students adhere to the Young Liberals or International Socialism or the Socialist Labour League, and a few still to the Communist Party. Others subscribe to the *New Left Review* or to *Anarchy*, and the hippies rather than the militants to the *International Times*. This multiplicity of allegiances makes it difficult to generalize about the political views of the student left, except to say that there is clearly not a single, coherent intellectual movement. Characteristically within one university there is a Socialist Society which acts as an umbrella organization for all or most of the left-wing groups. The extent to which these groups have a separate identity varies from university to university, but the larger the university the greater the chance of sectarianism. But all of them are generally prepared to act together over such issues as student power, Vietnam, Rhodesia, Biafra and so on.

The size of the militant group and of the penumbra of sympathisers who are prepared to take part in demonstrations also varies from university to university and from issue to issue. At one extreme are the small

1 Parkin, F., *Middle Class Radicalism*, Manchester University Press, 1968.

institutions, exemplified by Essex and Hornsey with some thousand students apiece, in which a majority of the students were actively involved in the disturbances. Partly because of this wide participation and partly perhaps because of the involvement of staff in the protests at each place, the controversies at Essex and Hornsey never took on an ideological or sectarian tinge: the themes of the debates were always rights and justice, educational issues and tactics, rather than alienation, the class struggle and so on. And though there was a wide gap between the most and the least militant, the militant were not composed of factions each with its own brand of the truth. At larger institutions, like Leeds, L.S.E. and Leicester, the situation seems to have been somewhat different. Active participants in the disturbances always remained in a minority, and there was a greater degree of ideological sophistication and differentiation.

However, it would be wrong to overestimate the ideological nature of the present ferment among students. Like the students in the U.S.A., but less like those on the continent, what British students have been making is moral protests: they have not been responding to any theoretical analysis of society. Theoretical analysis has indeed arisen from the protests rather than vice-versa.

This is not to say the students are without ideas. One touchstone of any left-wing movement is its attitude to Marx. Up to twelve years ago debates in Britain were primarily concerned with Marx's later work, notably *Capital*, in which Marx foresaw the growing immiseration of the working class at the hands of an exploiting bourgeoisie leading inevitably to revolution. The conventional social democratic riposte to all this was the assertion that the working class was well able to improve its position by legitimate democratic procedures. The fact that it has indeed done so, and today is quite lacking in militancy, has caused the left to shift its attention almost exclusively to the earlier Marx.

It is true that the more traditional Marxism still has its adherents among students, and they tend to be distinctly guarded about the significance of student unrest, since for them the true revolution must be a proletarian one. But this is very much a minority position. For the most part not only does the student left reject Stalinism, it shows little interest in the later Marx and has a deep-seated, anarchistic distrust of all formal structures, quite alien to the whole tradition of Marxist-Leninist political activity. Indeed the student left is extremely reluctant to accept any form of leadership, whether from individuals or from organized groups.

In his earlier writings Marx was making a moral condemnation rather than an economic analysis of capitalism: under a capitalist system of production the individual was dehumanized, unable to realize his true nature and hence alienated. The prevailing themes among the student left start from this point, and owe much to Wright Mills and Marcuse for their analysis of advanced industrial society, and to Debray, Guevara and Mao-tse-tung for their ideas about the Third World. The main emphasis is on oppression by the large bureaucratic structures of modern capitalist society. This focuses on two areas that might superficially appear some-what far removed – the position of the student within the university and the nations of the Third World, especially Vietnam and Bolivia where the United States is most actively involved in preventing the overthrow of the established order. But the two are linked:

examinations and support for the American policy in Vietnam both emanate from a certain type of society, from the same social set-up known as mono-poly capitalism.[1]

Thus the student left is marked in a somewhat paradoxical way both by extreme introversion and extreme extroversion. What links the two is the theme of oppression and liberation; to the student beset by a sense of powerlessness in the university the struggles of the Third World and its heroic figures – Guevara, Castro, Mao, Ho chi Minh – and the Black Power movement have a powerful symbolic appeal. So too the appeal of a writer such as Laing, who, in seeking to explain schizophrenia not in terms of individual pathology but as a response to intolerable social relationships, is pointing his finger at the oppressive and malevolent structures of modern society, especially the bourgeois family.

In this frame of reference the problems of British society have a curiously insignificant place: the student left of today shows none of that lively interest in redefining the issues of British political life betrayed by the New Left of ten years ago. Rather the present phase of left politics is essentially a student affair, in which the students find themselves to a remarkable extent isolated from all other sections of British society. In earlier generations the student left was always quite closely related to existing political parties or intellectual movements, and could look to the working class as the ultimate source of political salvation. Today some students make much of the temporary alliance forged between students and workers in Paris in May, but effectively the students are alone and are no more able to integrate themselves with the workers than were the Narodniks with the peasants in the Russia of the 1870s. At the same time they have a deep contempt for all forms of conventional politics; a powerful

1 Fawthrop, op. cit., p. 65.

distaste for the 'system', and show little interest even in the kind of broadly-based alliance with a programme represented by C.N.D. The achievements of C.N.D. were after all limited, and with it stands condemned the whole of the moderate, strictly non-violent trend that was dominant during the second post-war phase of left politics.

Thus the third phase of left politics has begun as a cry of protest against the inhumanities of the modern world. How it will develop remains to be seen. As one might expect the moderates among the students have a programme of university reform. They want more representation on university committees, more involvement in decision making and so on. The granting of such demands will no doubt bring about a greater responsiveness to students' needs and a greater recognition of student rights. But it is unlikely to satisfy the more militant students, who will see the student representatives as just another variety of bureaucrat. The militant students have slogans – 'student power', 'changing the structure' and so on – and a philosophy of protest, but hardly a programme. The question for the future is whether there are any reforms which can assuage or cut away the ground from beneath the militants. If this is not so, if the unrest is too deep seated for a straightforward cure, then we may be witnessing the growth of a permanently disaffected and alienated section of the intelligentsia, which 'seeking the totality of an overall conceptual reality'[1] will establish its own separate institutions and modes of living. This is what happened in Russia in the last century and what seems to be happening now in America. But in Britain it would be a new phenomenon with revolutionary implications, for our intelligentsia, though often critical or disaffected (as in the 30s), has hitherto always been ready to advance programmes for solving specific ills of society and to participate in movements and alliances designed to bring these programmes into effect.

1 Fawthrop, op. cit., p. 26.

Ernest Gellner

The panther and the dove: reflections
on rebelliousness and its milieux

An American professor, a man in no way lacking in sympathy for the
Protest Movement, a man with a fine record of active social commitment,
one of the main organizers of the national Teach-Ins, was describing to me
the state of mind of some 'activist' students he had been addressing. He
did not mind in the least that they were ignorant. He did not mind that
they could not tell a coherent argument from an expression of attitude. All
this could be remedied. What he did mind, he regretfully admitted, was
that they did not seem in the very least interested in such a distinction.

Yet this is a movement of intellectuals, and it passionately wills itself to
be a doctrinal one. The specific grievances it feels and the injustices it
champions are meant to be united by some common thread of doctrine.
Others have wished to be open-minded and were in fact doctrinaire: this
movement wills itself to be doctrinal, but is in fact doctrinally invertebrate. Such doctrines or rather slogans as it possesses ('alienation' and so
on) could endow no one with an intellectual backbone. Perhaps the best
way to approach the movement is through an attempt to understand this
paradox.

The movement is international, and its deepest roots are not geographic-
ally specific. Nevertheless, it may be best to begin with local sources. Two
intertwined strands lead up to the present: one can be traced from the
'30s, the other from 1956.

The term *intelligentsia* is hardly used in England to describe any local
phenomenon, and the term intellectual, as a noun, only with a feeling of
awkwardness. It sounds pejorative and foreign. 'Are we workers, peasants,
or intellectuals, Fotheringay?' asks one clubman of another, in an Osbert
Lancaster cartoon. A don is a don and not an intellectual. All this is
significant. An intelligentsia is by definition a class dissociated from the
beliefs and values of its own society, by virtue of a superior education.
In this sense, England has not had an intelligentsia for a very long time.
At some periods, it looked as if it might acquire one – but, in the end,
social conscience and criticism found channels for expression and action

within the existing structure. Intelligent awareness did not face a stale-
mate and did not need to face the alternative of either rebellion or inner
emigration. In all this, the situation differed markedly from that of other,
less fortunate lands. Even the secularized noncomformist conscience
learnt to speak Hegelian, and used this idiom to draft the foundations of
something as constructive and unrevolutionary as the liberal welfare
state.[1]

The real significance of the '30s is that they constitute an exception to
this happy state. In the '30s intellect felt both outraged and helpless. In
retrospect, the remarkable thing is not that some intelligent people became Marxists, but that some did not. The depression had unmasked the
economic reality behind liberal society. The fascist regimes, and the ambiguous attitude towards them of liberal states, had unmasked its political
reality. The façade was down, and what seemed to be behind it was not
pretty to behold. Admittedly, neither the very existence of the Soviet
Union, nor the political realities within it, fitted the Marxist analysis: but
these two solitary discordant facts could hardly outweigh the others.

Facing a terrible and in fact insoluble situation, the generation of the
'30s really did rather well. Looked at in detail, the antics of some of its
members may look comic; and some of them did not know clearly whether
they were opposed to fascism or to fagging in Public Schools, and had
some difficulty in distinguishing the two. But all this hardly matters.
There was *no* solution. Fascism could only be and was stopped by force,
and the force was in the end applied by those members of their own
societies who did not share their anti-military values, and by Stalin. The
only thing the intellectuals as such could do was to register a protest, and
this they did with lasting effect. Their protest left a deep mark, and affected
the collective conscience for good.

The real failure of this generation came not before the war, but after it.
Before the war, they had faced an impossible situation which had no
peaceful solution, and events moved faster than they could think. But
after the war, things were different and, on the whole, much better. Now
there was time enough, and a situation which, even if not satisfactory in
all respects, at least offered a basis from which to work. It was in this
situation that the real failure occurred. The interesting case is not that of
the Philbys who never extricated themselves from the '30s but of that
majority which sank back, exhausted evidently by their earlier exertions,
into an uncritical and indiscriminate complacency. The real work of
demolishing Stalinism intellectually had been done by others (Koestler and

1 Cf. Melvin Richter, *The Politics of Conscience.*

Orwell in literature, Popper in philosophy, Aron in sociology): if this lot joined in, they did not add anything, other than a kind of routinization.

The post-war rejection of left extremism was not, in England, marred by any McCarthyism. They came quietly and no one harassed them or called them to account. On the contrary: the movement was only eased along and gently lubricated by an organization financed, as we are now told, with the help of the intelligence services of the United States.

This second historic incarnation of the generation of the '30s, in the post-war period, is deeply significant. As I do not wish to be misunderstood, perhaps I may say that I consider freedom to be a supreme value; and that, in the modern world of massive organizations, I can conceive that it may need to be organizationally defended, and that its defenders may sometimes be forced by their opponents to be less than fastidious in their methods. The case against the Aparatchiks for Freedom Inc. and their clients is not what they did but how they mismanaged it. They were told to sell cultural freedom (admirable) and in so doing they sugar-coated it. Actually, the quality of the coating was remarkable: for instance, their intellectual journalism, though not sympathique, was of a very high order. What it did not do was to sell the idea of freedom. The case against the aparatchiks of freedom is that they did for *liberty* what the communists were doing for *peace*. They gave it a slanted image and a bad name. The sugaring was excellent but it only hampered the product.

The social reasons for this failure are mildly amusing. The days of the Anglo-American marriage (in a literal sense), in which a fortune weds a title, are probably gone and belong to the world of P. G. Wodehouse. Today, an American fortune is more plausibly incarnated in a Foundation than in an heiress, and the cachet is embodied not in a groom but in some person occupying a key position in that socially prestigious set of institutions and ambience which can surround intellectual life in England. Nowadays, organization is everything, after all: it is not a case of boy meets girl, but a person with access to institutional resources, above board or not, meets another with access to institutional prestige. The aparatchiks of freedom, who had the former, appeared to be recruited from some tough Budd Schulberg world, and in England they were liable to the same weakness as the English once displayed in the Middle East – they simply adored the Shaikhs. Here these sammies could indulge in fantasies of social grace for which they lacked the preconditions at home. This intoxication rather showed up in the sugar-coating they offered for liberty, and for this reason, one rather doubts whether any real waverer in the cause of freedom was ever seduced or fortified in his faith by them. Rather the reverse, one fears.

What of the outlook that was being sold under that coating? If any one slogan can sum it up, it is the 'End of Ideology' theme, the view that societies are best run on the basis of a pragmatic consensus and, above all, the negative view that the greatest enemy of liberty is general doctrine. The curious thing is that at that time, this kind of view did not need to be imported or encouraged: well before the official announcement of the End of Ideology, under that name, there had been local and spontaneous ends of ideology, springing unprompted from local and quite diverse roots, ranging from a local Hegelianism to radical empiricism. Views such as that social theories have no injunctive force, that theorizing must be separate from action and can only follow it, that theorizing must be quite distinct from social and other belief, that general theories and synoptic ideals are the very devil, were locally current and fashionable anyway. The official End of Ideology, so named, was formulated by sociologists, and had some interesting and concrete intellectual content. The informal versions were formulated by local philosophers and had almost none. The only role and logical status which social thought could still have, on these premises, was a kind of after-dinner exercise, and indeed the most characteristic academic political theory of the time did have a post-prandial quality. The various groups propounding such views rated their own originality, style and premises so highly that they did not always at once recognize the similarity of their own views to each other: nevertheless, the atmosphere generated by such ideas fused easily with the conservative-liberalism encouraged by the aparatchiks of freedom.

The trouble with this kind of conservative-liberalism was that the conservatism was quite unselective, whilst the liberalism was only too selective, or rather, not very searching, and hence in effect selective. Most sensitive to the danger to liberty from social doctrine, especially Marxist doctrine, it did not puzzle too hard about the conditions in which liberty must labour in the mid-twentieth century, or worry about other dangers to it. Its unselective conservatism was as regrettable as its selective liberalism. The point about our world is that a great deal of liberal affluent society is very much worth preserving – but omnibus, abstract, indiscriminate conservatism is absurd. Yet the social doctrines in question were quite unequipped to make subtle or probing or indeed any distinctions in their endorsements.

So much for the conservative liberalism, which the young rebel will encounter – if he deigns to notice it – as he charges against the Establishment. Neither the force or subtlety of its formulations, nor the stature or record of its carriers, seem likely to awe him or make him falter in his steps.

1956 is of course a crucial year in the history of contemporary protest and rebellion. One member of the editorial board of *The Universities and Left Review* put on record, in a letter to *The Times*, the as it were official view of what happened in that traumatic year: apparently, the twin shocks of Hungary and Suez awakened a generation, hitherto somnolent under the influence of the beginnings of prosperity, and brought home to it the need for political action. At the time, I asked the author of this letter to give me some names of young people who had been political vegetables prior to 1956 but were galvanized into consciousness by it. He could not recall any names just then, but promised to think of some. I still see him from time to time, but at the time of writing (1968), somehow no name has yet come back to him.

What really happened, from the viewpoint of the ideological evolution which concerns us, is somewhat more complex. Not Hungary alone, but Hungary preceded by Krushchev's speech, had liberated, on the far left, a reservoir of political and intellectual talent, hitherto frozen in the Stalinist ice age. One doubts whether Hungary alone would have freed any who had lasted that long: the self-maintaining circle of ideas would have absorbed this shock as it had so many others. But since Krushchev's speech, a charter for dissent existed *within* that circle, and once this was the case, the shock was able to make its impact. Thus, a talented political leadership was liberated.

It could meet, lead and enlist a new followership of a kind that had not been foreseen and which could *never* have been forced into the doctrinal or organizational strait-jacket of an old-fashioned extreme left-wing party: the marching-fodder of the new protest, the generous, free-floating, doctrinally amorphous young of the relatively affluent society. The leaders were now freed from the inept and restrictive discipline and directives of their erstwhile party, and this new liberty affected even those who had been enlisted in rival organizations. With the old restrictions, they could never have led the new social potential, not for revolution, but for protest. The leadership looked like a kind of disembodied party, and in its disembodied way it floated freely, breathing in the free air with commendable joy.

Thus a perceptive university administrator, observing the skilful exploitation of student unrest, could be excused for bitterly blaming Krushchev. If only Krushchev had kept his mouth shut at the XXth Congress, if only the extreme left could dissipate its energy in either maintaining an impossible faith or in denouncing it, the students might be that much easier to handle. It is not only in Prague that the thaw is troublesome. The organizationally and doctrinally manacled Stalinists were so much easier to handle. (In Paris this spring, the forces of order had good cause to be grateful for some surviving Stalinoid sclerosis on the left.)

Here the story must be related to the other one (the progression from the '30s to conservative liberalism). The leadership of the new left also had some roots in the '30s even if many of the leaders were too young to have been active then. Not all the leftists of the '30s had, after all, trodden the primrose path to anti-doctrinaire liberal caution. Some had stayed on the far left, no doubt with increasing discomfort – and now they were free at last.

They remained faithful to their leftism in considering doctrine to be important. Unlike their opposite numbers on the other side, they were not going to turn against doctrine as such. But which doctrine? One thing was close to hand: the woollier, more philosophical views of Marx's Hegelian youth, recently rediscovered, fed by other continental streams, suitable for fusion with existentialist and psychiatric themes, hallowed by the courage of East European liberalizers, and above all, loose enough to be usable with the new followers, who would never have put up with the rigid, scholastic Marxism of the dark ages. Marx's youthful MSS are obscure, their obscurity heightened by the fact that they were written against the assumptions of an age and with messianic expectations, which are not ours and which are neither shared nor understood in our time. But they make up in social importance for what they lack in clarity or merit. Being parts of the scriptures of a faith, they are the natural charters for any would-be reformers or liberalizers from within the faith. (In these various respects, there is an analogy between the MSS and the New Testament.)

An adequate account of the notion of 'alienation' is evidently beyond the powers of its users, but the ideological mechanics of its employment are perfectly clear. The rebels are such on behalf of the workers. The workers reject them and their views. This forces the rebels into a kind of ethical Objectivism – they know better than the workers themselves what is good for the workers. But the rebels cannot openly embrace such a Platonist ethic: after all, they belong to the tradition of the Enlightenment, they can only preach political values endorsed by the willing consent of the people. So the pseudo-concept of alienation enables them to bridge this gap, to preach an objectivist, platonist, paternalistic ethic, whilst observing the empiricist, democratic proprieties. To declare some class of people to be 'alienated' is to proclaim them unfit to recognize and articulate their own interests, and to appoint yourself their guardian. The period of wardship will end when they gratefully recognize the justice of your views. The result is well known: alienation is now as familiar as the Oedipus complex.

(I find it amazing to think that until quite an advanced age I had never heard of it and yet managed to keep up a fairly active intellectual life, and that in my youth I supposed Marxism to be about historical materialism and the Labour Theory of Value.)

All the same, this kind of philosophizing did not absorb all their theoretical energies. They must also turn to the real world, and here too, many at least remained faithful to the key concept of the radical left – revolution. But they could not and on the whole did not deny that revolution, in any ordinary and real sense, was unlikely. Leaving aside the device of exporting one's revolutionary ardour overseas, or what might be called the Che Guevara complex ('Thou shalt not covet thy neighbour's revolution' as a French technical assistant observed in Algeria), this only leads to metaphysics and circumlocution: revolution *is* conceivable but in some new and special sense; a revolutionary potential *does* exist, but in some very new sense and so on.

In fact, they know that the Revolution is dead, just as God is dead, and in similar fashion. (Some even took part in both.) The decease is in both cases accompanied by much publicity and is by some curious twist of logic made the occasion for a revival of faith. Just as the death of God is somehow turned into His latest manifestation, warranting increased theological activity and zeal, so the death of Revolution is made into one further complaint against society, justifying revolutionary protest. The machine, the cultural apparatus, affluence, consensus – these have deprived us of a dimension of choice, and thus call for one further denunciation, or so we learn from Professor Marcuse, who seems to have become the Billy Graham of this left revivalism.

The tacit or other recognition that revolution in any normal sense is out, has curious consequences for the kind of reward a revolutionary can expect. No doubt I may be misunderstood on this point, so I'd like to stress that I do not know, or believe, these revolutionaries (either lot) to be particularly self-interested. I imagine their motives to be humanly mixed, like everyone else's, and the distribution of ambitious and selfless individuals among them not to differ too drastically from that found in other groups. My point concerns not the existence of ambition, if any, but the nature of the objective prospects facing it, if and in as far as it exists. Here again there is a parallel with the Death of God situation: the old believer could expect his fulfilment to come in another world, but his modern sophisticated successor must seek the meaning of religious fulfilment here and now. The same goes for 'Revolution'. A revolutionary of the '30s, if he was ambitious, could look forward to power *after* the Revolution.

(This only came to pass for those who were East Europeans, who could be rewarded with positions in the new communist regimes. Some paid for it with their lives or liberty during the anti-intellectual witchhunts of Stalin's last years.) But if ambitious men exist among the leadership of the present protesting left, they cannot and do not expect rewards of this kind. But they can expect some rewards in this, pre-revolutionary world, whether they want them or not.

For the ironic fact is that the World of Protest is *not* alienated, whatever it says. Not only does it have its rich culture and shared norms which many of us, yearning for human warmth, may well envy; but also, it is a world continuous and overlapping with many other worlds, in that series of overlapping circles which make up British society. (America is different in this respect.) The worlds of pot, pop, and protest adjoin the world of culture, education, entertainment, and the mass media, and prominence in any one can easily lead to, simply, prominence. I repeat that I am not attributing motives, but only noting objective situations and opportunities.

Here there is a certain contrast with the earlier wave. The revolutionary of the '30s could only look to a reward after the revolution, if he looked to a reward at all, but he was, unexpectedly, rewarded by the pre- and non-revolutionary society when he returned to the fold after the war. The returning prodigal was welcomed back, and resources were made available to ensure his comfort. Not all those ex-revolutionaries had started off well-connected, but those who were and those who were not melded into a network, which may compare with or surpass in social importance some more familiar old-boy networks. There is an excellent thesis subject here for some young sociologist. This very important social function can still be performed by the organizationally disembodied left leadership of today, but it can no longer be quite so innocent: the this-worldly reward, whether desired or not, cannot any longer come as a total surprise, for they do not expect any other world to make its appearance. In some ways, the new protesters can retrace the steps of the old, but with far greater speed: the transition from the journal of protest to regular contributions to the C.I.A.-sponsored journal of consensus can be achieved not in a matter of decades, but a mere year or so.

In one of the earliest manifestoes of the new protest, one of its spokes-men claimed that English intellectuals are haunted by the thought of the fates of Keynes and Trotsky. As a statement of fact, this is quite untrue: few English intellectuals, even economists, are obsessed by the fate of Keynes, and fewer still by Trotsky. But as a confession of the Walter Mitty inner life of such a spokesman, mirroring the vistas as they appear to *him*, it was perfectly accurate. As he takes a little time off from a perfectly satisfactory and smooth academic career in the rotten society, to try to foment industrial strikes, and as he lifts the receiver, hears a click and fancies that his telephone is tapped, is it fear or is it hope that tells him that the end-point will be, not an ice pick in the skull, but perfectly comfortable success? Without quite endorsing the comparison with Keynes, one supposes that these fears of martyrdom-deprivation will prove entirely justified.

These, then, are the ideological leaders, who offer *encadrement* and doctrine to the young rebel, as he goes charging against the Establishment.

What of the followers, the erstwhile marching-fodder, now sitting-in-fodder? They are, after all, the most interesting, important, least understood element in the situation.

Perhaps the mystery is not so very great. Perhaps these rebels simply offer a foretaste, like those almost symbolic harbingers, the Swedish delinquents, of the problems of social control in affluent, liberal, welfare and doctrine-less society. When the new non-ideological consensus was being celebrated and the embourgeoisement of the proletariat commenced, certain inconveniences were ignored. After all, a part at least of the old bourgeois youth regularly went bohemian, in one form or another, and loudly repudiated the values of their fathers, whilst generally keeping open a line back to dad and society, the repudiation being verbally violent but neither total nor final. If the bourgeoisie and middle-class life styles spread through to much larger part of society, this type of ambivalent rebellion can also be expected to grow in proportion.

Of course, not all the rebels come from such comfortable backgrounds. Here again, something had escaped earlier notice. When people wrote of meritocracy, they generally expressed regret that the process of upward selection by education would deprive the discontented classes of potential leaders. On the basis of premature extrapolation from the first post-war wave of entrants, who seemed gratefully willing to swallow *anything* the universities dished up, it was much too easily assumed that all these would be digested with ease, that none of them would rebel during the very process of upward suction.

Social control in liberal, affluent, non-ideological society works under very special and restrictive conditions. It lacks a doctrine which would justify anything. It has deprived itself of the economic stick. If Marx were living in this hour – he would have no need to sponge on Engels. He could, like other authors of books on Marxism, obtain a subsidy from the Congress for Cultural Freedom, and if he refused to do this, it is quite easy to keep body and soul together in Kentish Town by, say, giving extramural lectures on economics and social philosophy for the University of London.

Whilst largely deprived of the economic stick, liberal affluent society is extremely inept in its use of the prestige carrot. It possesses an educational system whose nominal function is preparation for the full life, but whose latent function (which is perfectly manifest to everyone) is preparation for a privileged life and position. Those skills of lucid expression and essay-writing would be somewhat irrelevant for people to whom no one will listen and whom no one will read. At the same time, the society drastically expands the educational system: even allowing for changes in occupational structure, this means that for many who pass through the educational machine, it must appear that they are being prepared for something which they will not be allowed to enjoy. The fact that the biggest or initial rebellions took place at Berkeley and L.S.E. may be significant. In universities which are socially more prestigious, the majority of the students know that they can expect positions commensurate with their training. In intellectually less glamorous centres, appetites and expectations may be less titivated. But it is the middle area which is most explosive: here the students know that some, but some only, will make it, and they suppose that many of their teachers already have access to the perks of modern society, to power, the mass media, and so on. When the sweet smell of success constantly wafts through the overcrowded and anomic corridors, but it is known that some only will be allowed a bite, the irritation may become intolerable.

Modern society expands the educational system, and it wishes to make it egalitarian – which means, it endeavours to make entry into it and performance in it quite independent of the previous social niche of the entrant. At the same time, modern society, either side of the big divide, continues to be incurably *in*egalitarian with respect to the distribution of power, if not quite as necessarily or quite as conspicuously inegalitarian with respect to styles of life. If the (very partially implemented) *aspiration* to educational equality is taken in conjunction with the *reality* of concentration of power, we get something like a janissary or mameluke situation: the power-holders are to be torn from their social wombs and recruited as solitary social atoms. So far so good. But the societies which recruited mamelukes to rule over them had the sense to import only a limited number (if only because they were expensive) – and even so, they had their troubles with them. Modern society is like a mameluke-employing state which endeavours to import as many as it can, without counting the number of places available for them.

In America, it is customary to distinguish two types of rebel – the hippy and the activist. These are indeed good 'ideal types', and represent the classical alternatives facing groups which reject the values of the world and the dominant society: either to attempt to change the world forcibly, or to opt out into a haven of quietest withdrawal. (This dilemma faced the English noncomformists, and as David Martin has pointed out, they tended to choose quietism *after* their Revolution had failed. In America, the time-order seems curiously reversed: Beat quietism preceded the revival of activism.) The interesting thing is that, on the whole, these *are* only ideal types: most of the rebels are clustered not at the two ends of the Hippy/ Activist spectrum but somewhere along the ambiguous middle. A real activist, who fully believed his own rhetoric about the rottenness and ruth-lessness of the society he is opposing, would train, organize, and brace himself for the merciless struggle which is to come, and not waste his time on elaborating an absorbing subculture, which in its lack of discipline seems ill-suited for a social Armageddon. He would not solicit the support of the hippy, and a consistent hippy, withdrawing into his private world of sanity and freedom, would not be available for recruitment.

The interesting thing is how very few people are located at either of these logically consistent poles: the culture of rebellion is clustered in the middle, fusing both attitudes. This inner contradiction no doubt con-tributes to the doctrinally invertebrate condition of the rebellion.

Yet this very ambiguity, coupled with doctrinal and organizational formlessness, may well provide *the* type of protest and Fronde in contem-porary society. Various factors are conducive to such a condition. Tactically the best prospects seem to be available for small, determined, free-lance groups, unrestrained by a wider plan or discipline, moving invisibly like the proverbial Maoist fish in the waters of a wider population, such as students at large, which has both specific discontents and a general sense of malaise, and which can be led into action by such groups – if these are free enough, both in terms of doctrine and organization, to exploit oppor-tunities quickly, without reference to anything and anyone. And again, the social sciences may have reached a point at which they force political ideologies to 'demythologize': just as religion once contained, as an inte-gral part, doctrines concerning the *natural* world which, when proved to be false, were then declared to be inessential and peripheral (this is known as 'demythologizing'); so today perhaps it is no longer safe for an ideology to be committed too firmly to any specific views of the *social* world either. Nebulousness, in one case as in the other, is then a condition of secure conviction and effective operation.

Though not endowed with much of a theory, the movement does possess some nebulous outlines of an epistemology. The elements of this are somewhat different on either side of the Atlantic. In America, it possesses a theory of knowledge, and above all an associated style of expression, which goes back to populism and beyond it, presumably, to some form of popular protestantism. Its basic idea is that *sincerity* is the key to truth, and above all that any kind of order or structure is a betrayal. The view of truth manifests itself above all in the manner of its communication – that terribly *sincere*, carefully unstructured, conspicuously groping, free-associative style of speech, which has received so much confirmation from literature and some additional reinforcement, one imagines, from psycho-analytic theory and practice.

Despite the fact that the cis-Atlantic protest movement learnt a vast amount from the trans-Atlantic pioneers, especially in matters of tactics, it never quite took over this epistemology of sincerity, the manner of communication adopted by these inverted Babbitts. Another theory of knowledge can be discerned here. It runs in terms of 'theory and practice': the validity of thought hinges on being rooted in *practice*. In reality, this theory turns out to be a camouflaged version of an argument from authority. Everyone alive is involved in *some* practice: to make 'practice' into the legitimator of ideas is, covertly, to single out the practice of *some*, and to make their ideas sovereign. If those whom one likes, and wishes to enlist, turn out, despite their privileged practice, not to have the right ideas – if, to be specific, the workers are not revolutionary, and racialist into the bargain – well, then, this is known as the 'problem of consciousness', and can be discussed with much learned reference to Lukacs and Gramsci. The 'problem of consciousness' arises from the fact that the workers are known to have the right ideas, really, underneath, only sometimes these ideas remain latent and quite unperceived by their very owners, and then one has to wait for their awakening.[1]

This rather simple-minded circle of definitions and escape-clauses could of course easily be manipulated to justify anything. In its defence be it said that it does not differ significantly from an epistemology fashionable

---

1 In America, a variant of this doctrine has now assumed a very specific form: the ghetto has replaced the log cabin as the point of origin which legitimates the ideas of its possessor. The 'problem of consciousness' is, for the moment, ignored, for there is an opportunist alliance between the oppressed ethnic minorities, yearning for respect, affluence and respectability, and the activists, sated with affluence and respectability, and yearning for épatement. (As for the white workers, no one even expects them to be revolutionary – they appear to be lost to consciousness for good.)

on the philosophic right, which also values 'practical knowledge' above all else, and also defines valid social or political knowledge in terms of the practice, and hence the identity, of its bearers. The ideas of the leading conservative professor and of the local leader of student revolt are curiously similar. The privileged bearers and the type of practice are of course a somewhat different lot in the professorial case, and the nature of the practice-hallowed ideas is specified so little that the problem of consciousness hardly arises for his version. English philosophical conservatism of recent decades is remarkable in that it has worked out a populism-for-upper-classes: it reveres the inarticulate folk wisdom of a ruling class and seeks to defend it against the parvenu intellectualism of theorists – an amusing inversion of the usual pattern. Epistemology is only one of the areas where the protesters and conservatives mirror each other fairly faithfully.

The price of the doctrinal looseness of the movement, combined with the rhetoric of angry rejection, is of course a deep ambivalence. If you draw no fine distinctions, if the dissent is indiscriminate and vehement, it lashes out against society as a whole. But this total rejection, whilst it could be sustained by a tough, ruthless, determined, long-range revolutionary, is difficult to sustain for people who are nothing of the kind. If you draw no distinctions in isolating the *objects* of your emotions (and you cannot in fact have the same strong emotions towards everything), the inevitable consequence is that the emotions themselves become ambivalent: the distinctions which are not allowed to enter at the level of concepts make their surreptitious but uncontrolled entry at the level of feeling.

In California, the left activist Peace and Freedom Party is in alliance with the militant Black Panther Party, and the two campaign jointly and have issued joint posters, which can be seen in the windows of progressive people. On the poster, the symbols of each of the two parties is represented: the dove *and* the panther. That the symbol of gentleness and peace should lie down on one poster with the symbol of ferocious aggression is profoundly symptomatic. There are movements which are neither pacifist nor addicted to a mystique of violence. But this movement is not somewhere in the middle. It is in fact drawn both towards pacificism and to a romanticism of violence. The mystique of violence of course fits in perfectly with a vision of revolution which is expressive and not at all instrumental: to think of consequences of a revolution would be as sordid as drawing up a financial marriage settlement. Spontaneity is all.

Some coherence could be introduced into the attitude towards violence by saying that violence by the oppressed is legitimate, and violence by the possessors of the apparatus of oppression is not. But this does not quite capture the spirit of the thing. It might be closer to it to say disciplined violence on behalf of order is wrong, whereas spontaneity is its own justi-fication. (It is thus a neat inversion of the conventional attitude to violence and coercion, which sees them as necessary evils justified only by their contribution to order.)

The ambivalence manifests itself in that well-known phenomenon, the double moral standard of the extreme left. On the one hand, the least injust-ice or illiberalism perpetrated by the Establishment is vociferously decried (quite right, too – but it seems to imply that the Establishment can be ex-pected to be fair and liberal, and that there is some point in protesting *within* the order dominated by it); yet at the same time, a 'revolutionary' mystique, and in some (much smaller) measure, a revolutionary practice, are commended, on the argument that current institutions and legal proce-dures are *so* slanted that nothing can be achieved within them, and the only hope lies in bypassing them. Thus the current order is accorded a kind of sliding-scale semi-legitimacy. It is expected to protect carefully the rebel's legal rights, but at the same time to look on benignly and with affectionate understanding when the rebel bypasses legality in the interests of higher principles. It is expected to issue, honour and ensure a kind of Rebel's Licence. Thus not the revolution, but the *ancien régime* itself, is expected to be the midwife of the new order, and a most maternal and solicitous one at that. What kind of expectation is this? It has the mad logic of a family quarrel. These are emotionally most exhausting rebels. They demand to be loved by the order against which they are raising their hand.

Thus they wish to play within and outside the old rules all at once, according to convenience. Good luck to anyone who can get away with this: but what bothers me is the sociological self-contradiction. The premise for extra-legal activity is the prejudicial and slanted nature of current arrange-ments (which has a certain general plausibility, whether or not relevant at present – for in general social arrangements can be expected to favour their own perpetuation). The premise for appealing to the rules, however, is that the present arrangements are not so terrible after all, and can be expected to protect even those wishing to subvert them. This may or may not be true, but it is in blatant contradiction with the other premise.

This is true even of the extreme wing of the Negro Protest movement, whose members really would have good cause for genuine total rejection of society. Yet even their rhetoric is not accompanied by any corresponding consistency of attitude and feeling. The society which is declared rotten is also solicited for support, and failure to receive it, or enough of it, is bitterly resented rather than tough-mindedly expected. Some consistency can be introduced into this attitude by bringing in a time-scale: we are giving you one more chance to help us peacefully, and 'the fire next time'. But one feels that the inner ambivalence is there right now.

The French case has some special characteristics. Only in France did student action trigger off a wider response; yet in France, the working class also retains enough loyalty to a rigid Stalinoid organization, and the two things cancelled out. French intellectuals are permeated by a sentimental tradition of revolution. They possess a transmitted folk memory of barricades, of a kind which is absent elsewhere. The consequences can be curious. The revolutions of the nineteenth century tried to replay 1789, but for good, properly, with an extended social content and a successful outcome. This revolution, on the other hand, only tried to replay the unsuccessful efforts of the nineteenth century. It appears that barricades were placed, with an eye to piety rather than strategy, in the same places as they had been in 1848. It is also obvious, judging from the speed and size of the literary afterbirth, that the rebels took their typewriters along to the barricades. One trusts that someone reported to the General – Sire, not a revolution, a revolt! An interesting commentary on the events of May was the reaction of East Europeans resident in Paris: coming from a part of the world where politics are at present played for desperately serious and real stakes, they were appalled by this free indulgence in symbolism. Clifford Geertz has spoken of the theatrical, exemplary state in South-East Asia, of its 'exemplary' theory of legitimacy: here was a theatrical, 'exemplary' theory of counter-legitimacy. Instead of a theatre of revolution, they had a theatrical revolution. I am assured that the East Europeans' horrified reaction was shared, in equal measure, by both the émigrés-refugees and the official communist representatives. (One factor in the situation may be that a generation has grown up to whom Hitler and Stalin are no longer social realities, political possibilities, in the light of which current alternatives must be considered and evaluated.)

What is worrying about the student part of the movement is its occasional illiberalism. However libertarian its members may be about legalizing marijuana, they do sometimes put forward proposals such as the student control of 'what is taught and how'. It does not seem to occur to them that the implementation of this proposal would involve not the *transfer* of power from one set of people to them, but the *institution* of control where none exists at present. I do not wish to idealize the present situation: there may be junior teachers, without tenure, who believe that their careers hinge on pleasing their seniors. Sometimes they may be right. But at least in British universities, teachers obtain tenure very soon, and thereafter, though their promotion could depend on conformity, their security does not. They are safe and free to teach what and how they wish, and the students, who also complain, not without cause, of the quality of teaching, know that there is very little control of teachers. Those who demand control by themselves over 'what' is taught do not seem to realize the enormity, not of giving *them* control, but of instituting control *at all*, or rather, of replacing the present 'sociological' controls, working through indirect pressures which can be defied without excessive difficulty by anyone really wishing to do so – by formal and, presumably, enforced controls. The present pressures are limited in their effectiveness precisely because they are held to be illegitimate: they can only operate in camouflage, and this hampers them. But the rebels wish to institutionalize and legalize the controls which *they* would impose, and thus nothing would inhibit *their* effectiveness. They do not seem to have pondered the institutional implications of their proposals. What is to happen to teachers who disobey their instructions? One can only wonder whether they *do* know what they are saying, and are profoundly illiberal and totalitarian, or whether they do *not* know what they say, and the proposal is merely part of this generally invertebrate thinking.

These then are the rebels and protesters. Their economic base is the almost accidental discovery of the Beat generation of how easy it is to opt out and survive. Their social base is at least partly the uneven distribution of other goods. The movement generously concerns itself with real and specific ills, such as racialism, but, whatever its rhetoric, has quite failed to fuse its specific angers into a general, theoretical critique. It wills itself doctrinal and total: in fact, it is doctrineless and ambivalent.[1]

Perhaps a society gets the rebels it deserves. It is amusing to reflect in how many ways the protest movement is a fulfilment of the indiscriminate, doctrine-less or rather anti-doctrine attitudes of the end-of-ideology period.

That period preached the politics of pragmatic consensus, as against ideology. This had an element of novelty: past political philosophers had striven to give reasons why we should subscribe to this or that consensus. They said – the nature of things, or our interests, are such and such, and *therefore* we should all subscribe to a certain view or loyalty. The End-of-Ideology boys made consensus a premise rather than a conclusion, and

---

1 Cf. T. Bottomore, *Critics of Society*, Pantheon Books, N.Y., 1968. Arnold J. Kaufman, *The Radical Liberal*, Atherton Press, N.Y., 1968. Wolff, R. P., Marcuse, H. and Barrington Moore, *A Critique of Pure Tolerance*, Beacon Press, Boston, 1965.

preached it in a *l'art pour l'art* spirit. Consensus was self-justifying: not based on reasons, but a substitute for reasons.[1] Very well: but two can play this game. If consensus can dispense with reasons, so can dissent. And here it is.

Why should the devil have all the good tunes? Why should the conservatives have a near-monopoly of un-reasons? For centuries now, the left has, on the whole, been the intelligent party, kept on its intellectual toes both by its own super-ego (the left believes in reason), and by internal competition. The conservatives could on the whole make do without reasons, treating the *status quo* as self-justifying, and only offering indiscriminate, omnibus reasons for preservation or caution. But if, for instance, *intimations* are good enough for the conservative goose, they are now also good enough for the radical gander. The rebels, short on theory, are rich in intimations. One undisputable achievement of the protest movement has been to rectify this old injustice, and deprive the right of its monopoly of loose thought.

Or again, ponderous meaninglessness in sociological theory reached its height during the post-war McCarthyite period in America. At the time, it was natural to suppose that the two were connected: theories so lacking in clear meaning could not be subversive, or suspect as such. But today, the dissident potential of obscurity has been vindicated.

Thus in most ways, the rebels are a fulfilment of the end-of-ideology prophecy, if not exactly in the manner foreseen. In their doctrinelessness and ambivalence, they have paid liberal affluent society a far greater – because involuntary – compliment than the conservatives ever managed. Consider doctrine: when the Church faced the Reformation, when Absolute Monarchy faced democracy and constitutionalism, when feudalism faced egalitarianism, when capitalism faced socialism – in each case, there was a real contrast, and the old order had cause to tremble. But when alienated society faces the shining image of non-alienated society, one can only laugh. If this is the best (or worst) you can think up, the old order cannot be in any grave danger.

1 It is amusing to note that even the communist regimes have learnt this lingo. During the recent Czechoslovak thaw, the official line of the moderate liberalizers, who wished to move ahead without too radical a break with the recent past, ran as follows: We have now achieved consensus concerning the socialist basis of our society. *Hence* we may move towards pluralism . . . the implication being that the previous harshness, if not its excesses, were justified by the same principle as now requires more liberty. Consensus makes freedom possible; its absence makes it difficult or impossible. Did the communists who told me this learn it from the Voice of America, or did they work it out for themselves?

Nor is it. Society will not crumble under the impact of these rebels, not only because it is probably too rich, too resilient, too attractive for too many of its members, but also, and this is more interesting, because these rebels do not really wish it to. (They have no experience, and little imagination, of a genuinely revolutionary situation, when a social order is really losing all moral credibility for its members.) In a variety of ways, they refrain from cutting their lifelines to the established order, and thus belie the violence of their verbal, sartorial and pharmaceutical rhetoric.[1] This ambivalence is a greater compliment, just because it goes against the grain, than the subsidized, *voulu* conservative celebrations of consensus. The inability to choose between quietest withdrawal and revolutionary activism, and the fact that the quietism is anything but quiet, are further indices of this giveaway ambivalence.

It used to be a point of pride of the modern age that it had revolutionaries rather than rebels: that those who rose up against order did not merely (or at all) wish to substitute themselves for the previous power-holders, but wished to change the order itself – to abolish injustice, rather than just to reverse its distribution. We are now back in a curious situation in which, once again, we are without revolutionaries. But we have rebels who wish to act the part of revolutionaries. And the rebels are not mere rebels in the old sense either: they would be ashamed merely to be using rebellion to improve their position (though this will happen to some, whether they wish it or not). Past revolutionaries often – not always – started with a profound sense of the claims of past order, and were only pushed into outright revolution by the logic of events. With this lot, it is just the reverse. They start with a total mystique, and may end with a few reforms. They have failed to be revolutionaries, though their rhetoric aspires to it, because they have been unable either to conceptualize an alternative to the present order, or even to criticize it in any systematic fashion. There is no unity in their angers. (And the justified ones, such as the concern with racialism, are only sullied by running parallel with causes as frivolous, questionable and unimportant as the legalization of pot.)

But they have unwittingly held up a mirror to literally thought-less conservatism. The end of ideology has come home to roost. It is, I suppose,

1 One rebel set out to subvert what he considered a neo-colonialist African regime. When they put him in jail – he had left his schemes lying about in writing – he was outraged at failing to receive total and immediately effective help from the British diplomatic representatives (though these, presumably, must have been the puppet-masters behind that neo-colonial regime!). In trouble, far from being a revolutionary, he had the instincts of an English spinster of the Palmerstonian era: if you do not do as I say at once, I shall inform the British Consul!

too much to hope that either side will recognize its image in the mirror. But if unreasoning consensus, if rejection of general ideas as such, is legitimate for one side, then so is *l'art pour l'art* dissent. The new ultimate complaint is not that this or that deep ill calls for revolution, but that we are somehow deprived, through the very absence of a revolutionary situation and of deep pervasive ills. Self-sustaining revolt has answered the call of self-sustaining consensus. This will perhaps turn out to be its greatest achievement: by showing that the rejection of orderly thought and real distinctions can be used in both directions, it will remove one inducement to intellectual emptiness.

John Dunn

The dream of revolution[1]

Once again the spectre of revolution is haunting bourgeois Europe. The form which it takes in the west today is not, as it remains in the countries of the Eastern Bloc, a struggle for political liberty, but something more elusive and rather less dignified. The negro revolution and the student revolution seldom leave the front pages of the newspapers and the agony of Vietnam (which never leaves their front pages) is claimed optimistically by the students and the black militants for their own. In Western Europe and perhaps on the campus of Columbia University, history has taken once more to repeating itself as farce. The spectre which so many thought had been laid for ever has regained an improbable energy. What does it all mean? I'd like to try and explain why no one can yet know quite *what* it means, and to suggest why it was always a foolish belief that the spectre could be laid for ever.

It has long been part of the conventional wisdom of the western world that the promised revolution is not going to happen. Ever since Engels's secretary, Eduard Bernstein, pointed out that the Marxist scenario was not being enacted, before the twentieth century even began, the revolutionary dream has been peripheral to the development of western society. But despite this central fact, and despite the repeatedly proclaimed end of ideology which it is alleged to have brought about, the dream has shown a remarkable tenacity. The end of ideology seems as much as anything else to have been a function of the ageing process in the individual life cycle. Few ideologies can stand up to a lifetime's wear. Ideologies, like men, are always wearing out, but, as with men, new ones seem generally to be born to replace them.

The ideological enthusiasm for revolution today derives from what revolutions have come to mean in the twentieth century, which is something very different from what they meant in the nineteenth. In the nineteenth century, revolutionaries, particularly Marxist revolutionaries, saw their role as one of easing the birth pangs of the new society, bringing more

1 A talk originally given in the B.B.C. Third Programme, 29 September 1968.

deftly into the world a form of society already due to be born. The image
which best embodied the identity which they adopted was that of the mild
wife, the skilled human attendant at a quasi-biological event who merely
assisted the course which nature had already shown every disposition to
take. Today this picture has come to look excessively naïve. Neither nature
nor history any longer provides such crude evolutionary assurances about
the future. The Russian revolution was the last revolution to be made substantially within the framework of the older conception. Even the Bol-
sheviks derived their assurance in 1917 from the expectation that revolution
in Russia would spark revolution in western Europe. With the failure of
this hope and with Socialism in one country, revolution came to seem not
merely less reliable as an expectation but also less enticing as a prospective
experience. The more chancy it was that any particular revolution happened
at all, the more obvious it was that what was to become of any particular
revolution was a disagreeably open question. All political revolutions are
compounds of very abstract dreams and very concrete events. The abstract
dreams tend to be highly imitative. But the concrete events have turned
out to be in important ways unrepeatable. The morals which have been
drawn from this realization have been extremely diverse. The Leninist
moral, which was a necessary condition for the occurrence of the October
Revolution, was given extraordinary prestige by the idiosyncratic success
of that revolution. If history can no longer be relied upon to go one's way,
it is necessary to organize effectively in order, if at all possible, to compel
it to do so. Leninism as a doctrine of political action does possess a fairly
coherent political ethic. Lenin once said memorably to the Labour dignit-
ary George Lansbury, after being read a lengthy lecture on the bloodstained
character of the Russian revolution, 'I don't believe you can do it your way.
But if you can, well, do it.' It is a perfectly Leninist converse of this sneer
to conclude that if you can't, don't. And it is a converse which the communist parties of Latin America and Western Europe have lately drawn
with some clarity. But it is hard to tell for sure which way the moral applies
until you have tried and seen.

The five countries which have set the most unequivocal pattern of
revolution in the twentieth century – Russia, China, Vietnam, Yugoslavia
and Cuba – have nothing else in their experience which is common to
them all. And each of them has a great many features in common with other
nations which haven't generated such a revolution. In all of them a leading
role has eventually been played by the Communist party. But, except in the
Russian revolution, it hasn't been the superior historical sagacity of the
international Communist movement which has made the revolution

possible. It wasn't the international blueprint which the Comintern missionaries bore, or even the existence of the metropolitan church from which they came, which explained the success of these movements. What did in fact turn the determination of small numbers of revolutionary cadres to such remarkable effect in these countries is even now difficult to recognize with assurance and was in all cases impossible to know *a priori*.

So the morals which are drawn are likely to be morals which men wish to draw, rather than the morals imposed by the evidence. To mass parties in advanced industrial societies with the interests of millions in their hands, the moral drawn is likely to be the futility and immorality of adventurism. To the leaders of resistance to the surviving colonial bastions, as for instance to the late Frantz Fanon, it is more likely to be the social transformation produced by mass military insurrection. To the young and deeply alienated in more prosperous societies the moral drawn is even more abstract. Politely, it can be called the merits of voluntarism, of the role of the human will in history. Less charitably, it's simply a boundless hope, based insecurely on the understanding that the damnedest things can happen, because they already have done so, in Cuba. In itself this expectation is not an inspiriting example of political education. When allied, as it often is, with an ethic of pure intention, it can be very ugly indeed. Revolutions of the saints have an old hypocrisy to them. The belief that what matters is whom they are directed against (the wicked) rather than what they cause to happen, has always had to depend for its plausibility on more or less metaphysical theory. The evolutionary expectations of some nineteenth-century revolutionaries furnished a plausible theory of this type. Its phraseology has remained the phraseology of twentieth-century revolution. But the experience of twentieth-century revolution lends no authority whatever to the theory and exposes its contemporary believers as rankly superstitious or grossly dishonest.

At this point we may return to the student revolution. Why is it that the idea of revolution retains the appeal which it does for some students? The answer can hardly be, for instance, that their enthusiasm derives from a deep, sophisticated and informed delight at the social and political structure of the Soviet Union, let alone at its foreign military exploits. Nor is it because history appears to be going their way that they feel drawn to the idea. If anything, the appeal comes rather from a sense of heroic resistance to the tides of history. At one level it is appropriate to think of all this in the way in which an anthropologist might begin to analyse a primitive religion, to concentrate at first on the ritual. At this level, it is undoubtedly a middle-class version of the delinquent solution. Bashing a policeman for

Vietnam is a bourgeois surrogate for the rewards of Glasgow gang warfare. But every society to some degree deserves the delinquent solution which it gets.

All advanced industrial societies teach their citizens in childhood and adolescence a set of extremely elegant abstract moral values. No industrial society embodies these values in its social arrangements in any very literal fashion. In itself such a gap between proclaimed ideal and experienced reality doesn't provide the preconditions for social upheaval. If it did every Christian society in history would have been in a state of permanent social insurrection. In practice the reckless demands of the proclaimed values are effectively insulated for most citizens by a careful social training in relaxed cynicism. But under some circumstances the gap between ideal and reality can catch the attention of many and hence can become embarrassing or even intolerable. One of the features of advanced industrial societies is that they need a very high level of predictable behaviour from their populations in many different contexts if they are to operate with any tolerable ease. They are held together by the internalization of an extremely demanding set of performance values. Conscription, taxpaying, work discipline and public order depend upon a reliable acceptance of most of the social order by the great majority. The widespread chaos in America at the moment shows how easy it is for quite small numbers of determined men to disrupt the effective working of an advanced industrial society by pointing to the more obvious departures from its ideal values.

Another feature of an advanced industrial society is its increasing dependence on a massive sector of higher educational institutions to train the elites which manage and administer it. The university tradition in western societies is still sufficiently strong to ensure that the curricula of these institutions pay some systematic attention to the formal value system of the society. But this state of affairs might conceivably be reversed and in itself may be of no great importance. What is much more important and what is comparatively difficult, perhaps even impossible, to reverse, is the distinctive social character of higher educational institutions. Students are in many ways insulated from the rest of society, extracted from the constraints of the family, free from the rigid work discipline of an advanced industrial society and thrown into intensive and sustained contact with their own peer group in the daily discharge of their work requirements. This insulated but emotionally active situation can generate a remarkable corporate élan among certain groups of the students and can free their imaginations and energies to act upon the society at large with unique vigour. In the countries of Eastern Europe, for example, and eventually no doubt in Russia itself we may expect them to lead the struggle to recapture elementary human liberties for all. But in the societies of the west their role is a more isolated and ambiguous one. Many of their confrontations with the repressive apparatus of bourgeois society will take place over variously foolish or dishonest initiatives. But even the most corrupt may prove embarrassing to the authorities because the slogans under which they take place do claim the protection of the formal values of the society. And some will prove excessively embarrassing because they will claim this sanction with altogether greater moral authority than the repressive apparatus which confronts them.

However, there are certainly fashions in student interest and most students in Britain or America or Germany today are not much interested in insurrectionary politics. It is possible that that particular fashion will shortly fade away and be replaced by a decorous apathy or a sharp rise in Voluntary Service Overseas. But there is no particular reason to suppose that it *will* in fact fade away. It is interesting to consider what may become of it if it does not do so. At this point the change in the meaning of the idea of revolution becomes important. For the sense of quasi-inevitability, of reason latent in the course of social evolution, which was characteristic of the most impressive nineteenth-century revolutionary theory, has switched sides with some completeness in this century. The inevitable course of social development for western societies is posited with increasing assurance as an endless course of economic growth by means of an increasingly automated industrial sector. Production is to remain under the control of the kindly but firm paternalism of the highly technical elites who alone can comprehend the meaning of technical rationality in such a complex setting. Very few people in such a society are going to be well placed to see exactly how matters could be arranged differently and most of those who have passed through the institutions of higher education will be absorbed effortlessly into the elites which decide how matters *will* be arranged.

In this sense the political innocence of the student body, their most obvious disability, is also their unique advantage. In the immense intricacy of this future society only those who do not quite know why things are as they are are likely to be able to believe that they could in any important way be different. The twentieth-century experience of revolution serves as a powerful image of the openness of history, of the ways in which men can take charge of their social fate. It can give the student rebels the energy and the faith to doubt what the knowing know so well. But it cannot, of course, give them the intelligence or the information with which to know better. Indeed in itself it is unlikely to provide any very helpful directives on how to act. Che Guevara may be an inspiring image of youthful intransigence. But however deft an articulation it might have been of Bolivian social realities, taking to the Pennines with a rifle would not be much of a response to the political needs of contemporary Britain. Until they can elaborate a more purposeful picture of how their society might be better, and one with a wider social appeal than raising students grants, any increase in violence on their part is simply going to damage the better features of the existing society. A purposeful military challenge to the government by such a socially peripheral group in an advanced industrial society could not conceivably be successful. The Leninist moral, 'if you can't, don't', applies very fully. Societies of this type are not finally vulnerable to the conspiratorial pressures of a Leninist revolutionary party, still less to those of a Maoist or Castroite guerilla movement. They are too powerful and not directly oppressive enough. In any case, since there is nothing which the student militants abhor more deeply than authoritarian organization, it is not a Leninist challenge which they are going to offer their society, but something much closer to anarchist open conspiracy. A society which can withstand the Leninist threat with little effort is not going to succumb to the confrontation of anarchists. Revolutions involve the seizure and retention of *power*. Anarchism as a theory or a set of dispositions provides no resources for the retention of power and few for its seizure against effective opposition.

Because such a movement cannot conceivably seize power, its prospective political efficacy depends upon its retaining some legitimacy within the values of the existing society. The moral pretensions of liberal society, like most other forms of society, are not realized in its actual operations. This can be made dramatically obvious by determined resistance to the more arbitrary acts of its authorities. But a preparedness to tolerate the deliberate infliction of violence for political motives by private individuals could not be one of the moral pretensions of any industrialized society, nor is there the least reason why it should be. An anarchist open conspiracy in the name of the higher values of these societies might be able to force them up against these values as no other internal or external stimulus is likely to do. At best it might even compel them to live up to their expressed values. But if the behaviour of the student militants is seen to violate these values, its legitimacy will disappear and any potential power with it. Its consequences then may indeed be deplorable, may lead the society to diverge altogether more drastically from these values than it would otherwise have done.

The role which gives the student militants this power to exploit the distinctive vulnerability of an advanced industrial society is one which will demand extraordinary self-control and discipline on their part. On present showing it is only too likely that they will fail to carry it off. But if they do succeed in doing so they will be demonstrating the openness of history in just the same way as those who have led successful revolutions in this century. If they fail, they too will face the dismissive charge of having set themselves to oppose the inevitable. But in itself this may be no very dishonourable charge – as Van Woodward said recently, 'since the inevitable is generally unpleasant, it needs all the opposition it can get'. Certainly if it gets no opposition we shall never see how inevitable the inevitable was. By the time it becomes clear to the judicious how far the opposition has been tragedy and how far farce, the tragedy and the farce will not just be part of the past lives of a set of ex-students, they will be part of the future of all our societies.

Bernard Crick

The proper limits of student influence

The idea of a university

Universities are – this at least is not open to reasonable doubt – very *peculiar institutions.*[1] And yet, on immediate second thoughts, there are now some who have seriously argued that they should not be peculiar (even if they are), but should be – somewhat as Lenin saw the Communist Party – simply the vanguard and the speeders-up of an emerging social consciousness. When this Reformation is over, the universities will lose their 'splendid isolation', their 'selfish freedom' or their 'ingrained exclusiveness'; the 'ivory-tower' will then collapse, and its stones be used to build compulsive (that is both free and compulsory) educational nests or cells for all. Moreover, these same enthusiasts would wish to subsume or overcome (in some murky Hegelian sense), rather than simply destroy, all 'institutions'. This objective is, however, just intellectual muddle, for what is meant by 'institution' by any social scientist is no longer a fixed body of rules or visible edifice of bricks and mortar (full of signs saying 'Do Not Walk on the Grass' and 'No Writing on the Walls' – hence almost by definition 'bureaucratic'), but is the working of some associated set of concepts. Any university, in this sense, must necessarily be an institution, so that all we can intellectually ask of those who passionately want it to be some new kind of institution, something less peculiar (presumably more natural) than the present institution, is that they make themselves a little bit more clear than they have yet done about what it is precisely they want. 'The ethically desirable must be the sociologically possible.'

How precise one can be is, of course, a difficult question. But certainly it is no new thing for people to advocate very specific-sounding accounts of what 'the idea of a university' must be. For instance, it was once held that universities existed for the Glory of God. Then it was held that universities should exist for the creation of character – as by Mathew Arnold, in his

---

1 Some paragraphs in the middle section of this essay are taken from or adapted from my editorial, 'Student Politics', *Political Quarterly*, July–September 1967.

way, or John Dewey in his. A view arose, not necessarily wholly in conflict with these two views, that universities select and mould the governing
class – a view as much that of Bismarck and Stalin, in their different ways,
as of Macaulay and Trevelyan, both of whom saw university reform as a
necessary adjunct of civil service reform. Others at all times command
universities to be useful – a view in which Sir Paul Chambers and Prime
Minister Kosygin would plainly both concur (and which is probably at all
times the view that deserves to create the greatest fear). And now some tell
us that universities have a special mission to be the Godly Congregations
of some temporary revolutionary orthodoxy. The toughest form of this
latest 'idea' is that of the handful of tiny Revolutionary Socialist Societies –
of whom it is a gross flattery to be in the least fearful; and the gentlest
articulation, held by very many more, is that universities should be, no
longer the mentors of youth, but the *expression of youth*.

It is perhaps surprising that from all these various claims or assaults
could have emerged and be taken so much for granted: '. . . the concept of
universities as centres of education, learning and research' which 'exist to
transmit knowledge from one generation to the next and to seek new
knowledge and a better understanding of nature, man and society'; and as
institutions which '. . . can achieve these purposes only in a climate in
which rational discussion is universally accepted'.[1] The Vice-Chancellors
made a fairly good shot at a definition. It is, of course, an ostensive definition – it describes what is the case, or what is hoped to be the case; but it
does avoid the fallacy involved in that rather dreadful phrase, 'the idea of
a university'.[2] It would be better to say simply that universities are (or
should be) concerned with ideas, and the stress must be on the plural, just
as we had better claim to be many minds in pursuit of truths rather than,
the fault of all such general definitions mentioned above, to be a community
in possession of or in pursuit of the Truth. It is even to be doubted, if this
understanding is secure, why the Vice-Chancellors should have wanted to
insist that 'rational discussion is [i.e. should be] universally accepted'. For
it plainly is not, and nor should it be, unless they can convince us what we
should mean by 'rational'. It is apparent that all the above past and would-be
future authoritarian views still have some role to play for some people and
do, in fact, have some influence in many, if not most, actual universities.

1 From a statement or press release issued by the Committee of Vice-Chancellors
  and Principals, 17 June 1968.
2 I take this point from Peter Laslett in his essay, 'The University in High Industrial Society', in *Essays on Reform, 1967: A Centenary Tribute* (Oxford University
  Press, 1967); see also Lord Annan's excellent essay in the same volume, 'Higher
  Education', on the whole question of university reform.

Academic freedom is not the absence of authority but it is the arena in which rival authorities compete for allegiance. For this competition to be fair, the arena needs certain ground-rules and working conventions, but these rules and conventions are not ends in themselves – as some liberals suggest. This needs saying, even if it sounds banal, for one cannot beat something with nothing. Some toleration can be damnably condescending or utterly empty; and freedom needs exercise and activity, not eternal and unmolested repose. If authorities are untouchably secure in their own truths, their tolerance is unlikely to be morally acceptable – any man of spirit then wants to throw stones; but equally if they are tolerant because they hold no views themselves whatever, then their tolerance is likely to be rejected psychologically and denounced ideologically. If authorities are challenged by rival views, however wild or repulsive, and will not answer back then they are hardly likely to maintain their authority. It is less important for 'the authorities' to nerve themselves to deal with wild bulls in their china shops than it is for them to argue strongly and openly with the sacred cows, not just to pride themselves on their preservation. Press and television give extremists publicity, but it is only in the universities themselves that they can be argued back against.

On such grounds as these I will argue that the communication network is more important than the participation network. Increasing student participation is important: but it is less important than explaining much more and much more publicly how decisions are made. If university authorities do not understand this (which I think is elementary social science) they will be puzzled when they discover that the real steps many are now taking to increase student participation and to set up more and more staff-student committees, will be denounced as 'bureaucratic' by the very people they thought wanted them, and will not, of themselves, allay the present stirrings and discontents. Perhaps they should not hope for too much in any case, for many of the reasons for the present stirrings and discontents are quite beyond the control of the universities. Some of the causes are very general and we should not forget in all this discussion that in Churches, Trade Unions, Businesses, Firms, Banks, Local Government Authorities, and even in Parliament and Government Departments, people are beginning to demand greater consultation before decisions are made in their name or to bind them. The going will be rougher and less dignified for all these authorities, but, if they keep their nerve and play their hands properly, they may end up with greater effective power (if they can carry their constituents with them) rather than what is often at present an almost pathetically nominal power, unchallengeable but ineffective (which depends on letting sleeping dogs lie whose energies might, if things were done another way, be harnessed for common purposes).

The causes of the present discontents

The causes of the present discontents in England (I go no further) must be considered before considering how student influence may change, grow or become more institutionalized. I see at least fourteen different factors, and there may be more or slightly less according to definitions. To see their variety and multiplicity is important, although this is not to say that they necessarily 'add up' or are in any way systematically related – some are and some are not; and still less that they take the same form everywhere.

(i) The specific example of L.S.E. in 1967: genuine concern and bitterness in a highly cosmopolitan environment about the Government's Rhodesian policy, leading to a spontaneous, idealistic, ignorant, ungenerous and almost completely irrelevant outburst against their new Director's alleged record in Rhodesia; but after the fighting had broken out and had become frustrated of real enemies, new and slightly more rational sounding war aims were discovered to do, crazily, with 'student power' (an almost derogatory parody of the grim majesty of 'Black Power') or, more soberly, with student representation and influence – a long overdue (however muddled and rough) student interest in academic policy, syllabus, teaching methods and the examination system.

(ii) A more general sharing in international currents of 'Youth Nationalism' (more easily seen as 'anti-colonialism'), again a generalized cause searching for a local object: to this extent the 'generational argument' is true, that the cues for direct action tend to come from the international headlines ('They Stopped Berkeley, We'll Stop L.S.E.' or the ever memorable 'Paris Here') rather than from the exhaustion of local grievance procedures.

(iii) Local grievances, none the less, concerned with antiquated teaching methods, inexplicable syllabuses and, very often, overcrowding and neglect by teachers busy elsewhere on public business or just plain making money advising this or that or televising (two factors very evident at L.S.E.).

(iv) A generalized feeling that 'Youth' is, *a priori*, always right and should, *a fortiori*, should make itself heard on every great issue through what then becomes seen as their own institution, the university; and the university is then not a place of learning, but a stage on which one must develop one's distinctive and flamboyant personality – and if one hasn't got one, one has, none the less, money and leisure to dress the part and to learn, however painfully, some impressive and threatening imposture.[1]

(v) Alongside this, a bit of straight, old-fashioned trade union economic protest too: British student grants are *good*, both in scale and number, by any world or generational comparisons, but at half the national average wage students may well, without condemning them for arrogance or selfishness compared to working men supporting families in miserable environments, understandably feel some constrained itchiness of the purse, some frustration of expectations or sense of 'relative deprivation' – particularly as their age-group is the target of among the most poisoned shafts of consumer advertising: the plain style of dress, for instance of the Communist student leaders of the 1930s and 1940s has now given way to the extravagant exoticism of nearly all the new leaders, as dully fashionable and as restlessly trendy as any ad-man could wish (what old-fashioned Fascists would have correctly called, I suppose, 'decadent').

(vi) Some degree of genuine alienation from normal conciliatory politics among political activists, a real and wholly proper dislike of Mr Wilson and Mr Heath's tandem bicycle of consensus-politics (even if they are foolish to think that consensus as to ends necessarily arises from consensus as to means, and even if some of the alienation is largely self-induced – the paradox of the lads who say 'We are all brainwashed by the Interests', meaning that they are all responsible for their personal virtues but not for their common vices).

(vii) Incitement and conspiracy by 'Trotskyite' and other Revolutionary Socialist agitators: absurd as a general explanation, but not to be discounted in explaining the timing of some particular happenings – but it is always far more important to explain why such a few neurotic fanatics (who have always been around in one form or another, waiting for Armageddon) can now, in the right conditions, get such a large if temporary

1 The role of fantasy can hardly be exaggerated. Why do people dress like Castro or Guevera who have not the slightest intention of going to help in Cuba, or wear inconvenient and expensive Maoist jackets (made by capitalist clothiers and sold in boutiques), who never dream of going to fight in Vietnam? In the 1930s, there was an International Brigade; in the 1960s, a tortuous process of reasoning or sheer fantasy which identifies London Bobbies with Fascism, and which can chalk up nonsense like 'U.S. plus Napalm equals Fascism' – equals something morally terrible, certainly, but this slogan shows a complete misunderstanding of what Fascist systems actually were, how they worked, and hence how best they are combated or prevented. 'Role playing' is carried very far; one thinks of Hermann Rauschning's argument (a totally different substance, but a parallel social function) that many disturbed and rootless people marched in the Nazi processions and street demonstrations not because they already felt full of 'racial brotherhood' or 'party fraternity', but because they wanted to achieve such feelings (in his *The Revolution of Nihilism*, New York, 1939).

following of people who certainly do *not* share their specific opinions or general objectives (*pace* those journalists who are for ever talking about *the* views of *the* students, meaning the utterances of a few solemn madmen which are then built-up and publicized, often out of sheer laziness by journalists towards the problem of identifying opinions more typical of actual students and the many student sub-cultures).[1]

(viii) Also outside agitators and 'professional students' joining in for the hell of it; but students themselves, except when things have already got out of hand, are usually extremely suspicious of outside intervention (even Tariq Ali begins to look a bit old and Soho).

(ix) Mismanagement by academic authorities out of touch with (and much too busy to notice) ordinary student opinion, a peculiar academic pride that we all know intuitively what the students are thinking (so have no need to inquire formally or to survey scientifically); inconsistent handling of different cases which, whether Vice-Chancellors like it or not, are compared nationally, not according to local precedents (the great example of inconsistency being the indulgence of the L.S.E. authorities about responsibility for the Porter's death and then their attempted inflexibility in dealing with the nominal leaders); and an overall lack of wise public relations (students are not told enough or quickly enough and the press is something to be kept out at almost any cost).

(x) Universities are too paternalistic and interfere too much with the lives of their students (usually true for some, those in Halls or Colleges and for women generally, but not at all for others).

(xi) They are at the same time far too secretive and never explain what they are doing and why.

(xii) Random protest symptoms or mild delinquent behaviour as a result of either disappointed expectations about university life, or the complete lack in some of any kind of prior expectations at all (the ideal image is 'to play it cool' in such circumstances, but the actual strains are so great as to produce tantrums).

(xiii) The recent tradition of demonstrations and protest marches as the tactic of an alienated politics (not specifically student at all, except that

---

1 This may be pot calling kettle black, for very little academic research has been done in Great Britain into student attitudes or behaviour of any relevance to the present unrest – we have not, as social scientists, exploited our captive audiences or showed a scientific interest in them to anything like the extent of the Americans. An informal conference on 'Research into Student Unrest' in July 1968, arranged by the Social Science Research Council (in conjunction with the Department of Social Psychology at Brighton), concentrated wholly on plans for future research – since the subject is interesting; but there was little to report from the past.

students have more time on their hands and no jobs to lose by mid-week happenings); the reading of books and pamphlets and the drafting of programmes, even, is no longer fashionable compared with the joys and stimulus of 'direct action'[1] (and all such mass demonstrations, whether of Left- or Right-wing extremes, tend to become ends in themselves, happy just to be mutually provocative and mutually isolating).

(xiv) And, lastly, just plain, good old-fashioned student ambivalence to authority (L.S.E. students have usually been so terribly earnest compared to, say, the carnivorous-carnival spirit of Scottish student elections); and something still persists in the new demonstrations of the jocular, facetious and animal spirits of the post-war and pre-war student 'rags'.

If all these discontents and conditions came to a head at once – which is about as likely as 'if all the Greeks were to form one *Polis* they could conquer the world'. But equally nothing anyone can do, certainly not university statesmen, can cure or even very much allay some of these conditions. The beginning of wisdom in the practical implementation of some greater student presence or voice in university counsels is to realize that nothing can be done simply to avoid trouble; it had better be done to make universities better places anyway, and thus more able to sustain the periodic troubles and affronts which all major national institutions will now undergo, but of which universities will get a disproportionate share because of the unique force of 'youth ideology'.

The smoke and the flame

To realize that total breakdown is as unlikely as any return to a passive normal should strengthen resistance to some demands, which are either absurd or which threaten the freedom and the pluralistic nature of universities, but should make us accept the challenge in other directions of trying to make the students feel more of a community with the whole university. Such moves are not weakness if they attempt to restore, or perhaps to create for the first time, a sense of community which subsumes both the function of teaching and the function of learning.

1 One thing that needs to be researched, by political sociologists or political theorists using concepts from social anthropology and methods from empirical social surveys, is the character of the 'oral tradition' of popular Marxism and Revolutionary Socialism. I suspect that it depends very little on real Marxist writings, or any other, but has something of the spontaneity that its holders would wish to find in action, not in thought (but it may well have, if investigated in this way, a greater coherence than is apparent simply from reading the fugitive materials of the movement (or movements ?).

What are the most common complaints? Many students see the staff as too remote (although this can vary wildly – some see too much of them). The university itself is then incomprehensible and uninteresting as an institution. The syllabuses appear old-fashioned or, more often, highly random and fortuitous: they are changed without explanation: university or college statutes, ordinances and regulations are commonly set out in Calendars in such a way as to be totally incomprehensible to all students and to most members of Faculties. The course itself is always either (for one hears both) 'useless for the real world' or else 'cluttered up with practical stuff one can learn better on the job'. Readings lists are always too long and usually too unselective, and libraries are almost always too small and poorly stocked in multiple copies of much-used books.

Many staff see the students as unintellectual at the best and anti-intellectual all too often (as in the widespread craze to put juke-boxes in students' union common-rooms so that 'shop talk' is impossible). They are also often seen as lazy, purely career-minded and yet distrustful of any kind of authority (up to the moment of employment): more interested in buying a new shirt each week than a new book, a generation – it seems at times – who have had education thrust at them on a silver plate and lack seriousness. They pass resolutions about 'wanting more staff/student contact', but seven-tenths of them cut tutorials without warning, apology or explanation and teachers could 'keep office hours' for ever without most of the students even wanting to call to discuss their work. They demand 'student participation' but are not willing to trust their own elected officers and they demand that the university explains itself, but do not bother to read the statutes and regulations and the annual reports of Faculties.

These mutual complaints are a mixture of smoke and real flame: some of the wood is very damp – perennial complaints, part of an almost agreeable tradition of mutual grumbling. But some elements are more serious. They perhaps resolve into three factors. Let me neatly give great blame on each side for one of them, but see the third as a general folly of our whole educational system: that staffs explain too little about universities and take too little care to keep or remake the system comprehensible in realistic terms; that students expect too much to be done for them and too readily think of themselves as a community of age and not of function (hence leaders of the contemporary, fashionable but quite peculiar – historically speaking – 'youth cult', not fellow members of a republic of learning or a timeless universe of discourse); but that the laws and conventions of our society send people into higher studies either before they are old enough or in such a way that university seems to be only a peculiar and less well organized extension of school – British students, like those in the U.S.A., are nearly all too young, or too inexperienced in looking after themselves in a real work situation.

Far more could be done to explain what a university is: places that perpetuate traditions of learning and try to discover new methods of discovery. We are primarily interested in education for its own sake, not in training for practical ends. We need no longer pretend to be ancient Greeks; we see nothing base in interest in *techne* rather than in *schole*; but we must see it as something different. Frustration and incomprehension arise when the two are confused. This is easy to say, but hard to insist upon, as a rule, without at every step appearing to insult worthy colleagues; but it is a risk to be run rather than disappoint those students (for there are still some) who want to study 'the nature of things'. The disappointed are more dangerous than the indifferent or the purely mercenary.

Neither the Robbins report nor Mr Crosland's gloss on it help very much. Instead of there being a university reform movement, university teachers rallied behind their pay claim in 1963, behind the Robbins report in 1964, against the cuts in 1967, all quantitative and financial things; we tacitly agreed to close the ranks and not to purge them. Real issues of university reform (such as the rights of junior staff) and educational reform (such as the universities relation with the schools) were either forgotten or not publicly debated; the students wishing for 'reform' lacked their natural leaders – the university teachers themselves Robbins looked at as numbers and disclaimed any responsibility for what should be taught *and* studied and how; Crosland created or discovered a dual system of 'university' and 'technical' studies, but only for future members in search of a club: the existing confusion of functions is, if anything, made worse. More does not mean, as Kingsley Amis oddly argued, 'worse'; worse than that, it has meant 'the same'. 'Worse' would give some incentive for rationalizing the system drastically between genuine (and fewer) universities and more technical or multi-purpose institutions; but with 'the same' we can muddle on: with Accountancy, Social Work, Metallurgy, Business and Civil Engineering studies all casting their cultural influences throughout universities as well as technical colleges. And even amid the intellectual disciplines, why need nearly every university have a department in nearly everything however small and second-rate?

Perhaps this is baying at the moon. But even within the present department stores (and we all know what bookshops in department stores are like), simple reforms in the direction of comprehensibility could take place. How rarely are student editors encouraged to report and comment upon changes in building plans, the creation of chairs and alterations and innovations in courses: the stuff of modern universities. How rarely is the Annual Report written as something to educate the students in what they are doing and where they are, rather than as a ritual regurgitation by Vice-Chancellors and Deans of stuff too well known already back to their senior colleagues. And if the civic universities and London have achieved some remarkable reforms of syllabus, so that the old narrow single honours programme is almost everywhere under competition from dual honours or even wider programmes, they have seldom gone in for simplification and codification of regulations. And nor are the methods of marking, the way classes of degree are decided, nor even, very often, individual marks disclosed. Does such secrecy strengthen or weaken systems of government? These things remain mysteries to the average student. If he is not helped to take an intelligent interest in what affects him as a studious person, no wonder he often wanders off into the shadow politics of demanding 'equal student representation on all major committees'. Something approaching this could be given readily in most cases, and make no difference to academic authority whatever: the student generation is too short compared to the staff generation, and in a learned institution authority will inevitably flow from the learned.

False expectations and uncertainty

The real and the legitimate student demand is to hear and be heard on matters that affect him as a student or young scholar: not just on marginal things – athletics, lodgings and union premises. The protests and demonstrations against the raising of fees for overseas students stemmed from the whole university community – students and teachers together. But the student diminishes his authority as student when he demands a 'student voice' on all kinds of matters which are not university at all, but part of common citizenship. Every time a students' union racks itself with resolutions and counter-resolutions on world politics, it both diverts its members from their interests as students, and weakens its authority. By all means let students be politically active – no educational authority has any business intervening here (as Teachers' Training Colleges and others need firmly reminding), but active as members of the community in groups catering for all ages and interests – like, for instance, political parties. Perhaps when the voting age is reduced to eighteen, student politics may well divert itself to more concrete political issues.

One last point on expectations and comprehensibility: schools are much at fault in not preparing their potential university students more. Some do, most do not: students commonly come up with no idea at all what a university is like. They feel neglected if they are not lectured at: they are at a complete loss how to use a library and yet, breaking from home and school together, they want to assert independence even if many of these assertions, like beards, bizarre 'strong views' and public petting, are disappointingly superficial. But there is no sense in allocating blame: universities should 'spoon-feed', if that is what it is, by giving specific instruction on how to make notes, how to use books, how to use finding aids, how to prepare essays and reports. There is no longer a tradition about these things (if ever there was) and it does not 'rub off somehow'.

Students often expect too much because they do not know what to expect. It does go back to the school teachers. But it also goes back to tendencies in our modern industrial culture particularly disturbing to any social-democrat; we may not be getting nearer the take off point, but slipping backwards. The development of 'personality' is somehow deemed more important than the pursuit of objective standards of truth, beauty or justice. The philistine student will, indeed, not feel himself challenged in his values by a genuine university teacher: for he is armoured already to think of such people as 'characters', tolerable as such. And perhaps they make themselves 'characters' rather than appear to offer a direct challenge to the values of their students. Probably most student political activists chase false hares because their teachers disappoint them by their lack of dedication; but it might be nothing to the uproar if their teachers really did treat them as members of an intellectual community and refused to simplify, only to discuss and to dispute obsessionally. John Saville, Lord Halifax, wrote in *The Character of a Trimmer* that 'the struggle for knowledge hath a pleasure in it like that of wrestling with a fine woman'. The student should at least be encouraged, even by example, not to compartmentalize his life.

In this light it is interesting that those practitioners of student politics who claim to be Marxists commonly lack nearly all the energy in research and scholarship associated with Marx, but rather exhibit a romantic individualism, anarchism more than socialism or communism, which ultimately stems from Rousseau (the anti-scholar) and not Marx (the enemy of mere-scholarship).

One of the problems is plainly the rather lovely mixture of great expectations and little experience. Indeed 'experience' is almost a dirty word to many students; it means to them a cynical and middle-aged realism,

MAC

'worldly-wise' in the worst sense, the doctrine of civilization as it is, rather than of society as it ought to be. The political implications of this are obvious; but contemporary 'youth culture' and the 'cult of youth' add on even greater burdens diverting student from ever becoming scholar, or 'young man' from being man. It is widely and solemnly believed, for instance, that all pleasures of secular life, notably travel and love, must end by twenty-one or twenty-two – all have to be crammed into those long vacations and monstrously short terms.

On a more mundane level, the real youthfulness of students of seventeen and eighteen forces universities into a whole range of completely una-cademic activities, the grossest of which is the paternalism and the waste of money of Halls of Residence. If students were older they could either shift for themselves, which would have had some interesting implications for the location of new universities (or better, for which of the civic to have expanded); or else the university, if it had to be a builder of residen-tial accommodations, would limit its subsequent role to that of landlord and rent collector.

Any who remember the post-war generation of ex-servicemen and women or who regularly teaches some 'adult' or 'mature' students would argue that intangible factors of maturity do emerge with those extra years; that students would get more out of their studies had they done anything else for a couple of years between school and university; that they would have established a real personal independence from home and from school-habits (so be less likely to make aggressive and largely meaningless big gestures of independence); and that they would be more conscious of the privilege they enjoy and responsibilities they owe the community. Curiously, students think of such points as 'conservative'; I think of them as socialist. Some real experience of work in an industrial society would remove those, perhaps few, but shamefully evident, sections of universities which seem like indulgent and arrogant youth clubs in permanent session at public expense.

The remedy for the faults of the universities, which are faults of rigid and unexplained teaching, methods, and organization – not of political reaction – lies in the students' own hands. They can force the pace and show great gains when they will concentrate on issues that peculiarly affect them as students: people studying something as part of a wider academic community, not as a self-contained community in themselves.

Students have rights, which should be asserted: not to govern or share in the government of learned institutions, but to be consulted, to be told 'why' as well as 'how', and to be provided with conditions in which they can work effectively and syllabuses broad enough in which to study freely. But they have duties, too: to pursue their studies, to repay the community by useful service for what it has given them (at the expense of money from others and which might have helped others), and the duty to include even themselves in their pleasing scepticism at established authority.

For 'Youth' is no more acceptable as authority than 'Age': it is either adolescent or senile to think otherwise. We are all one of another. Rights and duties are reciprocal and authority is neither good nor bad as such: it depends on the uses to which it is put. Students should respect authority, but that authority must make itself both more comprehensible and more worthy of respect. Authority is relative to function: if we master our subject, we should yield to none, State, student or colleagues, as to how we teach it. But all authority is limited (except, some say, the authority of God and of the Revolution – but then absolute truth cannot concern us as truth-seeking and truth-doubting universities for that very reason). If we will not assert and publicly justify our learned authority, we deserve to be humiliated, but if we use it to pontificate or to intervene in the personal lives and beliefs of our students, we weaken it and bring it into contempt. The univerity is a community, but it is not a total community as both the old Oxbridge College mentality (even or especially in its Civic University form of departmental paternalism) and the new Revolutionary Socialist creeds would have us believe and act accordingly. But being a community, there are many matters of common concern, between university authorities, junior staff and students, which must be publicly discussed. Take, for instance, the small but deadly issue of those few who take flight from reality into forms of drug addiction. As teachers we should neither tolerate this on principle nor should we use disciplinary power to go beyond what the civil authorities can do; but we should stand up and argue, publicly and privately, what we may think, as much as they, is right. But we should do so because we think it right to do so as individuals, not in virtue of our office. The distinction is difficult in practice, of course, but it is clear in principle and should be stated.

Text and commentary

Now, to conclude, anti-climax. What changes are likely to take place and should take place? I know no better starting point than the astonishingly sensible and radical 'Joint Statement from the Committee of Vice-Chancellors and Principals and the National Union of Students' of 7 October

1968 – a document which must be brought to life and rescued, on both sides, from the instinctive but false feeling that it is likely to be (if anyone read it) but a string of vague compromises and platitudes.

Let me quote the four key sections and offer only a brief commentary on the text.

Student Participation in University Decision-Making

4. The National Union of Students seeks effective student presence on all relevant committees. Our discussions identified three broad areas of operation of such committees: (*a*) the whole field of student welfare – for example health services, catering facilities and the provision of accommodation – where there should in our view be varying degrees of participation of students in the decision-making process. Apart from this, there is the area which covers for example the operation of student unions and the management of a wide range of extra-curricular activities, in which most university student organizations rightly have long had complete responsibility, (*b*) that relating for example to curriculum and courses, teaching methods, major organizational matters, and issues concerning the planning and development of the university – where the ultimate decision must be that of the statutorily responsible body. In this area, we would regard it as essential that students' views should be properly taken into account, and (*c*) that involving for example decisions on appointments, promotions and other matters affecting the personal position of members of staff, the admissions of individuals and their academic assessment – where student presence would be inappropriate. Students should, however, have opportunities to discuss the general principles involved in such decisions and have their views properly considered.

The three categories are sensible. The first, (*a*), is obvious, although many local battles are still to be won, and beyond the universities this will and should cause constant trouble between Local Government Authorities, colleges in their sector pursuing university-level work and their students. If the second, (*b*), is taken seriously, a great change in atmosphere will take place. It is astonishing how little this is done, and it needs some modicum of formal institutions, it cannot be left to chance, sherry parties or to 'informal good relations'. Students must be given definite occasions on which they can put, either by staff-student committees or by general meetings (as they must themselves choose), questions, objections and reasoned alternatives to their teachers. This will lead to considerable changes, for there are some purely traditional elements in many syllabuses or types of teaching method which, if ever challenged at all, will surely change. It is always good to be forced to justify what one thinks one is doing. This will not, of course, always or often lead to changes so immediate that they benefit the students who make them – regulations cannot be changed overnight. But it will educate everyone in responsibility for the future years as well as to the past. One of the best methods of discovering 'consumer reaction', for instance, is obviously to survey students who have just finished their degree work, or some definite section of it. But then the results of such surveys must be fed back to the present generation of students, not kept as some secret of state or *arcana imperii*. From (*c*), matters of appointments and promotions of staff, students should be excluded; but they should be reassured that representatives of junior staff are consulted (even if the facts have to be changed to make these assurances true). If universities are self-appointing oligarchies, they are at least oligarchies penetrable by merit. The issue of wider consultation and justice being seen to be done in appointments and promotion is a clear case for university reform, not just student reforms.

Course Content and Teaching Methods

7. Discussion in this area must necessarily be subject to the clear right of the individual teacher, in consultation with his colleagues who by their scholarship in the relevant field of study have proved their right to an opinion, to decide on the way in which he presents his subject. Once this right is infringed from whatever quarter, from public pressure, from university governing bodies or from students themselves, the way is open to censorship and interference of every kind. We believe that the great majority of students are fully aware of the need to preserve this most essential of all academic freedoms. But we think that without any interference with this principle, it is possible and indeed right that there should be opportunities for students to enter into discussion about the content and structure of courses, about teaching methods in general, and about the effectiveness of the particular teaching which they are receiving. In general, the larger the university administrative division concerned, the more necessary it becomes that such opportunities should be offered through official committees at the appropriate levels.

Most of the above comments also apply here. And staff should brace themselves and their students to come to realize that public consultation is no meaningless substitute for direct participation in deciding such matters, but is usually a more effective control and always a necessary condition of public participation. The wild-men are quite right, in principle, to suspect that a few student representatives on university or department committees run the risk of being either bamboozled or, quite simply, Uncle Toms muzzled with discretion and self-importance. But the problem is a general one throughout our society: do all kinds of voluntary bodies really speak in the names of their members ? and how often does the apostle of publicity become the defender of secrecy once he is elected or appointed to the Board ? The answer, however, can never be more and more direct representation. Modern society is too large to go back to the market-place of the Athenian *Polis*. The more likely answer is to increase publicity and effective communication. Publicity is at least as important as electoral representation in the history of democracy. If some are rightly suspicious that there is emerging a new cant of participation which could well be mere 'public relations' by some Vice-Chancellors and Dons, or Mr Wilson's secret weapon for resurrection on the national level, they will have only themselves to blame if it so degenerates. The door has been, some will think, dangerously opened: it is now the obvious tactic of those genuinely interested in university reform, staff and student, to push hard for the nominal or official policy and to insist that open-government results from, and is not subtly frustrated by, formal institutions of participation and consultation.

Examinations

11. In the view of the National Union of Students, the traditional examination technique assesses only one aspect of academic worth. Different methods of assessment test different aspects of a student's ability and it is therefore to be expected that a mixed system of assessment would present a truer picture of total ability and achievement.

12. It was common ground in our discussions that more research and experiment on the subject of examinations are required. There was no question but that methods of assessment which recognize the very varied abilities of university students, and which are accepted by the public and employers generally, are an essential student interest. On this common foundation, we believe that useful discussions with the student bodies, nationally and in each university, can be continued.

Again, much the same general commentary, but the specific point that the dangers to 'individual independence' of continuous assessment must be considered in detail by the student body, quite as much as the prospects of greater equity and some release from the tension and fear of the 'all the eggs in one basket' of the traditional examination system. Here the students will learn that you cannot beat something with nothing, and they will need skilled study and advice from their National and local unions, and will probably come to find natural allies in the junior staff – which will at least do much to break down the irrational belief in a natural conflict of the generations and to recreate talk of 'univeristy reform', seen as a whole, not the inherently temporary victories of student power, necessarily based on all too short three year generation.

Freedom of Speech

22. Freedom of discussion is one of the foundations on which the universities have been built. All members of a university should be prepared to tolerate, and indeed protect, the expression of unpopular opinions. It is the responsibility of all to ensure that within universities there are appropriate opportunities for hearing all sides on matters of current controversy. The right to freedom of speech, however, must not be exercised in ways which infringe the rights and freedoms of others.

But freedom of speech, like all freedom, must actually take place on both sides and be exercised. If students want to challenge things, they must be answered. We as teachers must be prepared to carry the ball into their court, to challenge their assumptions, not simply to tolerate them liberally, particularly as so many of their own assumptions are the products of materialistic and consumption-dominated society – against which they are rightly protesting in general terms but are rarely pausing long enough to study it and think how to draw specific conclusions. All this, emerging from all these splendid, silly and muddled mixtures of stirrings and discontents, is something with which universities can cope while moving out from their present traditional framework into something far more genuinely a universe of intense discourse than has been the somewhat sleepy and complacent pattern of the past. The 'Joint Statement' deserves to become an historic document in British universities if it is used as a framework and starting-point for consequences yet to be made concrete.

John Sparrow

Revolting students?[1]

'Could it happen here?' people in this country have asked themselves during the last year or two, reading accounts of riots and disturbances in the Universities of California and Columbia, of Rome and Berlin, and, most recently, of Paris.

Well, it has happened here; on a small scale, but with ugly enough results, at the London School of Economics, for instance, and in the Universities of Leicester and Canterbury and Hull and Essex.

'Ah, but it couldn't happen *here*', people inside the grey walls of Oxford and Cambridge have reassured themselves, as they read accounts of what was going on in other British universities.

Well, during the last week or two it has begun to happen in Oxford and in Cambridge; and 'How much further will it go?' is the question that the dons have now been forced to ask themselves.

What is the 'it' that forms the subject of these questions? 'Student unrest', 'student protest', 'student riots', 'student violence', 'the movement for student power' – these are phrases that have been used to cover a wide variety of actions and attitudes and opinions; let us look at some of them nd see what they have in common.

In universities all over the world students – often with the help, open or clandestine, of junior teachers – have taken to the use, violent or non-violent, of force. This display of force has been directed sometimes towards political, sometimes towards academical ends. In the political field, the students' aim has usually been either to challenge the government and what it stands for (for instance, in the U.S., the war and the draft; in the U.K., 'biological' warfare and 'racialism'; in France, the General, the *régime*, and the *société de consommation*), or else to prevent others from expressing on such issues opinions that differ from their own; visiting speakers are howled down, threatened, or actually assaulted. In the academical field, the students' immediate aims have been various. Sometimes they are

1 A revised and extended version of an article printed in *The Listener*, 4 July 1968.

seeking to obtain remedies, badly needed in a number of universities, for particular deficiencies such as inadequate lecture-halls and lodgings and inefficient, uninterested or absentee professors and tutors. Sometimes they aim at effecting changes in the curriculum (e.g. more 'socially relevant' subjects, or the abolition of examinations), in the administration (e.g. proportional or majority representation for students on boards and governing bodies) or in the regulations governing student life (e.g. freedom from restrictions on indulgence in sexual intercourse). Sometimes, again, the display of force has taken place in an area where the political and academical fields overlap: an example in this country was the campaign in the L.S.E. against the appointment as Director of Dr Walter Adams on the ground (now admitted to have been false) that he was a flagrant 'racialist'.

All these manifestations have been characterized by one common feature: the students have relied not on pressure exerted along constitutional lines, nor on the backing of their claims by a majority, still less on reasoned argument, but simply on force or the threat of force: they seem to have learned the lesson inculcated in Régis Debray's *Revolution in the Revolution?*, that 'to show force is in effect to use it'.

In their encounters with authority students usually avoid being the first to have recourse to actual violence. Some of them, no doubt, are believers in 'passive resistance', but usually the predominant reason is a prudential one: it is better tactics to provoke violence than to start it; thus one creates martyrs for one's cause and justifies retaliation. Herbert Marcuse, however, on the plane of theory and Debray on the plane of practice agree that if the authorities will not respond to provocation it may be necessary for the student guerillas to initiate violent action themselves. To see how far students will go along that line one need only look at Paris, where their leaders were evidently trained in the tactics of a *force de frappe*, and acted in accordance with the precepts of Debray's guerilla manual. Nothing quite like the occupation of the Sorbonne has yet happened over here; but during the last year or so the character and scale of student protest in this country has undergone a sinister and significant change: the protest march – a mere declaration of opinion and display of feeling – has given place to the sit-in, which achieves its ends by force. The students, in fact, have made an important discovery, and it is this: a small but determined group, however unreasonable their claims and however slight the volume of support they command, can by deploying their strength physically at appropriate points completely paralyse the university machine, so long as the authorities in charge of that machine are not prepared to take strong action against them.

To exploit this discovery, to gain your ends by force and by intimidation and not by reasoned argument, is of course to substitute the methods of the bully and the blackmailer for the code that prevails in civilized societies and to challenge the order of values that universities, beyond all other institutions, are supposed to maintain and inculcate. But that is exactly what the strategists who direct the operations of Students in Revolt are out to do: 'We are not really protesting against Vietnam, we are protesting against Society,' said one student the other day. 'For long-term perspective – Marx; for contemporary orientation – Marcuse; for tactics – Debray', was the *confessio fidei* of another. 'Radical transformation of the *status quo*' is called for by a Jamaican leader of student revolt in Oxford, a Rhodes Scholar, who declares that 'student power needs for its completion a wider social upheaval against authoritarianism.'

For those who think in such terms, revolt in the universities is only the first stage in a comprehensive social and political revolution, and the students form the spearhead of a larger force engaged in bringing it about. This objective clearly inspired the student leaders from all over the world who took part in the recent TV programme *Students in Revolt*. The word 'liberalism', innocently let fall by the question-master, evoked growls of angry protest from the whole assembly, as if an obscenity had been uttered. Evidently for these students liberal reforms, whether in the state or in the universities, would only patch up a structure that they would like to shatter completely – how completely, appeared from the contribution of the English representative, Tariq Ali, who came out boldly in favour of the abolition of money. 'We are inventing a new and original world', said Cohn-Bendit's men in Paris; 'Imagination is seizing power'.

Most students in this country find such an anarchic and patently impracticable gospel difficult to swallow, and the engineers of revolt do not waste time attempting to indoctrinate them. If you are a rebel leader, you don't succeed by attracting converts, you attract converts by succeeding: revolution first, revolutionaries afterwards. But to stimulate revolutionary action in the universities you must find practical issues that will unite the students in opposition to authority: hence the need for grievances.

Grievances, however, are not enough: you must have a favourable atmosphere. Such an atmosphere exists today in universities, and not only in universities, all over the world. It has been generated by a mood that set in during the 1960s and now affects a large proportion of the young.

It is not an angry or a rebellious mood, but those who are subject to it offer an innocent and easy prey to the engineers of revolt. These potential rebels are not actively defiant or militantly hostile to their elders or to authority, personal or impersonal; rather, they are uncomprehending, alienated, and inclined to be contemptuous; for them, the generations confront each other not on a battlefield but across a gulf – the under-25s against the over-30s.

These representatives of the younger generation claim that boys and girls of eighteen are, nowadays, fully mature sexually and ought therefore to be treated in every respect as adult citizens. They are slow to take anything on trust from their elders, and feel a sense of solidarity with students of other universities and with the young of other countries. They see an issue of principle involved in every conflict with authority and are eager to take a stand upon it. Serious-minded and high-minded, they have no constructive ideas or positive ideals, beyond an eclectic pacifism (war is absolutely wrong, unless waged on behalf of coloured people), an egalitarianism that is simply humanitarianism in rational dress (all human beings should be treated *as if* they were equal), and a passion for justice that is not really a desire that people should get what they deserve, but a pedantic insistence on uniformity: it is unjust – they call it 'victimization' – to punish some culprits and let off others.

Like most of their contemporaries, these students are less interested in political than in ethical and aesthetic questions. In the field of morals they challenge not merely particular conventions but convention itself, which for them is something linked with the past, artificial, and tainted with hypocrisy. As for art, they care more about it than for it; indeed, the *avant-garde* among them favour 'anti-art', rejecting the hitherto accepted idea of art as a special form of conscious creative activity, in favour of Op Art, Pop Art, the 'happening' and the 'live-in'. Many of them find their spokesmen on ethical and aesthetic questions in the leaders of the pop groups and the pot groups. 'The Mona Lisa is a load of crap', said John Lennon, the chief of the Beatles, whose excursions into mystical philosophy are, it seems, taken seriously by the young. 'We are not old men; we are not worried by petty morals', declared Keith Richards, one of the Rolling Stones. 'I don't see what's wrong in going on trips' was the libertarian doctrine propounded by Mick Jagger, the handsome animal who leads the group, after his conviction on a drug charge. 'It's up to me to pick the things I want to do, and I will.'

Confronted with this sort of challenge, many of the middle-aged, whether dons or outside observers of the university scene, take refuge either in shocked horror or in affected toleration. Both reactions are mis-judged. You may lack sympathy with the students' ideas and the dress and style of life in which some of them express their protest against conven-tional respectability – the shaggy hair, the dirty jeans, the bare feet on the pavements, the sluts, male and female, making love (if that is the word for it) in the streets, the drugs, the pills, the squalor, the whole apparatus of the Dirt for Dirt's sake movement – that, after all, is only a matter of taste. But you should not conclude, because you find the fashion revolting, that those who follow it are in revolt; and even if they are, you should judge the claims of revolutionaries, like anybody else's claims, by the arguments that support them, not by the appearance and manners of some of those who put them forward.

Equally mistaken are the elderly ostriches, both inside and outside the universities, who pretend to themselves that nothing is really happening and see no more in it all than a superficial craze of no significance, like the fashions that flourished between the wars, the Oxford trousers and the Eton crop – 'the young have always enjoyed shocking their elders'. That is as great a mistake as it would be to equate the supra-political gospel of today's leaders of student revolt with the positive and specific enthusiasms of the 1930s for the ideals of the Communist and Socialist parties. No, the 'new wave' is really new; it gives expression to an undercurrent of feeling both genuine and deep, a dissatisfaction, inarticulate and often only half-conscious, with the whole of present-day western civilization. Such a mood, uncertain and lacking positive beliefs, can obviously be turned to practical account by engineers of revolution like the nihilistic leaders of Students in Revolt.[1]

The press and television – in this country *The Times* and the *Observer* are particularly bad offenders – have done much to exaggerate the myth of student power and to encourage a natural tendency on the part of stu-dents to imitate the exploits that they read about. With such assistance from the 'mass media', the militant activists can play on the prevailing mood and cripple a whole university by sheer force; but they will not maintain their momentum or keep their revolution on foot, provided the authorities meet them with decision, unless there are real and substantial grievances for their followers to complain about. A vice-chancellor, there-fore, who is apprehensive about an outbreak of revolt in his university should ask himself two questions. First, what proportion of my students are likely to lend an ear to the professed leaders of revolt? Second, do con-

1 See Note at end.

ditions in the university afford grievances that a responsible majority would accept as justifying direct action?

Let me try to answer these questions with reference to Oxford – and, like Henry James, 'when I say Oxford, I mean Cambridge', for, in this matter at least, what goes for one of the two ancient universities goes for the other.

In Oxford certainly there exists the same nucleus of extremists as in other universities, forming and re-forming themselves into committees that work 'Toward the Oxford Revolution'. There is also a much larger number who are indeterminate in their attitude, conscious of their status as students and very ready to challenge the authorities if an immediate issue arises, but feeling no *a priori*, doctrinaire, hostility towards them. Finally, there is an inconspicuous mass of ordinary undergraduates who are pretty well content with the syllabus, the administration and the conditions of undergraduate life in Oxford, and are frankly not interested in reforming the University. These last are quite out of sympathy with 'direct action', dislike violence, and resent being associated with the image of 'the student' that the extremists have foisted on the public mind.

What proportion do the last two elements bear to one another? It is difficult to say. But the other day an incident occurred that acted as a precipitant upon the mixture. On Whit-Monday some 200 students swarmed into the Clarendon Building, occupied the office of the Proctors and compelled them, after five hours or so, by force of numbers and refusal to budge, to withdraw a Proctorial regulation.[1] The rebels were exultant. 'It was because of the direct action we have taken that the Proctors gave in', they declared: 'Direct action works'.

Full publicity was given to this exploit in the press. What was not so fully publicized was the fact that a good proportion of the crowd were there out of curiosity or were actually opposed to the rebels, and that next day over a thousand undergraduates signed a manifesto deploring the action and dissociating themselves from it. (*The Times*, which gave headlines to the 'riot', reported the protest against it in small type at the bottom of a column.) A week later there appeared in *Isis* an article by an undergraduate criticizing the Proctors for appeasing 'petty dictators who want to force their ideas on the whole of student society',[2] and a letter from

1 The regulation forbade the public distribution of leaflets without prior leave; a handful of activists defied the ban; the Proctors, to their disappointment, let them off, promising to consider the repeal or amendment of the rule; and then, under the pressure of physical force, withdrew it entirely on the spot.
2 This sentiment earned for its author, at the hands of an activist opponent (Mr Michael Rosen, of Wadham College), the sobriquet of 'new-style jewish fascist' (*Isis*, 12 June 1968).

another undergraduate declaring that 'activism defeats its own ends' and suggesting that the retreat of the Proctors 'in the face of action from a minority' was 'sad, because it is the first step towards more militancy'. I believe that such protests represent feelings overwhelmingly preponderant among ordinary undergraduates, and that they are symptoms of a healthy reaction (called a 'backlash' – with a hint of the sjambok – by its opponents) against the use of force by student rebels.

Since this incident occurred, self-examination has quickened in Oxford: questionnaires have been circulating among undergraduates and dons, and in many colleges there have been meetings of the J.C.R. (Junior Common Room, not *Jeunesse Communiste Révolutionnaire*), all concerned with student conditions. The picture that emerges from it all is pretty clear. The physical conditions in which undergraduates and graduate students live and work, and their relations with the dons, are far, far, better in Oxford, largely through the operation of the College and tutorial systems, than in American and Continental universities and most if not all other universities in this country. Oxford students, before they complain, should compare their 'miseries' and 'sufferings' with those of the faceless hordes crowded out of lecture-rooms in the *universita di massa* in Rome, or of the unfortunates who try to find digs in Nanterre or a Liberal Arts tutor on the campus at Berkeley or a lavatory in the L.S.E.: they just don't know how fortunate they are. Most of them, however, do know it, and are in no hurry to follow the militants to the barricades in protest about the conditions under which they live and work; nor even, I suspect, in the cause of what the activists' committee delicately calls 'mixed visiting overnight in Colleges' – the item that heads their *menu* of outstanding grievances.

None the less, there remains a volume of undergraduate feeling that is dissatisfied about *something*, and it is to uncover the roots of this discontent and if possible to remove them that the University has recently set up a committee under Professor H. L. A. Hart, a jurist far enough to the Left in his views to satisfy all but the extremists (who of course write him off as an elderly liberal and his committee as a sham). A look at some of the draft submissions prepared by J.C.R.s for the Hart Committee, talks with representative groups of undergraduates and an analysis of the opinion polls that float around the University, reveal pretty plainly, I think, the nature of the trouble. It is a failure of confidence, and a double failure: the undergraduates seem to have lost confidence in the dons, and the dons to have lost confidence in themselves. It is the task of the Hart Committee to restore that confidence – to the dons just as much as to the under-graduates.

It is doubtful whether the J.C.R. documents represent the views of the generality of the students, but the main remedies that they suggest indicate what it is that worries such of them as are in favour of reform. They are concerned about work and discipline; they do not want to do away with examinations, to have a hand in appointing the professors, or to abolish the Proctors; but they feel that the authorities in Oxford should be more fully aware of the students' opinions, and that when changes are decided upon they should be put more quickly into effect. To achieve this, they ask for representatives, to be appointed by a Student Council, on University bodies controlling matters that affect junior members, and for elaborate legal machinery to deal with disciplinary offences.

The same demands, with special stress on the statutory recognition by the University of the Student Council as the representative body of all the students, are contained in a very ably drafted petition submitted to the Privy Council by a group of twenty-nine students, including the Presidents of several college Common Rooms.

There are two significant things about these demands. First, they relate to University and not to College administration; in the colleges, it seems, the relations between junior and senior members are on the whole close and satisfactory. Second, they evidently spring not from a desire on the part of the students to run the University themselves (a little experience of University committees would soon cure them of that desire if it existed), nor from an acceptance of the extremists' doctrine that in a truly demo-cratic university the undergraduates are entitled to representation pro-portionate to their numbers and their importance. In fact, the complain-ants ask only for token representation, and seem generally to be content that their representatives should have speaking but not voting rights, or should attend simply to be 'consulted'.

Both the form and the substance of the students' demand, therefore, suggest that its real purpose is not to seize power, but to remedy a break-down in communications: they want to be assured that those who are on the other side of the gulf that separates, or seems to separate, the teachers from the taught, really listen to their complaints, understand what they are saying, and are concerned about their interests. If 'representation' through a Student Council were the only method of achieving this, or of reassuring the students themselves about it, the University might be wise to accede to their proposals. But there are several reasons for hoping that

Professor Hart's Committee will find some other means of satisfying the student's wishes.

I pass by the practical difficulties, which are serious enough. The undergraduate representatives would change annually, for they would have to be drawn entirely, or almost entirely, from the men in their second year; freshmen would clearly be non-starters, while third-year men would be taken up with work for their impending Schools. The representatives could only keep in satisfactory touch with their constituents if they were briefed by (and reported to) the Council regularly on the many issues of concern to students that arise week by week in the University, and if the Council itself truly reflected student opinion on these issues. Those conditions might be fulfilled if undergraduates and graduates generally gave up a great deal of their time and thought to university politics. (What a pity, incidentally, it would be if they did! How much better that their Oxford days should be spent in work and recreation, and inspired by enthusiasms at once more human and more humane!) It is unlikely, however, that many of the young men could be persuaded to take a continuing interest in the business of the Student Council, which would almost certainly fall into the hands of a few barrack-room lawyers and professional student-politicians (many of them no doubt graduate students) who would not really represent the whole body of the students or communicate to the authorities the true state of student feeling.

There are more fundamental objections however, to representation through a Student Council than the merely practical.

To recognize a Student Council, as a body that through its elected members represents and speaks for the mass of undergraduate and graduate students, would be to introduce into the life of the University an element quite alien to a place of learning and more suited to an industrial enterprise, where workers' representatives bargain with the management in an atmosphere of mutual mistrust. The activists are already academic shop-stewards: do not let us turn the Colleges into students' co-operatives!

Furthermore, as the University itself pointed out in its reply to the students' Privy Council petition, recognition of the Student Council as the official representative body would lead to the by-passing of the more direct and sensitive channels of communication that already exist both inside and outside the Colleges. Recognition of 'one centralized representative body would, in the end', as the University's reply puts it, 'be bound to weaken the multiple structure of representation of junior members which now exists'. In other words, a single body, which spoke for at most a small 'political' element in the University, would in effect silence the voices of the generality of students whom it professed to represent. There is a further danger. What if those who represented the Student Council found that when they gave their advice their opinions were not heeded and that when they gave their 'token' votes on academic bodies they were voted down? They would not be slow to put forward the claim – illogical and unfounded though it would be – that the University, by recognizing the Council and accepting the principle of representation, had admitted that students are academically adult and therefore qualified to be consulted by their seniors and to sit side by side with them on the bodies that administer or actually govern Oxford – and if that is so, why (they would ask) should they be content with 'token' representation? Why should they not have seats in proportion – as the activist leaders claim they should – to their numbers and their importance (or their own sense of it)?

In fact, of course, students are not 'academically adult'; it is a purpose of their university education to make them so. To suggest that a professor or tutor is no better qualified to judge about administration, appointments, and curriculum than is the pupil he instructs is to confess to a failure on the part of the university that they belong to. A boy of nineteen, however sexually adult, cannot be expected to display the informed judgement or to possess the experience of the academic system (which is too complicated to be picked up in the course of a three-year sojourn) that would qualify him to sit side by side with his elders in consultative or administrative councils. There are, indeed, youthful students with judgements older than their years, just as there are dons who are mature in nothing but their age, and dons who in the course of years have lost all touch with the world around them; but these are exceptions that do not upset the rule.

If it is suggested that the undergraduates of the 1960s have a more adult sense of responsibility than those of earlier generations, the reply is surely that though the student of today may be far more serious-minded than any of his predecessors, to lack a sense of humour is not the same thing as to possess a sense of responsibility. For confirmation of that axiom one need only reflect upon the attitude of the 'teenage' generation on the question of drugs, and upon the readiness with which many of the students have themselves swallowed the nostrums offered by the leaders of revolt.

As for discipline: to attempt to reproduce within the University a counterpart of the criminal courts, with their adversary system and elaborate safeguarding machinery, would be doubly deplorable. First, the students would find themselves worse off for the change – for the complaints about the proctorial system are entirely theoretic: in practice (as the figures put forward by the University demonstrate), the system is most

NAC

sympathetically administered and has given rise in recent years to no specific complaints of injustice. Second, and perhaps more important, a legalistic system, with parties at arms' length, would replace the mutual confidence that should subsist between members of an academic community. Least desirable of all is the suggestion that the university should disclaim all responsibility for discipline, leaving its members, if they broke the law of the land, to the mercies of the police. The best solution is to be sought along exactly opposite lines – by placing greater reliance, for discipline as for consultation, upon the domestic machinery afforded by the Colleges.

The suggestion that student discipline is no concern of academic authorities well illustrates the difference between two kinds of university. On the one hand is the academic institute which exists solely to train its students for degrees, and regards them simply as citizen academic workers with whom it acknowledges no personal relationship and for whom it takes no responsibility outside the lecture-room, leaving discipline to the operation of the law. In Essex the other day three young students, having drunk two bottles of whisky (Grants whisky, one may presume),[1] stripped and brutally attacked a young girl; convicted of criminal assault, they pleaded 'the pressure of exams' and were taken back by the University. That is a good example of a non-collegiate university in action.

On the other hand is the collegiate university, which interests itself in the whole being and welfare of its junior members, encourages human relations between them and their seniors, counts mutual trust and loyalty as academic virtues, asks for a decent standard of behaviour from its students and treats disruptive activity as an academic offence. The students who complain of being treated as impersonal objects, mere 'degree-fodder', and at the same time resent 'paternalism' on the part of their seniors, are having it both ways. They want the indulgence accorded to a member of a family without any family responsibilities. 'Can't we discuss this as human beings?' asked a senior member in a 'provincial' university the other day, having reached an *impasse* in argument with a student leader: 'I am not interested in you as a human being' was the cold reply. It will be a

1 In the original text of this article in *The Listener* I gave 'Grants' an apostrophe, thus (it appears) obscuring a *double entendre* that, crude though it may have been, seemed to me obvious enough. Since, however, this play upon their name has caused embarrassment to Messrs. Grant, the famous distillers, I must explicitly declare that no serious reference to their excellent Whisky was intended.

Indeed, since in the Essex University junior instructors are, I understand, particularly active in support of student rebels and often act in concert with them, I might perhaps more reasonably have suggested Teacher's Whisky as the brand in question.

sad day when such an exchange takes place between an Oxford tutor and his pupil.

What is the lesson, then, that Oxford – 'and when I say Oxford, I mean Cambridge' – should learn from what has happened? First, it must not abandon the character of a collegiate university, a community interested in the whole range of its students' lives, and not merely in training them for a degree; second, it should make use of its collegiate machinery to maintain a channel for mutual understanding between teachers and taught; finally, when faced with force the authorities should not hesitate, after due warning, to hit back hard; calling in the police where necessary, and in appropriate cases expelling rather than rusticating serious offenders; plenty of substitutes will be found who will put their grants to better use. For such firmness the dons will find, not least among the undergraduates themselves, a volume of support that will surprise them.

Note

A typical case-history – pathetic, one would say, if it were not so alarming in its implications – comes from Paris.

In *Le Monde* of 4–5 August 1968 a young student of the Sorbonne, M. J. Postic, describes the process of his almost religious conversion to the cause of student revolt. Likes most of his comrades, he says, he did not at first know very clearly what were the purposes of the students' strike when it was declared on 6 May. But as soon as the strike actually started he recognized in it an opportunity – unhoped for (in his own phrase) except in dreams – of taking a stand against the daily academic round, 'contre la discipline astreignante . . . des cours, des repas pris à temps fixes, du travail personnel quotidiennement accompli.' Then came the actual experience of revolt. M. Postic found it intoxicating: 'Je vivais, je mordais sur mon avenir. J'étais comme un peu ivre.' He goes on to describe, with touching *naïveté*, the 'deux difficultés majeures' that confronted him and his friends as soon as the first flush of rebellion faded: they didn't understand the problems they were facing, and they were painfully ignorant of what it was that they themselves were aiming at: 'La première [difficulté] résultait d'une méconnaissance certaine des problèmes auxquels nous nous attaquions . . . Le seconde résidait dans une impuissance douloureuse à formuler ce que nous ressentions et voulions.'

It took only a week or two, however, for the young student's aims to formulate themselves: 'Vers la fin du mois de mai, je rencontrai en diverses occasions des membres des bourgeoisies lyonnaise et grenobloise. Avec foi jê présentai mes projets de société nouvelle, dont les maîtres-mots étaient participation et justice et où l'intelligence gouvernait.' A true democracy, in which justice and intelligence reign supreme, chimerical though the concept may be, is no ignoble aim, and the *bons bourgeois* of Lyons and Grenoble were not without sympathy for the young enthusiast. But the practical counsel that they offered him was not acceptable: 'Mon jeune ami', they advised him, 'retournez à vos études.' These wise words came too late: the revolutionary virus had already done its work. 'Mai mourut et juin naquit' – 'mai qui fut sans nuage et juin poignardé', M. Postic might recall, were he old enough to have faced real evil as an enemy – the democratic process functioned; the elections took place; and when on 14 July vent was given to the feelings of the vast mass of the nation M. Postic and his fellow-rebels tasted the bitterness of betrayal: 'Ces discours, ce pharisaisme m'ont laissé et ont laissé à beaucoup un goût de fiel sur la langue.' 'Rien n'est réglé', he concludes: nothing has been settled.

What of the future? M. Postic leaves us in no doubt about his own attitude: he has murder in his heart – 'comme une envie de meurtre qui monte je ne sais d'où'. If student revolt breaks out again, he and his friends (he tells us) will make no second mistake: 'Ce que je sais . . . c'est que beaucoup de jeunes, d'étudiants . . . s'ils ne savaient pas début mai pourquoi ils se mettaient en grève, ils le sauront parfaitement à la prochaine occasion.'

Could one ask for a more perfect illustration of the text suggested in my article – 'Revolution first, revolutionaries afterwards'?

Donald G. MacRae

Between commitment and barbarism

No history is more mysterious than the history of modes of thought and action. No constituents of history are at once more permanent and more protean than these modes. There is no paradox intended here, but the statement of a fact which involves a dilemma: how can we doubt the recurrences and re-emergences of ideologies and ideologically motivated deeds over long tracts of time and in diverse social contexts; how can we recognize with certainty unities in these matters where appearance so often belies reality?

The various varieties of historical and sociological determinism have their answers. For example: class-struggles are constant, ubiquitous and ideology and political style are their epiphenomena; the human personality is framed everywhere and always in the same tangle of frustration and aggression, guilt and desire, and must manifest itself in the same ways; the analysis of social structure takes advantage of the fact that only a very limited number of variables and patterns are available to men, and inevitably they return again and again to similar forms of action, just as only a limited number of throws is possible with two dice; and so on and on. The trouble with these answers is not so much that they cannot all be true at once, or that they are all (as is indeed the case) demonstrably false except for certain specific cases and circumstances, as that they do an intolerable violence to reality as we experience it in our own living out of events and as we strive to grasp its fabric either in alien places or other times.

We are, I think, concerned in the wave of student dissidence which began it is usually claimed at the University of California's Berkeley Campus in 1964, but which could be discerned in style and even concrete events elsewhere, particularly in Europe, certainly five or six years earlier, with a recurrence and even a continuity in thought and action. In saying this I am not trying to assert either of two often asserted things: neither that these transactions should be taken as a part of that series of conspiracies to overthrow an institution or a society the study of which begins at Corcyra with Thucydides, nor as asserting that these things are part of some jolly ragging student tradition going back to medieval Bologna, Paris or Oxford. (And how jolly was, or is, that tradition? How amusing was it in 1192 for the serfs of Saint-Germain-des-Prés to be involved in that fray with students which is almost our first clear intimation that the University of Paris existed – or for the citizens involved in that second battle of 1200 which resulted in the first recorded faculty strike?) The point rather is that we are seeing the restoration of a particular tradition of thought and behaviour which has been in the more advanced countries – whatever that means – suppressed or overlaid by other events, forces and ideas.

No doubt the events of the spring and early summer of 1968 at Columbia and, far more important, Paris will soon be reduced to order by research and assertion, and agreed versions will be arrived at. Already, only six weeks after the Parisian outbreak, I have heard an eye-witness put down and corrected in his account of his experiences there by a scholar who, like myself, had the advantage of not being present. An established fable will reign. Meanwhile the student revolt and the general strike seem to me extraordinarily reminiscent of an almost forgotten episode in modern history, the period which followed the general's rising and opening of the civil war in Spain. Paris in 1968 sounds very like Barcelona in the days of the F.A.I. – and it is not just that the black and red banners of anarchy appeared again in a significant context for the first time in a generation. It seems clear that the animating spirits of these days in Barcelona and Paris were alike. There was a faith in voluntarism, participatory democracy, the moral imperative of instant virtue, the creative élan of the workers, populism and primitivism, and the conviction that continuing revolution was itself a good – which is also presumably the Maoist view. And there was apparently in both contexts a hatred or contempt for the unspontaneous work of the mind, of scholars, teachers and intellectuals. Once again the revolution was declared to have no need of savants – nor in West Berlin, to have need of liberals.

Now this is very different from the authoritarian era which began in 1917. The essentially Blanquist idea of the mastering of an institution or a state by a disciplined cadre, exercising dictatorial power after its seizure of power was modified by Leninism and routinized by Stalinism. The lamentable fate of German Communism was one result. The enormous ineffectiveness for its declared purposes of French Communism was another. (Of course French communism *was* effective but in other ways. It was an obedient instrument of Russian foreign policy. It played a serious part in French local political patronage and intrigue. It organized major sectors of the French wage workers and peasantry in a manner that gave them ideological satisfaction, a connection with the Jacobins, and a feeling that in the end they would triumph, so now they did not need to bother too much with such transistory things as real events.) This tradition dominated the left until recently. No one can say with certainty how much influence it retains – it certainly has power in the straightforward sense that the U.S.S.R. has power – but an older tradition has reappeared and is challenging both the established universities and the public authority as well as the authoritarian left.

This is not to say that this new left (by which I mean very little to do with the learned and disillusioned Stalinists who were so central to the 'New Left' after the Hungarian revolt of 1956) is without totalitarian aspects. Nothing is more manifest than its readiness to impose its standards and its will (if they are known) on dissenters if only by the processes of endless debate and confrontation. One straw in this wind, by the way, is the contempt of students from Berlin to Berkeley for that great instrument of democracy, that enemy of enforced consensus, the secret ballot. But it is an authoritarianism of an older sort, one which however deviously, derives from Rousseau and from the young Marx. We are confronted by a restoration of an ancient, antinomian revolutionary ideological complex.

Men in positions of power, both in the universities and in public office, are to be found who approve at least some of this. Mr Short, Secretary of State for Education and Science, hedged his bets in Britain, but his basic position seems quite clear. He told a meeting of educators (*The Times*, 29.6.1968) that authoritarian regimes 'persist' in too many universities. There should be 'new methods of discipline that are more appropriate to the democratic context in which students will live their adult lives'. According to the reporter he criticized much of education as 'intellectual junk', and said it was 'more important to know all the facts about Vietnam than to know the details of the Wars of the Roses. . . . The apparent chaos and violence of student protest, rightly understood and used, could raise the whole quality of our democracy.' And so on: one could cite many examples of this, for such voices are to be heard in every level of the educational apparatus, and at many levels of government!

In all this we may be encountering a recurrent symptom of genuinely pre-revolutionary times. I refer to what Crane Brinton long ago called 'the transfer of allegiance' – the movement away from the accepted positions in ideological alignment of the intellectuals[1] by way of a period of disorientation and estrangement to one of new radically intransigent

---

1 I am not claiming Mr Short as an intellectual, and for all I know he might be made angry by such an attribution.

postures. But at least western society has been here before. There are
some new ingredients in the ideological cauldron, but most of them have
been familiar since at least 1848, and as I suggested above many have been
current fare since the time of Rousseau or can be found among the
Christian heresies of the sixteenth and seventeenth centuries. They were
the leading themes of rebellion, 'propaganda by deed', syndicalism, and
the aspiration of the non-social-democratic left until the triumph of
Bolshevism, and they continued to be of importance in the Catalonia of
Durutti at least until the very end of the civil war in Spain. In some ways
they seem peculiarly congruent with opposition to a régime such as that
of Napoleon III – and it may be no coincidence that they re-emerge so
strongly in the Fifth Republic. After all in many ways General de Gaulle
resembles Napoleon III – the former Prince President – in his rule more
closely than he does any of 'the forty kings who have made France'.
Plebiscitary affirmations and a 'liberal empire' are also *revenants*.

But whatever we may think of 'the transfer of allegiance', yet more
revolutions are attempted than succeed. The *émeute*, too, a ritual act of
propaganda as much as a serious enterprise, has a history even older than
the Fronde. Recent events certainly contain in their animating ideas
elements of primitivism and exoticism – Che Guevara and Mao, not to
mention the Freudian discovery of a primordial childhood for each of us,
an 'exemplary infancy' as Eliade somewhere describes it – which are
novel. And the emphases are often new. Yet to me it all seems genuinely
like a restoration and a return, even if we never *quite* return to the places
we once knew, to the traditions of an earlier rebellion with which earlier
generations were familiar.

The novelty lies, I believe, not so much in concepts as in the situation;
the new and central role of the universities, a novelty of claim by students
to which we will return, and a genuine cultural gap between generations
which is accentuated by the sheer proportional numerousness of the
student-aged population – a factor which, demographically speaking, will
reach its height for most advanced countries in the 1970s. I have tried
to deal with the third of these elsewhere.[1] That analysis turned on five
factors: changes in affluence, socio-economic status and aspirations; the
experience of 'contingency' in a world of rapid change and nuclear wars
where absolutely anything is possible; the politics of destalinization in
relation to youth movements; the energies released by decreased tensions
and guilts in the sexual sphere of life; and the devaluation of a tradition

1 D. G. MacRae, 'The Culture of a Generation: Students and Others', *Journal of
  Contemporary, History* Vol. 2, No. 3, July 1967.

of learning, logic and rhetoric essentially classical and verbal. In these matters I shall try not to repeat myself more than is necessary for my purposes here.

The new claim made by students is itself an interesting one, and is perhaps connected with the sense of the contingency of the world which I mentioned above. That contingency can result in feelings of an urgency towards immediate enjoyment – including our enjoyment of power – which goes beyond any of the usual reactions to the fact that youth's a stuff will not endure. Such an explanation may be too charitable. The central case is that a special indulgence, gratification and authority should be given to students *because on them the future depends*. This claim is a little like asking dividends first, capital to come later. Of course the future depends on people, for the future is a human category. Of course it will largely depend on the skills and attainments of these young people. But to blackmail the present in the interests of the future is a dubious practice, and not just for the good reason that too many crimes and errors have been committed by the future-minded in our century for one to have much confidence in this kind of arrangement, but also for the rather obvious point that skills and attainments likely to have a major social pay-off are not going to be furthered by the disruption of the universities in which, however badly, these skills are acquired.

Another argument for this claim is that only the young are truly contemporary, therefore only they can know what today and tomorrow both hold and need, therefore they have a right to a particularly powerful political influence and to, in the small world of the universities, a decisive say in the conduct of instruction. This is really part of the same syndrome. It has been grossly overblown by those publicists, older than the students, who constantly hold up their hands in wonder at the rate of change and who find a new industrial revolution twice a decade. It is so largely untrue that one is inclined to dismiss it, but it has some truth – enough, I would say, for an explanation and discussion of curricula to become a normal, if not too time-consuming, part of university procedures in so far as courses are not self-explanatory, as they often are. This part of the claim seems particularly important given the new centrality of the universities in society (which can reasonably be deplored but must be admitted) to the affairs of the state at the three levels of finance, faculty expertise, and the drive for economic growth by the massive deployment of higher education as an aid to technological and other efficiencies.

This restoration of an old tradition of strong dissent must affect different university systems differently. Certain points about the British system, points which are in many ways strengths, render it vulnerable to damage of a kind to which other forms of university may be less subject. I am not sure that discussions of the present situation have concentrated sufficiently on these characteristics of British universities. One reason for this failure has been that new modesty, that mini-Englandism, which is one of the more depressing features of these '60s. There is an unwillingness to accept that in any sphere of life our ways and organizations can possess unique merits of efficiency and economy. In fact the intense British three (and in some cases at Keele, Oxford and in Scotland four) year first degree is very remarkable as compared with other countries. Its intensity and the impartial rigour – widely deplored – of the accompanying examination system mean quite simply that we attain in three years what it takes a four year degree *and* a master's degree to produce in the United States. And, although examinations are arduous the mixed methods of instruction we use are on the whole among the most flexible, least bureaucratized in any part of the world. (To all I say, of course there are exceptions, but the general picture is true.)

Now for a country overburdened by the demands of the age this is all to the good. Whether students are numerous enough and in the right subjects are other questions, not for discussion here. The system also has a record (measured in terms of its resources) of producing much and good scholarship and research and an unmatched quantum of public service. But it is also a delicate and a nervous exercise. To achieve these things it asks more of students and dons than do its foreign alternatives. The dons, however badly, are also administrators. Increasingly they are the direct servants of the state – including the Mr Shorts – and their autonomy is bought at a price and defended with difficulty. If one cares for learning and freedom that price is not too high nor that defence to be abandoned in the interests of either a vision of the omnipotent state or of student communes.

In our time we have seen the re-emergence of an old and central theme of our civilization – a theme which derives from Christianity itself. Christianity simultaneously makes men both guilty, that is of uneasy conscience, and responsible. It also places the primary guilt out of time, in the primordial fall, but it constantly challenges men with the vision of the good and peaceable kingdom, unattained. With what relief then have we welcomed the idea – an inspiration of much sociology – that as individuals we are not responsible for our condition, but that the ordering of society is the decisive element in our lot. Both guilt and inevitable fate can then be shrugged aside, and society transformed or reformed. This idea has so much to its credit that one hesitates to question it – and hence comes that pervasive idea that one must have no enemies on the left. The attack on our relatively economic, just and efficient ordering of the universities which would transform them into perpetually smoking cauldrons of permanent revolution is possibly useful in pointing to genuine failures and grievances (which of course exist, and should be remedied) but is more likely to be merely destructive of a fragile set of institutions and devices. The restoration of the pre-Bolshevik revolutionary tradition is poly-centric, various, generous in intent, humane in many of its aspirations (although essentially inhumane in its tacit promise of human perfectibility, here, now) but it is fundamentally unrealistic in its neglect of opportunity costs in actual social situations. It is morally better than a decadent Stalinism, and much more attractive. It reveals certain forgotten continuities in our societies. It is attracted by sociology – and profoundly ignorant of the results of that disillusioning subject. Its rhetoric in word and deed should not be allowed to destroy what with difficulty has been achieved and maintained in higher learning – either directly or through the use that can be made of this movement by men who are essentially anti-intellectual and believe only in the power of the state. For, and here is a paradox, it is such men who, outside the universities in administration or politics, are most likely to be the beneficiaries of this dissidence which is at once old and new. It gives them cause for complaint and intervention, and it gives them a vocabulary. Of course it also threatens them as Paris showed, but the measure of that threat cannot be assessed without a metric which can give us a total accounting of the political and social potentialities of our specific societies and their interrelations. It would not be any great novelty if a revivified tradition of dissent and revolt advantaged only the barbarians of our time.

Peter Wiles

Die Bauchschmerze eines Fachidioten

The late 50s and early 60s were the golden age of the don. He researched, he published, he broadcast, he travelled, he sat on Royal Commissions. The B.B.C., the Ford Foundation, the University of California at Berkeley (yes, there was such a place), the United Nations, etc., paid him substantial sums to air his views. Everyone smiled to see this new character in the limelight, so witty and unselfseeking, so full of ideas and good will, so controversial and so harmless. Even the Press spoke of him respectfully. The old notion persisted that he had sacrificed a substantial salary to pursue learning, that he was unworldly. It is very pleasant to earn a lot more money than people think you do. It is not even unpleasant, when you get right down to it, occasionally to teach; but of course all this *brouhaha* got in the way of it – and the competition for us enabled us to bargain for lighter loads.

The new contact with the outside world created a market for works of imagination: *The Masters, Groves of Academe, A New Life, Accident, Who's Afraid of Virginia Woolf?* Dons, not students, were of course the subject – and why not? they are much more interesting. The public was fed with visions of Byzantine intrigue at the office, with couplings of Murdochian complexity to round out the full life. It admired these visions greatly, and somehow persuaded itself that they had no parallel at the works, in parliament, in the army. Or at least they were to be condemned in such milieux, while greed, slander, dishonesty and neglect of duty were merely amusing if their practitioners were learned enough. University life became news: to the educational correspondent was added the gossip column. The architecture and government of new universities were subjects of serious general discussion. The Vice-Chancellor elect of Essex (yes, there was such a person) even made them the subject of the Reith lectures, as if a combined common room were on a par with the discovery of D.N.A. or the liberation of Africa. Research was still an absolute good; intellect excused everything. 'This is the way to be, Peter,' an academic figure of world renown said to me as late as 1964, 'we live like kings'.

How dated all that is. I am older and more distinguished now, and occupy, as the saying is, the Pan-American Chair more often than ever. Side earnings come still easier than before. The intrigue is no less Byzantine, and I come out on top more often; though of course the passage of time is setting an expected term to the couplings. But I feel less like an ersatz king than a late pre-Reformation abbot. Time is running out. Three out of three French colleagues, due to attend a conference or write a paper this summer, have cried off, 'à cause des évènements de mai–juin'.

The student revolt did not start these misgivings, indeed has somewhat diminished them. I am not responsible, and am not held responsible, for so great a natural phenomenon; but rather regard myself, with renewed self-confidence and sense of purpose, as a public servant putting out a forest fire. To this we shall return. That uneasy 'pre-Reformation' feeling was induced, on the contrary, by just the euphoria of the previous period.

For universities are not all that important. Judge them first by their outputs. There is too much research. It is plausibly argued that if the human race is to survive it must produce no more ultimate weapons, and that means an end to progress in most natural sciences; while the social sciences are of doubtful validity and the humanities but a pastime with a weak claim on the public funds of a poor country. There is far too much publication; I am typically conscientious, but only read at the most a thousandth part of what comes out in my field. Teaching is vital and neglected, but it still matters who is taught what. Give Oxford philosophy to a Mormon and he loses his faith; give theoretical economics to the socially concerned, and they reach for sociology and paving stones.

Then there is the resource question: can we afford to tie up so much ability? 'Those who can, do; those who can't, teach' – but not since governments got the education bug. Now it is 'Those who must, do; those who can get away with it, teach.' Few people really want to leave a university. Lower seconds acquire tastes above their heads. Young revolutionaries linger in the only place where revolution has a chance, while their erstwhile contempt for academic values turns sour and threadbare. Civil servants pine for free speech, and wangle transfers. Under the pressure of an excess demand for teachers the *ewiger Student* has become the *ewiger Dozent* – or has been replaced by that contemporary archetype, the 'non-student', who uses the facilities without paying, and sleeps and reads at random.[1]

---

1 It is of course a truly excellent thing to read at random *sometimes*. Were it not for his defects of personality and low intellectual level, the non-student would be our only genuine Renaissance man.

Thirdly there is a moral or metaphysical issue. The public had an almost mystical image of the universities. They have, to revert to that pre-Reformation simile, been the monasteries of the modern world: great corporations with beautiful and expensive buildings, their denizens held in absurd respect by the outside world, eating up large tithes and rents, and justifying it all by a very peculiar *raison d'être*: they are storing up virtue for the population at large – a fine tale so long as the public believes it.

This scepticism is not anti-intellectual in the ordinary sense. I share in no degree the modern left-wing tendency to 'think with the blood'. It is on the contrary by the strict use of the intellect that I arrive at these conclusions. It is a square old-fashioned Utilitarianism, not some trendy Anarcho-Fascism, that persuades me we have overdone higher education and research in many fields.

For the signs of over-expansion are many. Our student population has grown many times without lowering standards, to be sure; but only because this undergraduate generation, revolutionaries and all, works harder, and because we have *excluded* the stupider members of the upper classes. The law of diminishing returns tells us that eventually More Will Mean Worse all the same. It is right to have Worse if More are really needed, but that question is not, as we shall see, easily answered. The decline of quality is already evident among teachers, and that too is not in principle wrong. But it is having an unexpected side effect in student discontent: whatever his politics and the degree of rapport he establishes, the young don's comparative incompetence is resented, for even if – nay particularly if – he is revolutionary, the student remains an intellectual snob. No great shakes himself, he has unlimited self-importance, and demands a range of qualities in his teachers that would fit each one of them for Prime Minister. We must at least concede that it is wrong for a student to go right through his higher education and have *no* contact with a first-class mind, or even with a broad and civilized mind.

Incidentally, the young don is often a revolutionary himself, or at least a fellow-traveller. It is not at all true that this phenomenon is due to the expansion of the university system, since ability is distributed among such people in much the same way as among other young dons. It was only to be expected that many, among the generation one or two years too old to have sat in, should have discovered in themselves similar attitudes *ex post facto*. Nay more, a milder sort of retrospective alienation is becoming common among dons in their mid-thirties. No shrinkage or expansion of the university system, no raising or lowering of the quality threshold, will alter this; it is simply a part of our times.

Reverting to quality, decline is even more evident among graduate students. They are not only less clever but also less dedicated, indeed hardly intellectuals at all. Again, why not, if they are needed? But the case has never been proved. If a man is to be a university teacher his job will deepen his knowledge of the subject anyway; he only needs a good first degree, a short course in teaching and a conscientious professorial supervisor. In many other careers too he can learn on the job; we are not all doctors. There is substance in Paul Goodman's accusation: prolonged study is an insult to virility, a sort of captivity.

To be sure, economic growth is *associated with* higher education, but which is cause and which effect? Who is to say that Enoch Powell is wrong? – higher education might be simply a consumption good for which rich communities develop a taste much as rich individuals like foreign travel. The so-called economic yield on higher education might be due to little more than this: clever people usually get more money than stupid people, but they will also compete for degrees, and pre-empt university places, once a prejudice in favour of degrees has been established. And such a prejudice might be initially due to nothing more than the convenience to employers of a free external testing system: the universities, already existing in adequate numbers, happen to be able to certify, at an absurdly great cost, which *are* the clever ones. So employers demand degrees, and from there on the whole expansion might be a vicious circle.

So I would have written two years ago – or so I think, for objective memory is rare. Upon this guilty splendour has intruded a new figure, the revolutionary student. I have the uneasy feeling that he is a very important figure, a harbinger of a new – and worse – society. He lacks at present 'credibility': he doesn't add up, least of all in his own eyes. Some aspects of him are transient, but which? – he also would like to know.

'*Larvatus prodeo*', said Descartes (masked, I go forward). His latter-day pupil applies this to human history in a famous passage:

We are never completely contemporaneous with our present. History advances in disguise; it appears on stage wearing the mask of the preceding scene, and we tend to lose the meaning of the play. Each time the curtain rises, continuity has to be re-established. The blame, of course is not history's, but lies in our vision, encumbered with memory and images learned in the past. We see the past superimposed on the present, even when the present is a revolution.[1]

Certainly nothing is more 'masked' than the present generation of revolutionary students. Principally we try to console ourselves that we have seen

1 Régis Debray, *Revolution in the Revolution?* New York 1967, p. 19.

it all before. But it is clear that the mask conceals at least a new combination of old ideological elements. It is also clear that the generation gap has
never been so great in human history. Furthermore, to come nearer to my
personal concerns, a great factual discovery has been made: universities,
unlike parliaments and armies, even unlike private and public corporations,
cannot easily fight aggressive non-violence – for of course 'non-violence' *is*
violence. Sit-ins pay. The majority of students weakly oppose them when
they begin, and strongly support them against police intervention. But
often only such intervention can defeat them. Therefore you must either
close down your university or give in.

It cannot be too strongly emphasized that this is a socio-military discovery, like the phalanx or the parachute brigade. One of the most irritating
things about being a modern don is those pompous leading articles on
university disorders. It is fine to be accused from the right of a failure of
nerve: many of my colleagues most scandalously lack nerve – that is why
they are in universities. It is fine to be accused from the left of lack of
imagination, failure to communicate and delaying necessary reforms until
they become concessions: that too is very just, though more surprising,
since many of us are social scientists and ought to know better.[1] But it
all leaves the essence untouched: I am never told *how* to cope with a
revolutionary movement that is determined not to be appeased, has a
serviceable new tactic and no scruples, and wants to bring the place to a
halt.

Very many others have dealt with the student revolt as such. It is not
directly our subject here, but what has to be asserted is that, if it has no
or only bad solutions, it has just complaints, both against the universe and
against the university. The former we shall leave aside. Many of the latter
I have listed above. One at least remains: internal government.

It is of course absurd to give students power over us. They are young,
emotional and transient. Mostly uninterested, they are powerless against
their own extremist minorities. In issues which excite these minorities
they are usually incapable of representative self-government: the wise and
the apathetic students alike simply stay away from the union. Student
power is thus a very bad idea, but is existing university government
better?

The public, that has made of the university a modern monastery,
demands that it be unusually well governed. And this public includes the
students. They come expecting a community of scholars, and what do

---

1 If the reader doubts my previous dismissal of the social *sciences*, can he explain
the failure of social *scientists* at all levels in university disturbances?

they find? They find in Britain – and I now consider only Britain – something much more boring than those splendid works of imagination referred to above. They find, precisely, a community of scholars. 'Community' of course does not imply equality of powers – a family is a community. I am amazed that this sincerely meant phrase should be used to prove my hypocrisy or argue for student power. But a community is pretty well by definition respectable, inefficient and slow. It is nearly impossible to change – everybody has a view and many have a veto, the army is all generals and no privates. It crawls with overlapping committees on which no one wants to serve. In other words university government is exceedingly democratic even where, outside Oxbridge, one-man-one-vote is not anchored in the constitution. Moreover – a separate point – it does indeed set a shining example of tolerance and civil rights in comparison with schools, enterprises, trade unions, political parties – virtually any group in the country. We do not enough consider, when we mouth the latest cant phrases about the Academic Gerontocracy, what it is like to be a Communist or a hippie or a homosexual or even just a little odd in a different kind of organization.

The surprising fact is that in their power relations with each other British dons do set the world a shining example. Within the ordinary limits of human imperfection they have very much to boast of: they are both tolerant and incorruptible – a rare combination. Let the reader contemplate the stuffy rigidity of a bank, the decadent mayhem of an advertising agency, the fraternal hatreds of the Labour Movement. Or let him consider, if he can bear it, foreign universities: the tyranny of American presidents and German professors, the malicious envy of Swedish doctoral exams. So long as we do not seek efficiency, we shall hardly find a more perfectly governed society than a British university.

What we do require, however, is that our perfections be more clearly seen. As a long-time admirer of Titoist economics, and a quondam fellow of two Oxford colleges, I cannot for the life of me understand why there should not be *formal* democracy among dons. It is useless to protest, correctly, that consultation is already very full and social tolerance complete: without being translated into power such assertions are simply not believed. As a good Machiavellian I must add that these formalities would make only one difference of substance: they would confer upon the young revolutionary don, that otherwise extremely dangerous figure, actual responsibility. It is not very risky to predict the outcome of that.

What, then, are my duties? Revolution quite apart, the university teacher faces an extraordinary number of small moral choices day by day:

OAC

more, surely, than anyone except the entrepreneur and the politician. This is due (in all three cases) to the undefined nature of his job. How much time do I owe this undergraduate? – is he only seeking to be spoonfed (10 minutes), or is his intellectual perplexity genuine (30 minutes)? indeed, does it mask spiritual trouble (seven sessions on his Weltanschauung at 30 minutes each)? Should these lectures be more perfect? – I could check that allegation in about three hours' work at the British Museum, but after all I'm not publishing it, it's only an illustration and I'll tell them I'm not sure. Is a letter to my publisher university business? Should I go to this conference in Michigan in term-time (they pay)? Why not, if I'm addressing Reading in term-time (and they don't pay)? Should I write this textbook on economic systems compared that is sorely needed (and may enrich me), or that work on Communist agriculture that would mean *really* learning Polish, and would 'expand the boundaries of knowledge' (but not my personal fortune)? I am a Liberal, and the Party wants my views on the economics of health: would typing the MS be university business? Should I join the admissions committee or found a new undergraduate programme? If the latter, it will lead to graduate studies in the same field one day, by mere *vis inertiae*: and that will cost the U.G.C. £5,000 a year. . . .

Perfect freedom is service indeed. Extremely few dons – and I speak as one who has seen many in many places and countries, and hired and fired them, and is naturally suspicious – are idle. But a professional code or Hippocratic Oath is needed, to control our use of our own time and other people's money.

Nor is that all. From playing around on TV, the licensed jesters and instant sages of the 1950s, we have been pitchforked into real history. A whole dimension of current social responsibility has been added to us: to bridge the generation gap, to defend free speech, to put down violence, to set an example of inter-personal behaviour, to reform our own institutions, to be ideologically responsive to large new discontents: in a word to be Renaissance men and preachers to boot.

'Each younger generation,' said an American philosopher, 'is a barbarian invasion.' The present one is a particularly virulent invasion, and if we do not domesticate it, what will society look like in twenty years' time when it has power? The Rome we defend against the invaders must at the same time be made worth defending. But that is a larger task, and belongs to all society. The smaller task rests squarely upon the university teacher, and it is more historically crucial than many admit. If he does not perform it, no one will.

He is ill prepared. He has, or can quickly get up, the required book-learning[1]; he is on an intellectual level with his charges. But he is, of course, a specialized person, too modest to indulge in bold general visions. He has learned disillusion and self-control, usually at the cost of emotional richness; whereas the quintessence of the New Left is the principled rejection of self-control. Again, he is not a politician: almost by definition he has renounced wider power, and mostly he is too busy and too interested in his job to care even about power within the university. Like those monks, he has shed responsibility. And herein lies selfishness, a selfishness highly characteristic of intellectuals, that the student – who accepts responsibility for the whole universe – is quick to detect. There must be both reform and resistance, but both are species of *action*. It is our incapacity to act that makes me wonder if we shall pull through.

---

1 A senior political philosopher of my acquaintance and age-group refuses to read Marcuse. After all, he might object, Louis XVIII had not read Rousseau.

L. C. Sykes

The new academics

How have academics changed in recent years? In order to answer the editor's question, I must observe the rules of the sociological game now so much in fashion. I shall have to pretend to detect uniformities in academics, and close my eyes to their individuality. Looking at them as members of a profession, I shall have to make believe that they are fashioned in its moulds. These moulds no doubt exist, and some of them are now pressing harder. Yet academics continue to enjoy quite extraordinary freedom to make of their profession what they will, to decide for themselves both what its obligations are, and how they shall be met. Generalizations are therefore peculiarly hazardous.

Happily the most objective statement I can make is also the one that provides the best basis for explaining the changes that seem to me to have occurred among academics in this country during the last ten years: quite simply, there are more than twice as many of them as there were in 1958. For in this decade nine new universities have been born (and never were births more public!), nine colleges of advanced technology transformed as if by magic into universities, and places found for double the number of students. This Robbins age has been a golden age indeed – in which the youngest academics might count themselves fortunate to secure their first posts far more easily than any of their predecessors, and the not-quite-so-young rejoice in unprecedented opportunities for advancement. Senior posts have multiplied not in the new universities only, but in the older ones as well. The typical Redbrick department that had a single professor ten years ago now has two, three or even more. My own department has probably changed and grown more slowly than most; but since 1962 four of its twelve full-time members have been promoted or appointed to senior posts, and seven have begun their careers in it. Our universities had three chairs of sociology in 1962; now they have more than thirty. A good time, you might say, has been had by all.

Public opinion approved – chiefly because it had allowed itself to be persuaded that only more and bigger universities could supply the scientific and technological knowledge necessary for economic growth and indeed (as the tiresome and thoughtless cliché affirmed) for national survival itself. There never were quite so many academics in ivory towers as the myth suggested; today only a few still reside there. The largest group of academics is made up not of humanists or social scientists or pure scientists, but of those whose disciplines – law, medicine and engineering for example – have immediate professional relevance, and who are thus brought into close and continuous contact with what another tiresome and thoughtless cliché calls 'the *real* world outside'; and in that world the scientist, the social scientist and even the humanist are less than ever strangers. The multiversities of North America, says ex-President Clark Kerr of California, serve society 'almost slavishly'. Our universities, as Lord Bowden is never tired of reminding us, are still a long way from doing so. That is none the less the direction in which they have markedly tended to move of late. For in an age that is perplexed by 'problems' and credulously inclined to suppose that experts can solve them, it has been discovered that universities can supply experts at a moment's notice (and oracles as well). Thus there emerges here a variety of the academic species already familiar enough (like other phenomena to be noted later) in North America: the professor who, no longer absent-minded, is simply absent. When you looked for him yesterday he was at home writing a piece for one of the weeklies. Today he's in town lunching with a higher civil servant or a tycoon. Tonight you can hear him on the radio – if you can't, as is more likely, see him on TV. He won't be back tomorrow, for he'll be sitting on a board or a council, a committee or a commission set up by the government, by a profession, an industry, a trust, a voluntary association. . . .

No university matters (says the head of a very young one) until two-fifths of its staff are airborne at any one time. Matters to whom? No university is likely to matter much, one may guess, to these winged academics themselves. What matters to them is their specialism: to it they owe the double blessing of intellectual fulfilment and professional repute. So, of course, did pre-Robbins academics, and most legitimately; but the academics of 1968 have more opportunities and more inducements to devote themselves primarily to research. The advancement of knowledge implies – perhaps not necessarily, but as it is usually understood – its fragmentation, invites narrower concentration; and both the fragmentation and the concentration have been facilitated by the recent rapid growth in the size and resources of departments. As they have expanded, it has been possible to recruit ever more specialized specialists, who are not required to do so much teaching as their elders once were, and are less often subjected to the distraction of having to teach outside their own small field. They have not only much more time for research, but much more money as well; and in their eyes the place where they spend the money and pursue their research is their department rather than their university. This trend has not gone quite unchecked. Here and there – as our Plateglass universities often like to insist – the walls have been blown up in explosions at 'the flashpoints of knowledge', or deliberately knocked down to create 'inter-disciplinary schools'. But in general the academic increasingly prefers the comfort and companionship of the departmental home. What's happening next door he scarcely knows or cares. His professional standing is determined by the esteem in which he is held by his departmental colleagues – and by his fellow-specialists all over the world. Unlike the foreigners in other departments of his own university, these are the people who speak his language. He will meet them at congresses in Tokyo or Chicago, Istanbul or Melbourne. On their good opinion he will rely for flattering invitations from across the Atlantic, and all the other honours and perquisites of academic fame and VIP treatment.

What more particularly of the younger academics of 1968 ? Still in their twenties or their early thirties, these newcomers of the last ten years now outnumber their elders. They have mostly arrived in the universities along a path which, if not smooth, was undoubtedly less arduous than it had ever been before: they had obtained postgraduate awards quite easily, and had not had to wait long for their first appointments. A few even came straight from finals to assistant lectureships; many more, conscious of their 'scarcity value', have expected early promotion and have been granted it with an alacrity hitherto unknown. Of the appointments made to junior posts in the '60s, some have unquestionably been poor. The exact proportion is all the more difficult to estimate because it has certainly not been the same in all disciplines and all universities. My impression is that it represents a minority not so large as to be gravely disquieting, yet not so small as to be altogether reassuring. The rest have been good or better than good: most of the younger academics know their stuff, and often know it admirably. And yet . . . Here I hesitate . . . for if I express some reservations, they will be justly suspect, as the opinions of seniors about juniors always are. Besides, exceptions spring so readily to mind that I am even less sure than usual about the validity of my generalizations. It does however seem to me that the academic profession tends to be held in less esteem by its recent recruits, and that the intellectual and personal contribution they are able and willing to bring to it tends to diminish.

Older dons, of infinitely less distinction than Mark Pattison, have none
the less known the emotion with which he recalled the November morning
in 1839 when he received news of his election to a fellowship at Lincoln:
'No moment in all my life has ever been so sweet.' Brilliant or mediocre,
our new academics do not appear to look on admission to the profession
as a privilege: the very idea would, I suspect, seem to some absurd. The
profession itself is less for them a style of life (as, surely, it once was, and
not so long ago?) than a career, which they have chosen not indeed
absent-mindedly, but with no marked sense of vocation or even any strong
preference. They will satisfy its requirements, as they understand them,
with earnest conscientiousness rather than spontaneous and whole-
hearted commitment. The application of the mind to a particular task is
something they well understand: much less, the delight of its mere cultivation. Even an aggressive and self-conscious philistinism can sometimes be
observed; more common is a certain unadventurousness not of mind only,
but of manner too: as has more than once been remarked, the 'migratory
élite' to which young academics belong is surprisingly uninventive. And
this having been said, I emphasize that I speak here of what I think are
tendencies, not of the many exceptional individuals who do not conform
to them – like the young men who give up well-paid posts in colleges of
technology and take ill-paid posts in universities, because they hope to
find there better opportunities of becoming the thoughtful scholars they
want to be.

They will find those opportunities; but not, I fear, the satisfaction of
belonging to a coherent society in which all are truly members one of
another. As our universities have grown, they have more and more lost the
characteristics of communities and acquired those of organizations. (In
this respect the older collegiate universities are doubtless exceptional, and
so also, I hope, are the new ones that are similarly constituted.) Within
them personal relationships remain generally pleasant, and often as
eminently civilized as they should be: they range less freely and have
become more tenuous. The full sense of the loss thus entailed could be
conveyed only by describing innumerable changes of circumstance and
attitude, each trivial in itself but made significant by accumulation. Ten
years ago I often had lunch with a physicist, an economist, a biologist. I
can't explain briefly how it has come to pass that this rarely happens now,
or why I feel myself so much the poorer for the lack of their conversation.
They and I are no longer the close colleagues we were once. There are
indeed many members of the senior common room that I can't really call
colleagues at all: I don't even know their names, any more than they know

mine. If I who have been about the place for twenty years often feel myself a stranger there, can the new assistant lecturer be expected to feel that he belongs to it and owes it loyalty? Should anyone be surprised if (as I was suggesting) the profession means less to him than to earlier recruits – or if he seems slow or reluctant to make its values his own? In this morning's paper I read of a suggestion that a code is now required setting out the duties of university teachers to their students. That is the way things go. Tacit understandings used somehow to be acquired unconsciously, in the informality of easy converse among men who had time to get to know each other well. Now they must be replaced by statements on paper in which the letter is plain enough, but the spirit faint. And since the wholeness of the university can no longer be perceived, the groups to which *we* belong and *they* do not define themselves more sharply, and misapprehensions multiply marvellously.

In the bigger universities of today we, the academics, and they, the students, tend to move further apart; and they too have changed. Few have ever shown sufficient zeal to fulfil the doubtless unreasonable expectations of their teachers. Nevertheless the majority have been willing to learn, if not eager, and in this all-important respect at least they have been on the side of the academics. Happily they still are today. But lately there has been – in my opinion – a disquieting increase in the number of students who do not want to learn, and make learning more difficult for the rest. In lecture-room, tutorial, library and laboratory they are bored and ill at ease. They applied for admission because it was expected of them, and it was easier to go on sauntering along the academic road than to choose any other. Since they do not lack ability, it would have seemed unreasonable not to accept them. But by the time they have passed through a sixth form they have really had enough of study, and find no reward in the effort of sustained and serious thinking that the university must require of them. The present unrest among students admits of no single and simple explanation; no elderly don who remembers his own long-lost idealism will be altogether out of sympathy with some of the political and social discontents that provoke it. But in England, where substantial grievances within the academic field proper are rare, the complaints of students seem to me to be in large measure the unconscious projection of a conflict between role and inclination. I could even find some significance in the fact that the favourite manner of protesting is merely to sit down and just go on sitting.

Students influence their teachers. As their average intellectual temperature falls, so academics – especially the senior and the more able, energetic and ambitious – tend to find good reasons for turning aside from the ungrateful task of undergraduate teaching and for seeking satisfaction in more congenial pursuits. That is what has happened in the big American state universities; and that is what is beginning to happen here – the more easily as it becomes more than ever apparent that professional advancement and prestige are the rewards not of teaching, but of research, or of activities carried on outside the university, or (as commonly happens) of both. Obstinately there on the campus (as we have all now learned to call it) the student still remains; and I think there are as yet few academics here, even among the most passionate researchers and the most assiduous frequenters of the world outside, who would want to ignore his presence altogether. Nearly all are well disposed towards him. There are even some who go on believing that Newman's idea of a university is the finest ever conceived and who, with all the diffidence proper to so delicate an undertaking, would like to contribute to his education. So strong is the persuasion that teacher and pupil ought to meet face to face as persons conversing together, that every British university now has to promise to provide tutorials – though just what that means in practice remains uncertain. Investigations into methods of university teaching proliferate, and suggestions for their improvement abound; and if, believing that good teaching depends infinitely more on men than on methods, one is a little sceptical about the good that will come of them, one may nevertheless be gratified to recognize that they are prompted by concern for students.

How best to give effect to that concern today is the most perplexing question any academic can ask himself – and perhaps the most important: each must decide for himself. I end where I began. No change of circumstance, no new difficulty, opportunity, pressure or temptation has yet deprived the academic of his freedom to make of his profession what he will, or can absolve him from responsibility for the consequences of the choices he makes.

David Martin

The nursery of revolution

A Satirical Comment on the L.S.E. Student Left
(with apologies to all those students to whom it does not in the least apply)

Ever since Imagination seized Power in England's premier school of the social sciences the overheated air of that institution has been thick with immodest proposals for the abolition of this and the total transformation of that. One of the most intriguing has been the suggestion that the London School of Economics be converted into the Croydon Finishing School for Young Socialists. Another pleasing possibility put about by a student newsheet is that the college should be recreated as the London School of Untrammelled Desire. According to this proposal the motto 'Rerum cognoscere causas' should be immediately replaced by 'The Only Law is – "Do what thou wilt".'[1] But the most interesting of all the plans for a yet more glorious future has been the setting up of a Houghton Street Day Nursery of Revolution. Here indeed is a new and exciting concept of the modern role of a university and one to which we have already made so much progress that little more may be required than a simple change of name. Since the concept is so potent and the realization so nearly achieved one or two comments and queries are hardly out of order.

One of the consequences of this recent development has been, for good or ill, that academics now barely experience any awareness of a change when they pass from home to work or from week to weekend. Previously a weekend with the children was very different from a week at the School. At home the children were fascinating creatures, exposed to every irrational whim, quite amoral and charmingly spontaneous. One moment they would bury their heads in your bosom, the next beat you unmercifully between the eyes. Students on the other hand appeared as responsible adults, apparently well able to look after themselves without detailed supervision, and content with reasonable fulfilments of academic duty. At home the children wanted to be loved; at university the students

1 'Beaver', 24 October 1968.

wanted to be taught. The transition from one to the other seemed clear. Then quite suddenly all was changed. The façade of disciplined student endeavour was rolled away revealing an entirely new scenario in the making: the Houghton Street Day Nursery of Revolution. The young adults disappeared into the wings and in their place there entered a new set of fascinating creatures, quite amoral and alarmingly spontaneous, demanding at one moment to bury their heads in your bosom and the next beating you unmercifully between the eyes. The very revelation of this new scenario tore off the scales from the vision of the academics and achieved one major objective of the revolution: the abolition of the difference between home and work, labour and leisure. The life of the academic became all of a piece: he just moved from one nursery to another.

Academics are, by habit, disinclined to believe their eyes, but a whole series of changes confirmed this original impression. The first was a barefaced disregard for truth on the part of his charges. Whereas the adult student had always been slightly shamefaced about fabrication the denizens of the Day Nursery of Revolution positively celebrated it. They claimed that the invention of truth was better than reality – as indeed it was.[1] In their view the great defect of bourgeois science was that it could not make the truth up as it went along. The older type of student had only done this under pressure in examinations: he had hardly thought of making it *the* principle of scientific activity. It had not occurred to him that he was actually superior to the sordid requirements of mere objectivity and the heavy chains of bourgeois logic. But in the Nursery such things only weighed down the achievements of the imagination. The child constructs his own world. Anyone who contradicts that world he treats with a knowing grin of superior ignorance.

Apart from the new found power of fantasy the Day Nursery revealed an incipient thuggishness. It appeared that occupation was nine-tenths of the law. Wants and demands varied violently from one moment to the next. Egocentric autonomy co-existed with instant recourse to the maternal breast. Academics were required to be immediately available but not to interfere. The Nursery was *their* territory: there was no notion of neutral space. All the toys and apparatus belonged to the children by absolute right and they might use them if and when they wanted: the adult world owed them not merely a living but a leisured existence. All adult rules were resented but no one doubted the adults would appear with the goodies when the proper time for them came around.

The main activity of the Nursery of Revolution was drama. In the

1 The invention of truth is *their* phrase.

darkest corner of the Nursery is to be found an Old Theatre,[1] so called because the same childish scenes are re-enacted there year after year. There the children use their imaginations and play at revolution. They never tire of these endless scenes and enormously prefer them to contact with the outside world. This pleasure in make-belief explains phrases like 'Storm the Reality Studio' and 'Retake the Universe'.

Now that the principle and practice of the Nursery is so well established the L.S.E. academics naturally vary in their reaction: some for example are very reactionary indeed. Other academics have been so sheltered from reality by longish sojourn in the university that the Theatre of the Absurd does not strike them as in the least peculiar. This type of academic has the kind of centre which always has a soft spot for the wet left.

Yet other academics desperately wish to join again in the great dramas of youth. Some very curious symptoms follow as a result. For example they suffer acute confusion between paedogogy and paedophilia. To take another example they become unable to distinguish being lit-up from being enlightened. To join in the spontaneous life of the Nursery seems to provide the best guarantee against crabbed age and dull responsibility. They even develop a positive preference for ignorance and immaturity.

In a sense some academics discover in the Nursery a new version of *in loco parentis*. Nevertheless the role of the parent who indulgently eggs the children on to new forms of high-spirited and lovable mischief is not an easy one. He is only really wanted when there is some danger the mischief will annoy the neighbours to the point where they will do something about it. Apart from this the 'old boy' is dispensable. In any case the new version of *in loco parentis* is not really just what the old academic might wish. The real desire is less for an indulgent parent than a kind of private tutor: the sort of hapless scholarly attendant who waits upon the impetuous whim of the young master. This may suggest a new interpretation of the famous remark 'We must educate our masters'. The Nursery is indeed gradually moving towards this particular revolutionary notion of the academic role: one student actually complained to me that after having got excited about a book in the library he was unable to discuss it with his tutor for *a whole week*.

The capacity of the Houghton Street Day Nursery of Revolution to create a reaction has already been referred to. Those who 'react' are known as 'reactionaries' and are the embodiment of Incarnate Evil. They may be politically well to the left but a reactionary is currently defined as one who thinks 'we are none of us infallible, not even the youngest of us'. These

1 *The* Old Theatre where most of the student revivals occur.